# THE
# GREAT THORPE
# RAILWAY
# DISASTER 1874

## HEROES • VICTIMS • SURVIVORS

# THE GREAT THORPE RAILWAY DISASTER 1874

## HEROES · VICTIMS · SURVIVORS

### PHYLLIDA SCRIVENS

PEN & SWORD
HISTORY

AN IMPRINT OF PEN & SWORD BOOKS LTD.
YORKSHIRE - PHILADELPHIA

First published in Great Britain in 2021 by
PEN AND SWORD HISTORY
An imprint of
Pen & Sword Books Ltd
Yorkshire – Philadelphia

Typeset in Times New Roman 11.5/14 by
SJmagic DESIGN SERVICES, India.
Printed and bound in the UK by CPI Group (UK) Ltd.

Pen & Sword Books Limited incorporates the imprints of Atlas, Archaeology,
Aviation, Discovery, Family History, Fiction, History, Maritime, Military,
Military Classics, Politics, Select, Transport, True Crime, Air World,
Frontline Publishing, Leo Cooper, Remember When, Seaforth Publishing,
The Praetorian Press, Wharncliffe Local History, Wharncliffe Transport,
Wharncliffe True Crime and White Owl.

*For a complete list of Pen & Sword titles please contact*
PEN & SWORD BOOKS LIMITED
47 Church Street, Barnsley, South Yorkshire, S70 2AS, England
E-mail: enquiries@pen-and-sword.co.uk
Website: www.pen-and-sword.co.uk

Or

PEN AND SWORD BOOKS
1950 Lawrence Rd, Havertown, PA 19083, USA
E-mail: Uspen-and-sword@casematepublishers.com
Website: www.penandswordbooks.com

# Contents

# List of Plates and Illustration Credits

## Cover

Gravestones in Rosary Cemetery. (© Carol Gingell)

Peter Eade. (The Autobiography of Peter Eade 1916)

Train in Storm. (© The Victorian Picture Library)

## Plates

*The Pictorial World* 19 September 1874. (With Permission from Vintagedition.com)

Queen Victoria, 1875. (© National Portrait Gallery, London)

Arthur Duke of Connaught, 1879. (© National Portrait Gallery, London)

The Construction of Thorpe Station 1843. (© Norfolk Museum Service (Norwich Castle Museum & Art Gallery)

Foundry Bridge Norwich Thorpe Station. (© Norfolk Museum Service (Norwich Castle Museum and Art Gallery))

Norwich Thorpe Railway Station 1845. (*Illustrated London News* © Mary Evans Picture Library)

Industries on the River Wensum. (© Norfolk Industrial Archaeological Society)

Great Yarmouth 1878. (© istock by Getty Images)

Artist impression of Vauxhall Station, Great Yarmouth 1874. (© Phyllida Scrivens 2020)

# LIST OF PLATES AND ILLUSTRATION CREDITS

South Quay at Yarmouth. (© Norfolk Industrial Archaeological Society)

Passengers on a train, 1870s. (© istock by Getty)

Brundall Station c. 1915. (© Brundall Local History Group Archive *(www.brundallvillagehistory.org.uk)*)

County Lunatic Asylum by G.F. Sargeant. (© Norfolk County Council)

Norwich Thorpe Station interior 1863. (© Norfolk County Council)

Cooke & Wheatstone needle telegraph Yarmouth and Norwich Railway 1845. (© World History Archive/Alamy)

The Crash Site, *Illustrated London News* 19 September 1874. (© The Victorian Picture Library)

The Rescue Mission, *Illustrated London News* 19 September 1874. (© The Victorian Picture Library)

Accident Truck arrives clearing wreckage. (© The Victorian Picture Library)

The Three Tuns on the River Yare, with railway bridge. (© Norfolk County Council)

Mail train from Lowestoft to Norwich. Model similar to No.54. (© Science Museum Picture Library)

Express from Norwich to Yarmouth. Model similar to No.218. (© Science Museum Picture Library)

Consultant Medical Staff, Norfolk & Norwich Hospital, c. 1871. (© Norfolk and Norwich Hospital)

Ellen Eugenie Ramsdale and her fiancé, 1882. (By permission of Kathleen Irwin, OldPhotosFound.blogspot.com)

Sir Charles Rackham Gilman. (© Norfolk Industrial Archaeological Society)

St Andrew's Church, Thorpe-Next-Norwich 1880s. (© Norfolk Museum Service)

Mourning Card for Thomas Clarke. (© Norfolk County Council)

Mourning Card for James Light. (© Norfolk County Council)

Sir William Grove, Judge at Manslaughter Trial. (© National Portrait Gallery)

Walking stick believed to be made from wood taken from collision site. (© John Bolle)

The Rushcutters (formerly Three Tuns) in 2020. (© Phyllida Scrivens)

Crash site in 2020. (© Phyllida Scrivens)

# Foreword

The 1874 rail disaster at Thorpe has fascinated me for decades. I first encountered it in a piece from L.T.C. Rolt's 1955 book *Red For Danger*. It had been reprinted in a 1963 edition of *The Railway Lover's Companion* edited by Bryan Morgan.

The initial fascination, for my then schoolboy self, was that such a momentous event had happened in my home city. The drama had been played out on the station that I already knew well. What's more, this story, rooted in Norwich, was so important that here it was in books of national significance.

As time went by I became ever more interested. When I'd acquired enough knowledge, and formed my own opinions, I wrote a couple of magazine pieces about the 1874 crash.

By the time I'd dug even deeper I wanted to tell the story in a more comprehensive way. I wrote a screenplay about it. I pitched the film, *Sixteen Minutes*, to Mustard TV. They liked it, and in turn pitched it to the BBC. I presented the documentary when it was broadcast on BBC One.

Casting modesty to the winds, I think that my film set out the narrative of that dreadful September night as clearly, chronologically and comprehensively as any account had managed until then.

But it was a narrative of that dreadful night. Indeed it was a narrative of sixteen crucial minutes of that night.

What we have now is Phyllida Scrivens' unprecedentedly comprehensive, all embracing, account of the Thorpe Rail Disaster.

It's books like this one that make a difference. Now we get to meet the people involved. We see the backdrop of the context in which they lived and worked. The context in which some of them died.

This account lifts the 1874 disaster out of the genre of railway history, takes it beyond a wider analysis of what happened and how, and transplants it into a valuable piece of social study.

That does not mean that the broader brush stokes result in a loss of detail, nor that the book is drily academic. Quite the contrary. You will find more detail in here than I think anybody has ever gathered together on this subject before. You will find a narrative that does not fall short in delivering tension. This is an immensely readable book.

In these pages you will discover how a disparate group of people found themselves involuntarily drawn towards one shattering, shared moment. You will discover that, as this book's title tells us, there were on that night, heroes, victims and survivors. You will discover how the moment of impact between two trains sent shock waves rippling outwards, causing a seismic impact on society.

I have always thought that, when it comes to the Thorpe rail disaster of 1874, there was a bigger story to tell, a more in-depth examination to be carried out. Phyllida Scrivens has not only, through her assiduous research, proved that; in this outstanding book she has, through her writing, delivered that.

Personally, I can't pass through Norwich Thorpe station without being aware that my feet are following such tragic footprints. I have stood, for research purposes only I hasten to add, in the very dock, in the courtroom, where some of the protagonists in this drama stood; my feet occupying precisely the space that theirs once did. It was one of the most extraordinary sensations I've ever experienced. I felt I knew these people. I knew their story. It seemed they were somehow part of my life. If, unlike me, you are unaware of their story, then Phyllida Scrivens' book is about to change your life.

The events of that night in September 1874, and their aftermath, will never be forgotten. There will, doubtless, be more research, and maybe more discoveries. I think though that it will be a long time, if ever, that a piece of work emerges to replace this book as the definitive, and enthralling, account of the Thorpe railway disaster.

Pete Goodrum
November 2020

Pete Goodrum is a successful author and broadcaster, appearing frequently on BBC local radio, covering topics ranging from advertising to music and social trends. He also writes and presents TV documentaries. His best-selling books include *Norfolk Broads: The Biography*, *Norwich in the 1950s* and the sequel *Norwich in the 1960s*, and most recently *Jarrold 250 Years, A History*. Pete has a real passion for the history of Norwich and Norfolk and lives the centre of the city with his wife Sue.

# Author's Introduction

I first moved to Thorpe St Andrew, two miles east of the city of Norwich, in 2004, unaware of the local legend about a Victorian railway disaster, a dark tale of death and destruction, totally at odds with the tranquil riverside village I was now proud to call home. Over the years, while working, studying and writing, I took time to learn more about the local history of the area, soaking up the presentations and guided walks organised by the enthusiastic members of Thorpe History Group. Every autumn, articles about the Great Thorpe Railway Disaster of 10 September 1874, seemed to proliferate in the local press and on blog posts, often involving a long list of the dead and the injured. Finally, the mystique peaked my curiosity; who were these individuals, brought together that night in the tempest of wind and rain? It was only once I'd moved to the other side of Yarmouth Road, into a house overlooking the River Yare, with its view of the Rushcutters pub (formerly the Three Tuns), and directly next door to The River Garden, previously The King's Head, that I resolved to write this book.

It has taken over two years for me to gather together the mass of research material and images essential for retelling this true life story as a blend of facts and speculative dramatisation. My aim was always to honour the memory of those poor souls involved, revealing the lives behind the list. They were real people, covering the entire spectrum of Victorian society, each with a past, present and for some, a future. There were many to choose from. Sadly there was no time or space to include all those who were injured. Their lives mattered too.

I will admit that I am no railway expert. I like to think of myself as a story teller. As such, I hope the lack of technical information within these pages will not disappoint those who cherish that particular passion. For me it is the heroes, victims and survivors who call out for our attention. This is their story.

# Acknowledgements

I should like to thank the following individuals and organisations for their support with this project. Without their time, expertise and knowledge I don't believe this book would have been possible.

Dr Paddy Anstey, Louise Atkins (descendent of John Devonshire), John Bolle, Lyn Brooks, Brundall Local History Group, Judy Fry (descendent of John Beart), Mary-Anne Garry, Carol Gingell, Pete Goodrum, Great Eastern Railway Society, Barry Jackson, Rachel Job, Richard Johnson, the late Graham Kenworthy, Bill King, Malcolm Martins, Lynette Millington (descendent of William Bransby Francis), Helen Murray, Norfolk Heritage Library, Norfolk Museums Service, Norfolk Record Office, Norwich Writers' Circle, Barbara Parry, Carol Rawcliffe, Richard Slipper (descendent of Robert Ward), Catherine Smith (Charterhouse Archive), Tim Smithers (descendent of Thomas Clarke), Michael Sparkes (descendent of Stephen Field), Thorpe History Group, Philip Tolley, Adrian Vaughan, John Watling, Alan Wheeler, Nick Williams, Dale Wiseman and Beverley Woolner. And finally, my love and gratitude go to my husband Victor Scrivens for painstakingly proofreading the numerous drafts, always an arduous task.

## NOTES

Sums of money detailed in the text are followed by the equivalent sums as in 2019, as estimated on the Bank of England Inflation Calculator at bankofengland.co.uk.

Further information, additional images and research references can be found at thegreatthorperailwaydisaster1874.com

# Prologue

## Thursday, 10 September 1874, 9.20 pm

Two massive steam engines, each travelling at thirty miles per hour. Visibility poor due to blinding rain and squalling winds. Two frustrated drivers, racing to make up time, both men aware of running late due to delays beyond their control. Both drivers unaware that the two trains are travelling on the same single line, on a catastrophic collision course. The mail train from Yarmouth passes by the eerie buildings of the Norfolk Asylum, gas-lit windows offering little respite from the pitch-black night. It then thunders towards the wooden bridge over the River Yare at Thorpe-Next-Norwich. The express from Norwich enters the same bridge, towering high above the lights from the Three Tuns pub on the riverbank below. Both crews on the footplate instinctively sense that something is fast approaching through the gloom. Despite every effort, they realise with horror that it is far too late to apply the brakes.

Inside the carriages the lights go out. A rush of noise envelops the 220 passengers, deadening other senses, the impact hurling them from side to side. Desperately they reach out for support as the structure around them creaks and cracks apart. The funnel from the mail train instantly sears. The express engine rears over its assailant. Twisting and screeching, the carriages whiplash into the air. The trains cling together, the summit some sixty or seventy feet above the ground. As the resulting pyramid settles, the wreck sways, threatening to collapse onto the tracks and river below.

# Chapter 1

# The Opening of the Yarmouth and Norwich Railway

## Tuesday, 30 April 1844

> Upon the whole, it may be said, that this line of railway
> will, for its length, be one of the most picturesque of any
> in the kingdom. Running upon an embankment through the
> beautiful valley of Thorpe, it cuts through the high ground
> at Postwick, and emerges into a rich and highly cultivated
> country, with the river winding gracefully on the right.
> Passing through the cutting at Reedham, it runs along an
> embankment, embracing a very extended landscape, until it
> reaches Breydon, when Yarmouth appears as seated on the
> waters, and reminds the traveller of the approach to Venice.
> (*Norfolk Chronicle*, Saturday, 1 July 1843)

From first light, along the banks of the River Yare in Thorpe-next-
Norwich, hundreds of enthusiastic locals waited. Thrilled by the large
marquees being set up in Thorpe Gardens, everyone was anticipating
the much publicised firework display that evening to celebrate this
momentous event. In the city of Norwich and villages en route, curious
and excited citizens, from errand boys to lawyers, flocked to find the
best vantage points. At Carrow, Whitlingham, Brundall and Reedham,
crowds jostled for position. All along the recently completed Yarmouth
to Norwich railway line, they craved a glimpse of a real railway train.
This modern wonder of travel was coming to Norfolk.

Fourteen years earlier, on 15 September 1830, the Liverpool to
Manchester Railway Company introduced the first ever timetabled
passenger rail service. From then on, it became the tradition to hold

1

ceremonial openings over a period of two glorious days, the first reserved for directors, shareholders, dignitaries and journalists and, barring incident, the second specifically for the public. But on that lovely April morning, it was Norfolk's turn and 200 privileged citizens were invited to ride the twenty-five miles from Norwich to the coastal town of Great Yarmouth.

For many it would be their first time on a train. For some it was a daunting prospect. Discussions over breakfast tables may have included recollections of past rail accidents, sensationally reported in the national press.

"Berkshire only four years ago, when the driver fell asleep. He was killed with his guard, smashed to atoms."

"And that dreadful business on the Great Western on Christmas Eve '41, near Reading wasn't it? A train derailed because of a landslide?"

"Eight good people crushed under the goods waggons, dead at the scene."

"Barnsley, only last year, when fog caused a terrible collision, carriages smashed to pieces, someone's head cut completely off. God protect us all."

Only two years earlier a young Queen Victoria, in her fifth year on the throne, took her first journey on the railway. Allegedly, she was deeply concerned about the prospect of travelling at unprecedented speeds. Her enthusiastic husband, Prince Albert, an avid supporter of new inventions, persuaded her to board the Fire-Fly class locomotive *Phlegethon,* for the twenty-five minute trip from Slough to London Paddington. The engine was capable of a normal speed of forty-three miles per hour, but the nervous monarch insisted that the driver kept it down to thirty. The royal saloon carriage was opulent and comfortable, with a padded silk ceiling and blue velvet sofas. On the footplate that day was the famous engineer Isambard Kingdom Brunel, responsible for the very line on which the royal party travelled. Later, in a letter to her Uncle, King Leopold of Belgium, Victoria admitted she was, 'quite charmed by this new way of travelling'. The international press carried the story, increasing the confidence of many sceptics.

It had taken fourteen years to bring the railway to Norfolk. From the beginning, while others saw the potential for making a fortune, Norfolk gentry, landowners, and the new middle classes, remained stubbornly traditional, resistant to change. Many were dismissive of this new-fangled method of transport, considering it an innovation too far, commercially unviable and potentially ruinous for the rich agricultural landscape. For over 200 years, fleets of black-sailed trading Wherries had successfully moved goods from the coastal harbours of Yarmouth and Lowestoft to the inland port of Norwich. These large open barges, their hulls traditionally blackened by tar and fish oil to protect them from the unforgiving North Sea winds, were capable of carrying 25 tons of merchandise, including grain, wood, coal, potatoes and fish. But the speed of progress along the narrow rivers of the Yare, Bure, Ant and Chet, was predominantly dependent on unpredictable tide and wind conditions. When the breezes dropped, the crews of tough, resilient wherrymen were compelled to propel the vessel manually, using only the heavy wooden quant pole, designed to reach the riverbed easily. Why would anyone want to disrupt this ancient trade and potentially destroy livelihoods?

At the Theatre Royal in Norwich, nine years earlier, the audience was treated to an unveiling of the latest Grand Moveable Panorama from the theatre's celebrated set designer, Mr Thorne. Billed as, 'Liverpool and Manchester Rail Road, with its tunnel, excavations and bridges', the expansive scene, painted in meticulous detail upon one long continuous reel of canvas, each end rolled around two large spool-type mechanisms that when turned, caused the canvas to scroll across the back of the stage. The excited theatregoers experienced an illusion of movement and an unnerving sensation of travelling through space. They watched agog as an immense steam engine appeared to roll along the railroad, pulling passengers, goods and even livestock in a variety of carriages. But despite this, Norfolk folk remained circumspect, watching and wondering, reluctant as yet to embrace the persistent rise of railway mania.

Eventually, on 19 February 1836, there came a breakthrough. A bill was presented to Parliament proposing the formation of a new company, Eastern Counties Railways. Objections were lodged and time-consuming legal claims for ownership of land were made, resulting in a delay of nearly five months. On 4 July, the necessary Royal Assent was granted. The *Norfolk Chronicle* of Saturday, 6 August could finally announce that:

> Eastern Counties Railway Company, incorporated by Act of Parliament for making a Railway from London to Norwich and Yarmouth, by Romford, Chelmsford, Colchester and Ipswich.

The race was on to bring the advantages of the railway to Norfolk. From the summer of 1836, Members of Parliament, railway barons, engineers, lawyers and landowners attended countless table-thumping meetings in gloomy gas-lit rooms. Surrounded by clouds of pungent cigar smoke, sustained by glasses of Madeira, they discussed contentious issues far into the night. Finally, shortly after Christmas 1840, a summit was held at the East India and Colonial Club Rooms in Pall Mall, London. The aim was to settle the gridlock once and for all. Having agreed to purchase shares in the project, and reassuring each other that any proposed route would not, 'pass through any gentleman's park or pleasure grounds', the meeting agreed a completion target of 1843. Progress at last.

By 1842 there were fifty-eight operating railway companies covering the entire country. On 18 June, The Yarmouth and Norwich Railway was added to the list, plans for the first railway line in Norfolk finally authorised by an Act of Parliament. The contractors Grissell and Peto were commissioned, one of the largest building companies in the country. Their engineers would work closely with inventor George Stephenson and his son Robert, to design the line through the rural Yare Valley.

One of the early challenges identified by the engineers, was the need for the line to cross a loop of the River Yare, within the environs of the picturesque riverside village of Thorpe-Next-Norwich. A canal was designed, referred to as the New Cut, with a wooden railway bridge at each end, so creating an island over which the railway line would run. A number of wealthy, influential landowners from Thorpe were vexed to learn they would have to sacrifice land and even their homes, the resulting compensation claims lining the pockets of local solicitors. At the eastern end of the village, the families of Robert King, a former Mariner, and those of naval Captain Thomas Blakiston, were forced to sacrifice their homes and gardens. Colonel John Harvey, a gentleman textile manufacturer and banker from Thorpe Lodge, lost one of his many farms on the outskirts of the village, with the tenant, Mr Woodrow losing his livelihood.

The local press continued avidly to report on progress with the new railway line. On 6 May 1843 the *Norfolk Chronicle* stated that the excavations for the new channel had commenced. A week later another under-whelmed editor described the scene:

> On the meadows of Trowse, described as being 'one continuous surface of vivid green' various large black masses

have arisen, forming a barrier and adding nothing to the pristine beauty of our universally admired Thorpe scenery.

(*Norwich Mercury*, Saturday, 13 May 1843)

Tensions were just beginning. Not everyone welcomed the railways.

Working on this project were at least 500 men, itinerant labourers known as Navvies, invading the Broadland villages accompanied by their wives and children. During the mid-eighteenth century, the beginning of the Industrial Revolution, these 'navigators' were responsible for digging the early network of canals, crucial for the improved transportation of goods throughout the country. With the emerging railway companies, the navvies' skills were once more in high demand. These men were not afraid of hard work, receiving substantial wages in return for toiling long hours in all weathers, facing constant dangers and living in often appalling conditions alongside the tracks. Gangs of around forty worked under the supervision of a self-appointed 'ganger', whose responsibility was to negotiate a price with the contractor for constructing the line section by section. By mid-June, despite a period of heavy rain, the New Cut took on the appearance of another river. The noise created by driving piles deep into the riverbed to accommodate an enormous draining engine, necessary to pump away the relentless water from the tidal river, led to angry complaints from local residents. Three miles east towards Yarmouth, work was also advancing, with a raised embankment now complete between the County Asylum and the river. Ditches were filled, bridges were nearly ready and small workshops for carpenters and blacksmiths were springing up along the line. Temporary rails were already in position, over which teams of horses pulled wagon after wagon of soil to where it was next required.

The navvies proved controversial, a source of fascination for the public and the press, objects of curiosity and admiration, distaste and anger. Renowned for having 'splendid muscles and brawny limbs, immense strength, skill and dexterity', as well as for foul language and partiality for the evil drink, it proved inevitable that the curious ladies of the city would orchestrate surreptitious glimpses of these strapping workmen, by taking constitutional strolls or, if wealthy, riding in their Phaeton or Landau carriages. For the best views, the route from Norwich took them well beyond the city walls, past the site of the emerging railway station, heading east along Thorpe Road. But as months passed, there were increasing suggestions in the local newspapers that some labourers were downing tools and harassing 'genteel ladies' while begging for money.

By late summer, much to the relief of Thorpe residents, it was announced that the New Cut was almost finished. High tides during July had caused the water meadows to overflow their banks alongside the new line, but the contractor's steam engine proved itself efficient and successfully cleared the flood. By 11 September the contractors were so confident of imminent completion that they held an auction at the King's Head pub in Thorpe Road, offering for sale the very same steam engine, along with its 27ft-diameter water wheel, sluice gate, driving gear and boilers. The event offered an ideal opportunity for members of the recently established Aquatic Club to gather subscriptions for a grand regatta planned for the beginning of October. Led by Mr Cattermole, then landlord at the Three Tuns, it would be a celebration of the New Cut and a promising future.

Over the winter of 1843–4, the rails were laid, bridges and station buildings completed – finished six weeks ahead of schedule. Opening dates were agreed, catering organised, invitations sent out. The region was enjoying one of the driest springs in living memory; so it was with good cheer that on the morning of 30 April 1844, a procession of carriages and cabs clattered over the Portland stone toll bridge known as Foundry Bridge. Anticipation was intense as grand ladies and gentlemen arrived at Norwich terminus to join the inaugural journey. They found a fine modern building, set in a wide-open space, neatly surrounded by iron railings. The distinctive Italianate tower was decorated with celebratory flags, banners, laurels and evergreens. All the inevitable rubbish, rubble and building equipment had been cleared away. Visitors hastened to explore the two long platforms, one entirely designed for the loading and receiving of goods, with three lines of metal rails between them, all covered by a grand arcade lit by gas lamps. Looking up they could admire the double roof, some 25ft above, supported by rows of decorative iron columns. Visitors squeezed into the passenger waiting room, before viewing the booking office, with its fascinating printing machine capable of producing thousands of passenger tickets every hour. Most intriguing of all was the Telegraph office, with the shiny new Cooke and Wheatstone 5-needle telegraph equipment, visitors proud to learn that Norwich was the first railway station to install one.

Outside, just a few yards away, they marvelled at the engine shed, where cleaning and maintenance of rolling stock would take place. Some 123ft long, it housed an enormous tank, said to hold 14,000 gallons of water. A series of pipes allowed the engines to be supplied in a few seconds. Most notable among the luminaries from Norwich were the Mayor, William Freeman and the Sheriff, George Coleman, accompanied by their wives. They greeted contractor Mr Samuel Morton Peto, and one of the inventors of the telegraph machine, Lieutenant William Fothergill Cooke. Conspicuous by their absence was Peto's partner Grissell, booked to open another new railway the following day, and George Stephenson, who was unwell.

Just before 10.00 am a bell rang on the platform, the signal for everyone to climb aboard and claim a seat in one of the fourteen six-wheeled carriages. The procession was made up of ten composite carriages, containing sections for both first- and second-class travellers, and four third-class carriages, open to the elements and resembling goods wagons. In one of these, just behind the engine, stood members of Howlett's Brass Band, struggling to play rousing tunes while packed closely together and desperately trying to keep their balance. Behind them a further open wagon was crammed with gentlemen and members of the press, dressed in Sunday best, vying for the best position, clutching their hats to avoid losing them. The fourteen carriages were bookmarked by two engines, one to pull and the other to push. Once the platform was clear, the assembled workmen gave three hearty cheers, the band struck up a lively rendition of 'Rule Britannia', and the train slowly moved away, the deafening steam whistle threatening to drown out the musicians. Picking up speed, the train passed over the first bridge on Carrow Road, welcomed by hundreds of cheering spectators. Children raced the train along the meadows, soon to be left behind, panting and puffing. As the train rattled over the bridge spanning the River Yare, they could see down the whole length of the New Cut, and down at the tranquil water of the River Yare, before looking up again to take in the approaching views. The journalist from the *Norfolk Chronicle* was effusive:

> The view was splendid; not a finer one is to be seen near any large town; hill and dale, meadows and woodland, a river on each side, and plantations in the distance right and left, presented a magnificent coup d'oeil.

Passing the riverside village of Thorpe-Next-Norwich to their left, the passengers were greeted by yet more spectators, waving handkerchiefs, hats and parasols. Flocks of greylag geese took flight, disturbed by this unfamiliar sound. As the County Asylum came into view, farm workers stopped to stand and stare as horses, cattle and sheep, alarmed by the deafening whistle and clouds of steam, scampered into adjoining fields. By now the engine was starting to achieve its full power, reaching about 25mph. For the passengers the experience roused a mix of emotions. Some became increasingly anxious, literally fearing for their lives as the train rumbled and rattled along, making a fearful racket. Others, fuelled by adrenaline, relished this unaccustomed sensation of speed, finding it quite different to riding a galloping horse. Passing through the deep excavation at Postwick, travelling under bridges, the train slowed down at the approach to Brundall, the tiny rural station platform lined with enthusiastic villagers.

Passing yet more farming land passengers were entertained by the sight of working horses bolting in fear, dragging their ploughs over the mud at a rapid rate. As the train neared the village of Buckenham, the River Yare once again came into view, the passengers enthralled to see the magnificent Steam Packet, continuing its journey down river. It had left Norwich two hours earlier, but was already being overtaken. Some queried why anyone would now choose to spend four hours travelling by river from Norwich to Great Yarmouth, when the rail journey takes only fifty minutes?

The skyline of Yarmouth came into sight, the huge central tower of the Parish Church of St Nicholas appearing on the horizon, along with fragments of the ancient town wall and the Norfolk Naval Pillar. Seagulls soared above, replacing the geese, ducks and swans of the river, welcoming the visitors with high-pitched cries.

As the strong easterly wind swept inland from the North Sea, those riding in the open trucks regretted any decision to travel without a topcoat. Those who had taken that precaution quickly buttoned up against the sudden cold. Smut marks and slight burns on their clothing caused some dismay, no one had warned them about that possibility. On arrival at the station, the railway servants of the Eastern Counties helped the ladies to disembark safely, the unpleasant smell of burnt coal lingering on their fine clothing. They were, however, delighted to find that the doors, pillars and ceilings were sumptuously decorated in a similar style to Norwich. The church bells of the town rang a merry peal and the Norwich and Yarmouth bands were in position, with a lively repertoire of musical airs. Outside the station a number of carriages, cabs and omnibuses waited patiently to convey the guests over the suspension bridge into the town. After some light refreshments in the booking office, provided by the Victoria Hotel, the passengers were free to discover the highlights of the town.

On reaching the suspension bridge, which had spanned the River Bure since 1829, there was a short delay due to a misunderstanding over the requirement to pay the usual one penny toll, due to be waived on the following day. Once this was resolved, the travellers found much to enjoy in Yarmouth, including the ruins of the thirteenth-century Greyfriars Cloisters, the jetty where Nelson had landed in 1800 after the Battle of the Nile, and the glorious tall ships moored at South Quay, a scene only marred by the pungent smells of fish, tar and pitch.

Just before 2.00 pm, the visitors made their way back to the railway terminus, delighting in the welcome given by the people of Yarmouth, gathered in Symonds' Gardens and around the railway station. Dignitaries from the town, including the Mayor, joined them for the return trip to Norwich. After a forty-five-minute ride, the party disembarked, many taking a cab home to prepare for the celebratory 'Dejeuner', beginning at 4.00 pm at the Assembly House.

The conversations that evening included businessmen rejoicing at the prospect of completing their business at Yarmouth and still arriving home in time for supper. Fishermen and farmers were bound to benefit, and surely the new line would open up Yarmouth as a leisure destination for everyone, rather than it being the preserve of the aristocracy and gentry. And this was only the beginning. Once the additional proposed lines were completed, travellers could be in London in just five hours. And from London, connections to great cities such as Birmingham, Manchester, Southampton and Exeter would open up the country, offering opportunities for both business and pleasure. These were exciting times indeed.

At 7.00 pm, as the visitors from Yarmouth took the return train home, the evening celebrations at the Three Tuns in Thorpe-Next-Norwich, were just beginning. Extra barrels of beer were on standby, the hired band was in position under the marquee and a brilliant display of fireworks was billed for 9.00 pm. It did not disappoint. The following day the new railway line was opened to the public. By the evening, everyone had safely returned, the public houses full of revellers sharing railway stories, those patrons fortunate enough to ride the train that day, each hailed as a hero.

# Chapter 2

# Thirty Years Later

## Thursday, 10 September 1874
## Norwich

> I could have stayed a long time in Norwich – it is like
> Bristol, an old city and not a modern town – and it stands so
> picturesquely, and has so many old bits, and the water winds
> about it so and its cathedral and thirty-eight churches make
> such a show, that I got at last quite the feeling of being in
> some old town on the Continent.
>
> (Poet and Critic Matthew Arnold, July 1861)

The city wakes to yet more rain. It is proving most vexing. August
had been pleasant, dry and sunny, but eight days ago the weather
changed for the worse, with torrential rain, high winds and sporadic
thunderstorms. In the more respectable areas of the city, three eminent
medical men prepare for their respective days out. The most senior
of the three, at 59 years old, is Mr William Bransby Francis, a well-
loved General Practitioner of Colegate Street. A portly man with a
kindly and genial nature, he is greatly liked by his many friends and
held in high esteem by professional colleagues throughout the city.
With the British Medical Conference, held in the city during August,
now a distant memory, William can finally devote more time to his
wife Jane, his passion for botany and experimenting in the emerging
miracle of photography. Today he is taking the train to Lowestoft to
attend the annual Flower Show, along with his wife, before leaving
her to spend a few days with friends at the coast. Tonight he will dine
alone.

\*\*\*\*

To the west of the city, in the sought-after area of Eaton, stands Heathfield House, the stunning family home of the White family. In the late 1860s, Dental Surgeon Richard purchased a home to suitably reflect his professional status and success, employing four servants to wait on the family's every need. Richard White senior resides here with his wife Anne, six daughters and three sons. The eldest, Ellen, at 27, is as yet unmarried and their oldest son, 26-year-old Richard Wentworth, affectionately known as Wenty, works with his father in the family practice, having graduated from the University of London in June 1865. The youngest of the brood is little Bertha, just 7 years old. As the children were growing up, their father built up the dental practice, while writing a pioneering book on dental care, *Advice on the Management of the Teeth,* covering topics such as milk teeth, extractions and even toothbrushes.

In recent weeks Wenty has given his parents cause for concern. During the medical conference in August, their headstrong son was involved in a disturbing incident, resulting in him being charged with cruelty to dogs. Wenty was among a group of five medical men who witnessed Dr Eugene Magnan of London allegedly injecting alcohol and absinthe into the veins of some sorry creatures. It was meant to be a bit of fun but senior doctors and veterinary surgeons had not been amused, preferring a charge against the perpetrators. Today, in spite of the weather, Wenty has business in Yarmouth. He is in good spirits, despite still awaiting a date for the trial. Once that is over, he will have his whole life before him.

*****

In Essex Street, a recent development of elegant brick built terrace houses, set in the fashionable Unthank Road area, widow Mary Ramsdale looks forward to welcoming home her 18-year-old daughter Ellen Eugenie, following an overnight visit to her guardian, Mr Rose, in Great Yarmouth. In three years Ellen will come of age and inherit her late father's auction house fortune, kept in trust since his death in 1859. Ellen is developing into a headstrong and independent young woman. Mary constantly worries that her daughter may be vulnerable to the attentions of unscrupulous fortune hunters. Ellen is not due back into Norwich Station until 9.40 pm. In the meantime Mary will make up Ellen's bed; her daughter will sleep in fresh linen tonight.

*****

John Willis Betts, a stoker with the Great Eastern Railway, established on 7th August 1862, is gleefully anticipating a rare afternoon off work. With his eldest son turning three only eight days ago, it is time to celebrate. A day out at the seaside will do nicely. Six weeks ago John's family had become four, with the birth of baby William. It's disappointing that the rain refuses to let up, but they are not about to let the weather spoil their fun. John is determined to offer his boys a better start in life than he had. He remembers only too well how, aged 10, he was sent to work in the local silk factory, close to his family home in Hadleigh in Suffolk. His father, John Betts, was a pig dealer and by 1861 had six children to feed. It was his eldest son's responsibility to contribute as soon as possible to the family's meagre income. John junior had married Elizabeth at the end of 1870. He was just 21, his bride a little older at 25. The family are now living in the village of Lakenham, close to Thorpe Railway Station where John is based. But today he can forget work. Once his morning shift is over, he will meet the others and climb aboard a train to the coast.

*****

Colour Sergeant Robert Ward, Norfolk-born and voluntary member of the West Norfolk Militia, rose before light at his home in Cherry Street, Lakenham. He tried not to wake his wife Eliza and their four children, Robert 18, Eliza 13, Edward 11 and Martha 9. Robert had spent last evening preparing the contents of his wicker fishing creel, sorting his collection of wooden reels with horsehair lines, his favourite wood and leather fishing priest – a truncheon like instrument for killing the fish quickly – his hand painted wooden and reed floats and bags of lobworms and breadcrumbs. This morning he added bread and a chunk of cheese to the basket. Pulling on his well-worn army boots and oldest coat with the largest pockets, he takes his wide brimmed fishing hat from the hook. Tucked under his arm are his favourite cane rods. As he sets off on the twenty-five-minute walk to Thorpe Station, he eagerly anticipates a record catch of bream or roach, maybe even a pike.

Robert has arranged to meet his friend and colleague Sergeant Major Frederick Cassell and together catch the 7.50 am train to Yarmouth. The two men greet each other warmly, anticipating a day of shared yarns and memories, while pitting their wits against the fish at their favourite spots on the Yare and the Bure. On the journey, they occasionally stand to peer from the high tiny window in the third-class carriage, spotting windmills or the black sails of passing Wherries. The weather is certainly disappointing, but rain never seems to bother the fish. As long as the two friends are on the train arriving back in Norwich at 9.40 pm this evening, their wives cannot complain too much. Especially if they can bring home some supper.

\*\*\*\*\*

Another early riser is 23-year-old James Light, a fireman with Great Eastern Railway. His home is at Wilderness Place, just off Kings Street, adjacent to the River Wensum. He lives with parents Isaac and Lucy and two younger brothers, Richard and George. Today James is rostered to be on the footplate of a variety of engines travelling between Thorpe Station, Lowestoft and Great Yarmouth. His first shift begins with the 7.50 am out of Norwich, heading for Yarmouth. GER rules stipulate that a fireman should arrive at work a minimum of forty-five minutes before his train is due to leave, appearing on duty as clean as circumstances will allow. His first task this morning was to ensure that the first engine is in proper order to go out, carrying sufficient supplies of coke and water.

James' walk to work takes him along the banks of the Wensum, past Colman's Mustard Factory and into the brewing area of King Street. He hardly notices the smells of fish piled high on the moored Wherries, mixed with those of mustard seed and hops. James is proud of his achievements since starting his railway career by cleaning engines in the sheds. He has been promoted to Fireman's Assistant, but has ambition to progress further, maybe even to Driver. That morning, James is looking forward to sharing the footplate with Driver John Prior, a man he respects and much admires.

\*\*\*\*\*

General Physician and Surgeon Dr Peter Eade is a busy man. Once he completes his morning surgery, he plans to take a train to the stormy east coast to consult with a patient, long neglected since before the medical conference. Peter is well known in the city for his heavy dark sideburns, boundless energy and, at 49 years old, his slight athletic physique. Every morning Dr Eade devotes some time to preparing his monogrammed leather Gladstone bag. He makes sure to include the basic necessities such as an ear trumpet, bottle of opium for pain relief and another of 'Calomel', a mix to aid evacuation. Other essentials include a small kit of scalpels, syringes and needles, a 'cupping' device and a number of assorted leather straps to use as tourniquets. His elegant home is in St Giles Street on the edge of the city, referred to as 'The Harley Street of Norwich', for its proliferation of residents representing the medical profession. Peter purchased this house in 1865 from a leading Norwich physician, when he, ironically through illness, was compelled to relinquish his handsome residence. At the time, Peter was uncertain whether his professional earnings 'scarcely justified so bold a step'. The family venture proved successful and his two spinster sisters joined the household, who were all delighted when Peter's list of wealthy private patients rapidly began to increase.

Taking his black umbrella and gabardine overcoat from the arms of the housemaid, he bids farewell to Ellen, his dear wife of only two years. Stepping out into the street he finds the cobbles to be glistening with rain. Hailing a hansom, he instructs the driver to take him to Thorpe Railway Station, about fifteen minutes across the city. Passing St Giles Church, with its imposing bell tower, the horse-drawn cab proceeds in front of the Norfolk Hotel, a group of elegant four-horse carriages lined up outside. The narrow alley between the Public Library and the flint Guildhall involves a steep incline and the horse slips a little on the wet ground. Just before entering London Street, if he glances to his right, Peter will catch sight of the life-sized bronze statue of Wellington, complete with cannon, set on a granite plinth and unveiled on the market place some twenty-two years earlier in 1854.

The cab shakes its way around the mound of Norwich Castle, home of the County Gaol, past the County Police Station and the very muddy Cattle Market Bullring, and into the imposing Prince of Wales Road, just one of the many impressive entrances to the city. Originally fields and marshland, used for growing hops, vegetables, fruit and flowers, this fine broad highway was raised in 1862 to connect the busy cattle market to the expanding Thorpe Station, sited on the other side of the River Wensum. Towards the end of this afternoon's ride, Peter's cab rattles between Lefrevre's Engine Works and Messrs Hill & Underwood's Vinegar Works, crosses Foundry Bridge, and takes a sharp right into the entrance yard of the Great Eastern Railway terminus.

Striding through the station entrance, Dr Eade buys a first class ticket to Great Yarmouth, a journey of around an hour, his plan to administer to his patient before returning home on the mail train, due to leave the coast at 8.40 pm. That should allow enough time to share a light supper with his Ellen before retiring.

# Thursday, 10 September 1874
# Great Yarmouth

When we got into the street [...], and smelt the fish, and pitch, and oakum, and tar, and saw the sailors walking about, and the carts jangling up and down over the stones, I felt I had done so busy a place an injustice; and said as much to Peggotty, who heard my expressions of delight with great complacency, and told me it was well known [...] that Yarmouth was, upon the whole, the finest place in the universe.

(Charles Dickens, *David Copperfield,* 1849)

George Womack steps aboard the morning train from Yarmouth to Norwich with a heavy heart. The proprietor of a popular city drapers' store, known as G.R. Womack, his extensive business is conveniently situated on the corner of Dove Street and Lobster Lane, attracting wealthy and prestigious clients following a visit to the Corn Exchange. Until 1862 George had been the 'Son' in the family firm of 'Messrs Womack and Son'. But in the May, his father, also named George, unexpectedly died following a short but painful illness. George senior had been a popular businessman, honoured by the City with the role of Sheriff in 1852. Many still feel his loss. The business had been doing well and George senior left his widow Ann well provided for. From then on George had managed the store and staff, continuing to sell Deer Stalkers, rolls of poplin, taffeta and velvet, quality ready-made clothing, hosiery, caps, tasteful carpetbags and, especially, hats from Paris.

But George's personal life is going through a difficult period. His fifteen-year relationship with his wife Emma has been deteriorating recently. A short while ago he met an enchanting young woman from

Great Yarmouth, with whom he struck up a 'friendship'. Events took their course and it wasn't long before George packed his bags and left the family home in Lakenham to live with his lady-friend by the sea. But getting to the store now meant an early morning train journey daily. Exhausted and unsettled, George is plagued with doubts and second thoughts. He misses his comfortable Georgian home, his two little daughters, Lena and Mildred, his four servants, and yes, even his wife. Just two days ago, George wrote to Emma asking that they might get back together, and to show good faith offered to guarantee her as the sole beneficiary of his estate should he die. As yet he has received no response. Emma must be still angry with him. George resolves to return to Yarmouth this evening on the 9.10 pm express and tell his mistress that it is all over between them. Meantime he has well-to-do discerning customers to attend to, if anyone should decide to venture out in this monsoon.

*****

At the Bath Hotel in Yarmouth, set high on the clifftop known as The Denes, proprietor George Colk ensures that his gentleman guest from London enjoys a hearty breakfast. George has recommended that he perhaps visit Norwich today, especially in view of the inclement conditions. George is proud of his establishment, built in 1759, boasting seawater baths and an assembly room for tea parties and balls. His guest had registered as Richard Slade, an architect, staying for just a few days. Most probably in his thirties and travelling alone, Mr Slade had yesterday swum in the sea and taken the air on Wellington Pier. As he left for Yarmouth station this morning, he advised his host that he would return on the evening train from Norwich, and could a light supper be prepared for his arrival? It would be George's pleasure. The pair bid each other farewell.

# Thursday, 10 September 1874
# Thorpe-Next-Norwich

From the very first I took a great liking for Norwich, which the lapse of time did not diminish – in fact, I believe that had there been a wider choice of employment I should have settled down for life under the shadow of the cathedral. I found much solace and delight in the surrounding country; in particular the village of Thorpe appealed to me with ever-fresh charms. I have always regarded it as the prettiest village in the country. The charming old church, the red-tiled houses, the green slopes running down to the river's edge, backed by high wooded land, with Whitlingham in the foreground, all combine to produce a scene of exquisite peacefulness and beauty. Even today, after a lapse of forty years, I can never pass the view without renewed admiration.

(Henry Broadhurst MP, *The story of his life from a stonemason's bench to the treasury bench*, 1901)

Pub landlord John Hart almost despairs as he surveys the raven skies looming over the river. Since the good weather broke, a week or so ago, his takings are well down. It looks as if the summer is over. John took on the reins at the popular Thorpe Gardens and Three Tuns in 1868, when landlord Charles Miller sold up and left. The pub is well known throughout Norfolk for its extensive riverside gardens; a favourite spot for locals and visitors alike since around 1830. The public events held at the pub are legendary, especially the annual summer Thorpe Regatta, in 1856 reputedly attracting a record crowd of 7,000 people. From his second summer at the pub, John had carried on the tradition, until two years ago when a crowd of unruly drinkers got out of hand and spoilt it for the rest. Today, with this rain, he'll be lucky to attract even his regular drinkers. If business doesn't improve he might consider closing up early.

Every day trains thunder across Thorpe Island along the single line track, slowing down to cross the 200ft wooden bridge, set directly above his pub, then picking up speed as they progress towards the coast or city. There has been considerable activity on the bridge of late. Gangs of workmen have been removing the railings, while they lay iron girders, required to accommodate the much-anticipated second set of rails. Once the inspectors pass these as safe, the racket from the passing trains will inevitably increase, as they cross each other on the new double line. John is not looking forward to that.

John Hart's friend and neighbour, Master Boat builder Stephen Field, is equally despondent about business prospects today. Not much chance of anyone hiring his pleasure boat. Thirty years earlier Stephen had been a proficient sculler, winning trophies and cash prizes, but even *he* wouldn't risk taking a boat out on the river in this deluge. But he has plenty of work to see to in his boathouse. At least he'll be dry and far from the chaos of his home life. His wife Maria had been coping with the five children admirably, but since the arrival of 9-month-old Frederick, any routine was proving increasingly challenging. Stephen had once enjoyed a thriving boat-building business over at Carrow Road, before Jeremiah Colman and Eastern Counties Railway between them bought up the land. Not that he was bitter; he enjoyed village life. From his workshop on the opposite side of the railway line, just east of John's pub, Stephen can hear the trains travelling to and from Yarmouth. First one way, then the other. The sound always strikes a nerve. Maybe he will join his friend John Hart later that evening for a jug of his best beer. That was something to look forward to.

*****

Further east still, stand the imposing yet intimidating buildings of The Norfolk County Lunatic Asylum. Dr William Hills has been the medical superintendent since 1861, appointed when just 33 years old. Later today he is expecting a special visitor, his new friend and colleague Dr Charles Owens, all the way from Diss in South Norfolk. The two men had first met during August, at the memorable grand dinner to celebrate the end of the medical conference, hosted by Jeremiah Colman at his factory School House.

Dr Hills had been asking colleagues about young Dr Owens, discovering that he had been born in Montreal in Canada to British parents. His impressive string of medical qualifications result from studies in Brussels, Dublin and Edinburgh and he had begun his medical career as a house surgeon at a hospital in Dover. Now he is the junior partner at old Dr Barton's practice in Stratton St Mary and, interestingly, a keen member of his village cricket team. Dr Hills looks forward to sharing an excellent port and indulging in a cigar later that evening, while exchanging views on medical matters of the day. He is convinced that there is plenty more to learn about his young visitor. Particularly, does he bat or bowl? But first, Dr Hills has to see to his morning rounds at the asylum. Duty before pleasure, that's the thing. This evening he can relax.

18

# Chapter 3

# Collision Course

## Evening – Thursday, 10 September 1874

If there is one thing that schoolmaster Reverend Horace Booty cannot abide, it is foul language. Particularly within earshot of his good lady wife Sarah and their impressionable 10-year-old son, also named Horace. At Yarmouth station it is just past 9.00 pm, the platform is filling up with men, women and children heading home to Norwich. As the Booty family huddle together in a draughty third-class carriage, awaiting the departure of the 9.10 pm service, the blaspheming from a group of particularly rough fellows leaves Horace no choice. As Master of the Norwich Presbyterian School in Calvert Street, his duty is to protect the innocents. With just moments to go before the flag is raised, the good Reverend bundles his charges out of the carriage, into the pouring rain, stumbling towards the rear of the train, anxiously looking for vacant third-class seats, while pleading with the guard to delay the off. It takes Horace some time to catch his breath.

In another third-class carriage, just behind the brake van, squeezed onto the hard narrow benches, sit a disparate group of weary and wet travellers. William Green, 49, a bookseller and stationer, stocks anti-popish books in his shop in White Lion Street in Norwich. He is returning home, accompanied by his wife Susanna and her two spinster sisters, Caroline and Harriott Dent. Caroline is 45 years old, a governess working for a wealthy farmer in the parish of Earlham, just west of the city. Her much younger sibling, 26-year-old Harriott, is a schoolmistress visiting from her home in Preston Deanery near Northampton. Throughout the long day, Mr Green has suffered the constant chatter of the three sisters, each of them seemingly unperturbed by their mud-splattered hems, or limp feathers and ribbons hanging from their bonnets. His wife's white Holland dress had looked most attractive first thing this morning. Not so

19

anymore. It is difficult to get comfortable. The carriage appears full of damp, steaming overcoats and despite the definite chill, the glass on the tiny windows drip with condensation, the smell of body odour and stale tobacco obliging the ladies to clasp lace handkerchiefs to their nostrils.

*****

Unfortunately for Mr Green, there are two other members of the fairer sex in his carriage. Two attractive young ladies are conversing, their voices raised over the howling gale outside. That which Mr Green can overhear, he finds both charming and distracting. Miss Ellen Ramsdale is 18, described later in the *East Anglian Handbook for 1875*, as possessing 'considerable personal attractions'. She has enjoyed visiting her guardian, Mr Rose and is content to pass the tedium of the return journey sharing light dialogue with fellow female passenger, Miss Elizabeth Smith, a 24-year-old dressmaker from Regent's Park in London. Ellen is fascinated to hear about the emerging fashions in the capital, finding Elizabeth happy to share the gossip. However, it is unlikely that Ellen will share family secrets with a stranger, especially concerning her mother's chequered past.

Ellen's mother, Mary Ann (née Dawson), was a Yorkshire girl born in 1830. Her father was a 'Gentleman', quite possibly living off investments or income from land or property. As a young woman, Mary moved south to East Dereham in Norfolk, a small town just four miles to the west of the magnificent fifteenth-century Elsing Hall, the ancestral home of the Browne family. Just five days before Christmas in 1852, the unmarried 22-year-old Mary gave birth to a child, her confinement taking place in Great Yarmouth, over thirty miles from her home. The baby's name was recorded as Amelia Mary Ann Browne Dawson. Was there a whiff of scandal in the village of Elsing surrounding the fine young man living at the big house?

Twelve months earlier, having just reached his majority, on the death of his father, Richard Charles Browne became the Lord of the Manor, inheriting Elsing Hall along with 345 acres of prime farming land. He immediately instructed prominent architect Thomas Jeckyll to renovate and redesign the property, adding tall Elizabethan style chimneys and decorative flint work to walls. As a landowner, Richard's life became one long round of social commitments, staffing issues, tenants and paperwork. Only a year or two later, he was made a Justice of the Peace. It is unlikely that anyone knew of Richard's clandestine life. Once Mary had given birth to his illegitimate daughter, Richard arranged for her and his baby to live in a modest house at 50 Queen's Road, Yarmouth, cared for by a maidservant. They were geographically close enough for Richard to visit, but far enough away from East Dereham so as not to arouse suspicion. When completing her entry in the 1851 census return, Mary gave the baby's name as Amelia Dawson, her official birth name of Browne discreetly excluded from the detail.

Meanwhile, in East Dereham, Robert Ramsdale, the 31-year-old unmarried son of a retired leather worker, still lived with his parents Thomas and Margaret, and his two siblings in Quebec Street, East Dereham. Robert was a successful coal merchant, employing two local men, while his older brother Matthias had followed their father into the leather trade. The circumstances of how Robert and Mary-Ann met are unknown, but meet they did, for by the autumn of 1855, Mary, already a single mother, was pregnant again, this time with Robert's child. Robert had now improved his position, becoming not only a promising and ambitious auctioneer, but also the local agent for the Phoenix Fire Assurance Company. It was imperative that the couple avoid any scandal. A discreet notice of a marriage appeared in the Norwich Mercury dated 15 December 1855, stating: 'Lately, at St Peter's Cornhill, London, Mr Robert Ramsdale of East Dereham to Miss Mary Dawson.'

The newlyweds returned to East Dereham, where Mary's second daughter was born early in 1856. They named her Ellen Eugenie Ramsdale. Robert was now supporting a wife, a stepdaughter and a baby. Amelia, although the eldest child, could never be Robert's heir. Whether Robert was aware of the identity of Amelia's father, or if Richard Browne ever visited his child may never be known. Despite these complications, Robert continued to build up his East Dereham auction business, dealing in all types of properties and land. But tragedy was not far away. When Ellen was only 3 years old, her mother was widowed. Robert died unexpectedly on 25 November 1859, after a short illness. He was not yet 40. His final wishes were laid out clearly in his will.

> I give and bequeath all the residue of my personal estate, whatsoever and wheresoever situate unto my dear Wife

Mary for her own absolute use and benefit. ... and to pay the residue of all rents and profits unto my said Wife for her life for her own absolute use and benefit independent of any husband with whom she may hereafter intermarry and without being in any manner subject to his debts, control or engagements.

(Last Will and Testament of Robert Ramsdale,
dated 8 November 1856, Norfolk Record Office.)

Was Robert referring to Amelia's natural father as he wrote those words? He also provided for any existing and future legitimate children, monies and properties to be held in trust until they were 21. Ellen was his sole heir, her destiny to inherit a substantial income once she reached her majority.

The census for 1861 provides further evidence of Amelia's paternity. On this occasion, now a widow, Mary transparently registers her eldest daughter as Amelia M. Browne. At Elsing Hall, Richard Browne was living the life of a wealthy eligible Lord of the Manor, providing a home for his mother and two sisters. Three years later, Mary was pregnant once again. The child was a boy, born in Ipswich in Suffolk on 26 December 1863. The boy is recorded as Anthony Charles and the identity of the father set down as Richard Charles Browne, a Land Owner. Although their relationship has most definitely been rekindled, the couple now having two children, class divides and social conventions make it inconceivable that Richard and Mary could ever become husband and wife.

By the end of the 1860s, Mary has either bought, or been gifted, a house in the new development of Essex Street in Norwich where she resides with her three children. In the 1871 census, Mary records her 7-year-old son, as her 'Godson', maybe unwilling to, or prevented from, admitting her boy's illegitimacy. No, Ellen would certainly not be giving away details of her family history to her inquisitive travelling companion.

*****

Sitting behind the two young women, are the two NCOs from the West Norfolk Militia, Robert Ward and Frederick Cassell, discussing the day's sport. Although not wearing uniform, it is clear from their bearing, distinctive facial hair and topics of conversation, that they are military men. They have enjoyed some success while angling, despite the challenge of discriminating between fish rings and raindrops. The fine specimens of bream and roach, wrapped inside newspaper, tucked safely inside their cloth tackle bags, are testament to that. There had been plenty of tales to tell over the long hours on the damp riverbank.

# Colour Sergeant Robert Ward

Robert was the third child of Robert Ward, a gardener from the ancient Suffolk market of Harleston. Already having two daughters, Robert senior and his wife Rebecca were delighted, at last, to produce a son. In 1822, the town was a bustling place, with a popular Wednesday market. Situated on the main coaching route from London to Great Yarmouth, there were good number of thriving hotels and inns. Robert was baptised, not in the parish church as were his two elder sisters, but at the Congregationalist chapel in nearby Mendham.

For much of his life, Robert had helped his father with gardening and odd jobs around the village, until around 1844 when he took an oath of allegiance to the Queen, signing up for a twenty-one-year period in the celebrated Coldstream Regiment, posted to the 2nd Battalion. By committing to such a long period, men were guaranteed a pension on discharge. As a new recruit, Robert earned one shilling a day, from which he was expected to pay for rations, clothing and medical services. In March 1849, Robert, now ranked as Corporal, was billeted at The Tower of London, the 2nd Battalion kept there in readiness to intervene at any outbreak of civil unrest.

In July that year Robert married Ann Cornett, a woman nine years his senior, born in Devon and now a domestic servant working in the quiet village of Cricklewood. The ceremony was held just a mile from the Tower, at the parish church of St Leonard's Shoreditch. As a country girl, Ann would be overwhelmed by its soaring steeple, giant Tuscan style portico, parish stocks and whipping post. Robert and Ann spent the next two decades following the Army's six monthly routine of battalions moving between barracks, including Wellington, Portman Street and

St George's in London, as well as Windsor and Winchester. Very few wives were permitted to live in barracks, soldiers were expected to arrange accommodation for their families. In 1851, Ann was lodging two miles from Wellington Barracks, at 90 York Street, Westminster. On the day of the census, 35-year-old Ann had a visitor, her spinster sister-in-law Eliza. It is likely that the two women offered each other support, company and conversation.

From February 1854, Robert's colleagues in the 1st Battalion of the Coldstream Guards, mobilised by ship to Malta, as a show of force in anticipation of hostilities between Russia and Turkey. The men of the 2nd Battalion were ordered to remain at home on domestic duties. There is no evidence that Robert ever saw any action overseas. By the spring of 1855, now aged 42, Ann was finally pregnant, their son Robert John, born during December. Tragically, she died only a few weeks later, Robert passing the infant into the hands of brother Edward and new wife Elizabeth.

Four years later, on 11 July 1860, Robert remarried. His bride was a younger woman, 28-year-old Eliza Stribblehill, the daughter of a Marylebone watchmaker. With a new mother for his son, Robert reclaimed 4-year-old Robert John from his brother. Whether Robert requested a transfer to Norwich is unknown, but by 1861 the family of three were living in Union Place, off Rupert Street in the Heigham District of the city. Robert was now recorded as holding the rank of sergeant, most probably engaged in training members of the Norfolk Artillery Militia. Although he would have spent much of his time at the recently opened barracks at Ivory House in All Saints Green, Robert was able to increase his family; Eliza giving birth to three children over the next four years.

In January 1865, while Eliza was pregnant with her third child, Robert's twenty-one-year term with the Coldstream Guards came to an end. He had received five good conduct badges, never been entered in the Regimental Defaulter's Book or tried by Court Martial. Had he stayed on, he could have expected a further promotion. Instead, he applied for a voluntary discharge, taking a pension of two shillings a day. Over his time in the British Army, Robert had kept his nose clean and avoided overseas action, disgrace, injury or, most importantly, death. He was now a free man. That summer, daughter Martha Louisa was welcomed into the family. Sadly the year did not end well, when Robert's octogenarian father died in November, the result of an unexplained accident in Suffolk. After a lifetime spent in Harleston, the old man's funeral attracted many mourners.

Having officially been discharged from the British Army, Robert applied to join the 1st Battalion Western Regiment of the Norfolk Militia, known more simply as the West Norfolk Militia. He was given a brand new uniform and the rank of staff sergeant, at a salary of 16 shillings a week. He could choose to supplement his income by training new recruits, each man earning him 5 shillings. Occasionally, he was sent away from Norwich on a recruitment mission, his expenses paid by the government. One of his duties was as a marker during rifle practice, repeatedly setting up targets against mounds of earth known as butts. For performing this somewhat perilous task, Robert received a further 5 shillings a day. An industrious and hard-working man, Robert also took on work as a gardener at two shillings a day, and saved money by repairing the family's shoes and boots.

At the end of 1873, it is probable that Robert was among those at Chapelfield Road Drill Hall, welcoming a new volunteer, Sergeant Major Frederick Cassell. Frederick may have been impressed by this cavernous building with its vaulted beamed ceiling and impressive balcony, decorated with regimental badges, from where the officers looked down upon the men. Frederick was nine years younger than Robert but senior in rank, recently discharged from the Grenadier Guards. The two men quickly discovered that they shared a passion for coarse fishing. So their friendship began.

# Sergeant Major Frederick Cassell

For Frederick Cassell, life began in 1831 in the small rural community of Islington in West Norfolk, set in remote marshlands on the west bank of the River Ouse, a two-hour walk south from King's Lynn. The son of labourer George Cassell and his wife Honor Claxton, at 20 years of age Frederick joined the legendary 1st Regiment of Foot Guards, colloquially known throughout the world as The Grenadier Guards. With the minimum height requirement for the 1st Foot being 6ft 2in, we know that Frederick was a tall young man. The Army recruiters preferred the country recruits; their strength and 'slow turn of mind in keeping with the requirements of a private soldier'

(The Diehards.co.uk). Within a year, Britain and France were at war with Russia, a conflict that became known as the Crimean War.

In November 1854, following his basic training and a year after the onset of war, Private Cassell was deployed overseas to join his company, the 3rd Battalion Grenadier Guards, along with soldiers from companies such as 1st Battalion Coldstream Guards and Scots Fusiliers. Frederick's world became one of drill, marching, boredom, perishing cold, flies, vermin, inadequate pay and rations, grumbling, drunkenness and indiscipline, outbreaks of disease including cholera, witnessing colleagues imprisoned or flogged, sleeping in stinking clothes under bell tents, constantly faced with the real threat of bloody injury or death.

Frederick arrived too late to see action at the successful battles of Alma and Inkerman, or thankfully the defeat at Balaklava. Instead he was deployed to assist with the legendary Siege of Sevastopol, already two months in, an effort by the Allies to take this strategic Russian port, the home of the Tsar's Black Sea Fleet. Frederick took his turn, often under cannon- or rifle-fire, to dig trenches and erect gun batteries on the approach to the city walls, his grey woollen greatcoat offering no protection against the heavy rains and snow of two seasons. Following a devastating winter, conditions improved in the spring of 1855, leading to a further six months of mixed fortunes on both sides before, on 11 September, the Russians burned the remaining ships of the Black Sea Fleet, essentially showing the white flag. The siege was effectively over. For the part he played, Frederick was awarded both the Turkish medal and a Crimean Medal, including a coveted clasp for his time at Sevastopol. However, despite those honours, Frederick did not come out of Crimea with a totally unblemished record, his name appearing twice in the Regimental Defaulters Book and being twice convicted by Courts Martial.

Frederick's overseas service 'in the East' is recorded as being some 221 days, terminating on 1 July 1856, three months after the Treaty of Paris, resolving the Crimean War as a victory for the Allies. Immediately on his return from the Crimea, Frederick found himself about to be a father. We must assume that he had been granted some home leave at the end of the Sevastopol Siege, when he came to 'know' a young lady, the result being that his first child, John, was born in Knightsbridge. The baby's mother was Eleanor Sebbage, a domestic servant working in St Pancras in London for a wealthy Scottish publisher and bookseller.

Frederick and Eleanor were married on 19 January 1857 in All Saints Church, Westminster, when their baby was about 6 months old. It is unlikely that the young woman was fully prepared for the life of a soldier's wife. Eleanor was intimately familiar with living 'downstairs' as part of a group of domestic servants, but she faced the very different prospect of travelling the country, living in lodgings or in overcrowded barrack buildings. Here, privacy was limited, separation from the ranks achieved only by blankets slung over a line. There were merely basic amenities and as a woman, Ann was expected to take on her share of domestic duties, such as laundry, on behalf of dozens of men. In March 1859, with Frederick billeted at the dilapidated Portman Square Barracks in Marylebone, his son Frederick William was born.

By the time of the 1861 census, both Frederick and Eleanor are recorded as living in barracks in Mitcham Road, Croydon, along with 6-year-old John, Frederick William 2, and Eleanor 9 months (born in Dublin during an earlier posting). It is probable that their daughter died shortly after her birth. For many years ahead, the daily lives of Eleanor and her children were dominated by the sound of marching boots, rigorous daily routines signalled by deafening bugle calls, sergeant majors shouting instructions, horses, barking dogs, boisterous young men returning drunk after dark, noisy band practice and the stench of the shared latrines.

By January 1862, with his promotion to Sergeant, Frederick and his family was transferred again to St John's Barracks in London, where another daughter, Emma, was born and baptised. Four years later, while posted to Windsor, as part of the protection detail for the royal family, the Cassell family is complete, with the birth of George William.

When Frederick's eldest son John reached 14, he chose to train as a drum-boy under the protection of Colour Sergeant Edward Bishop at Wellington Old Barracks. When his parents were transferred yet again, John did not go with them.

Frederick's 21-year military career was coming to an end. On 20 October 1873, Frederick received his discharge papers. He received a severance gratuity of £10, twice that of Robert Ward, reflecting his seniority and medals for active service. Frederick was awarded the rank of colour sergeant, an honour reserved for senior sergeants, with only one allowed in each company. This accolade, and a pension of two shillings a day for life, marked the end of Frederick's long service to his country.

Around the end of 1873, Frederick moved his family to Norwich, joining the West Norfolk Militia as a sergeant major, his rank and experience meriting a payment of £1 *2s 6d* a week, his new friend Robert Ward, following his promotion to colour sergeant, was earning only 16*s* 4*d* a week. Frederick and his family moved into quarters at the Militia Barracks in All Saints Green. Again, there would be little privacy but this was balanced against free rent, rations, fuel and no taxes to pay. With his income looking good, Frederick was confident of creating a comfortable future for his growing family.

# Jane Ann Faulkner

Domestic servant Jane Ann Faulkner rides alone in a third-class carriage. Life has not blessed her with wealth or status, but she has recently improved her situation. She is now a general servant working for Robert Rust, the respected proprietor of a Stone and Monumental Masonry business, trading out of Prince of Wales Street, Norwich, where he employs eight men. Jane was born in January 1843 in the village of Sprowston, just outside the city, her parentage uncertain. With no legal requirement to register a birth until 1875, information on Jane is scant, but it is likely that she was the illegitimate child of Jane Ann Faulkner, the daughter of Elizabeth Faulkner, an impoverished widow, originally from Kent. We can speculate that both women cared for little Jane Ann until she was 5 years old when her mother died, leaving her grandmother to raise her as her own in Sprowston. Jane Ann faced further heartbreak at the age of 9, when her grandmother Elizabeth died aged 76, worn out from a lifetime of hardship and loss.

It is uncertain who then cared for the child, but by the time she was 18, Jane was working as a house servant in the Sprowston Road, home of Lime Burner Paul Edwards. Here Jane attended not only to Mr Edwards and his wife, but also their married son, his wife and two small children. Ten years on and Jane was lodging with an elderly widow, in the St Michael Coslany Alms Houses in West Pottergate Street, eking out a living as a charwoman. This new post with Mr and Mrs Rust is a real step up and Jane is confident that life can only get better.

# Russell William Skinner

Russell William Skinner would dearly love to read his newspaper. But apart from the fact that there is no light in his second-class carriage, he also finds himself alongside two of his business friends, brothers George and Alfred Page. It would be most ill-mannered to remove himself from the conversation.

Russell's story begins at the Swaffling Rectory in Suffolk, during the summer of 1839. His father, Reverend Russell Skinner, had been Rector for just four years. Russell was the third child, growing up with two older sisters in this small rural village, situated in the beautiful valley of the River Alde. His father's marriage in 1834 to Violetta Williams had united two great dynasties. Reverend Skinner was descended from an ancient Norman family, mentioned in the Domesday Book, whose close relatives included a number of decorated high-ranking officers in the British Army. Violetta's family were landed gentry, originally from Oxfordshire. The combination of inherited wealth meant that, on his arrival in Swaffling a year after his wedding, the new vicar could easily afford to immediately set about restoring the church, adding a vestry, building a school and enlarging the rectory house and grounds. During his forty years serving his parishioners, he was well loved and admired, later described in his obituary as being 'singularly, transparent, childlike and trustful'. (*Ipswich Journal*, 20 August 1881)

Russell junior was sent to boarding school in Brighton, before entering Clare College, Cambridge in 1858, the same year as his sister Lucy married coal merchant and businessman Edmund Harnick Marriott. Three years later Russell's university studies were interrupted, when Lucy died aged just 24, giving birth to her second child. Her passing was a terrible shock to family, friends and the parishioners of Sweffling. Her parents naturally gave refuge to their grieving son-in-law, offering him and his two tiny children a home in the rectory.

Despite this family tragedy, by 1868 Russell had achieved both a Bachelor's and a Master's degree. While at Cambridge he met Annie, the daughter of the late Henry Foster, a successful brewer of wine and spirits. The couple married at St Andrews Church in April 1869, the service led by Annie's Uncle, the Principal of Brighton College, with Russell's father proud to assist at the ceremony. Now his marital status was secure, Russell set about taking on his most ambitious project yet: the treacherous sea voyage to Argentina in South America; his dream was to buy land and breed sheep.

By early 1871, Russell was making a success of his venture, able to buy a property in the fashionable area of Eaton, on the edge of Norwich. Within two years the couple were blessed with two children, a daughter Maude, and son, Russell Foster. When Russell was attending to his farms in Argentina, Annie remained at home, caring for her children with the help of a young nurse, housemaid and cook. In August 1874, Russell returned to Norwich, glad to be home following an extended business trip.

Having once again spent the day away from home, he is looking forward to spending time with his wife and two young children. Tonight he hopes Maude and Russell will be allowed to stay up beyond their usual bedtime, so that he can say goodnight.

# George and Alfred Page

Russell's companions, George and Alfred Page, despite being brothers, are two very different individuals. The younger of the two, Alfred, is lively and light-hearted, full of conversation and fun. George, on the other hand, is more introverted, often morose, seemingly carrying the cares of the world on his shoulders. From the age of 14, George worked in his father's expanding leather business, starting as an apprentice and becoming a full partner at 23. Conditions for the workforce were challenging; tanning, cutting and shaping animal hides, while the foul, pungent and penetrating smells of urine, rotting flesh and stagnant water filled their noses and their lungs. George would not have chosen this profession, but as the eldest son he had no choice.

As the younger son, Alfred was free from any such obligations. At 20, he joined the respected Norwich brush maker Henry Rogers. Henry had two daughters but no sons, and as he approached 50 he sought a reliable younger man to learn the brush business and ensure the continuation of the business after his retirement. Alfred accepted Henry's generous offer and the Wensum Street brush factory became known as Rogers & Page, employing twelve men and two boys. Over the next few years Alfred worked hard, learning all there was to know about treadle lathes, turning tools, warming pitch, positioning bristles and book-keeping. While

George worked reluctantly in the leather trade under the watchful eye of his father, Alfred began his rise through the layers of Norwich society.

Whereas George was a lifelong bachelor, his brother Alfred married Priscilla Alexander in May 1861. The bride was an excellent match, the daughter of an Independent Minister from St George's parish in Colegate. Five years later the couple had a daughter, Ethel. With business doing well, Alfred bought a grand house on the fashionable St Clement's Hill, employing a general servant and a nursemaid for 5-year-old Ethel. Their neighbours included the cream of the Norwich upper classes including gentlemen, landowners and solicitors. Rogers & Page rapidly expanded, by 1871 employing thirty-three men, nineteen boys and thirty-eight women. George, on the other hand, lived more modestly, in the middle-class area of Unthank Road, supporting his two spinster sisters with the help of one domestic servant.

Following the death of senior partner, Henry Rogers, in March 1874, Alfred now struggles to juggle his responsibilities. Not only is he in complete charge of the brush business, but also remains a joint trustee for the family currier business and is a conscientious Liberal councillor. It is local knowledge that Alfred is the more savvy and successful of the two Page brothers. Alfred is conscious of this too, carrying a burden of responsibility for his somewhat inept big brother, who is constantly suffocated by the overzealous supervision of their aging father. The brothers have a lot to discuss on their way home to Norwich this evening.

# John Beart

A successful draper from the pretty Suffolk coastal town of Aldeburgh, John Beart is travelling in the relative comfort of first class, heading towards Norwich. A genial, portly gentleman of middle years, John has a smile for everyone. Living on the edge of the North Sea means he is well acquainted with squally weather. John was the fifth of six children, born in the small Suffolk town of Wickham Market, twelve miles inland from Aldeburgh. When he was about 20, around 1836, John moved to Aldeburgh to join his older brother James, who for eight years had been trading as James Beart, Grocer and Linen Draper. Here he met Mary Hunt, the eldest daughter of a self-made shipbuilder, making her his wife at the end of 1837.

With the rapid expansion of this historical coastal town and its rebranding as a seaside resort, John and Mary, despite having no capital to speak of, were opportunist in setting up their own small grocery and draper's business. James lent them some money and initially John rented Rowley House, on the High Street, at a cost of £35 a year (£4,000), keeping just one apprentice and one servant. The house needed much improvement, so they set about refurbishing the living conditions, in readiness for starting a family. First to arrive was Edward in 1839, followed by Henry in 1842, George two years later, Ada in 1845 and Charles in 1846. Rowley House quickly became too small to sustain either the growing family or the business, so John stretched his resources and rented one wing of the extensive Crabbe House, in the High Street, adding a plate-glass front behind which to display their superior wares to passing customers. The move to be proved profitable, with John adding millinery, dressmaking and wine to his list of services, very quickly becoming the principal business in Aldeburgh. Crabbe House became the central hub of the family businesses, acting as supplier to brother James' shop, with John responsible for negotiating, purchasing and keeping the books. The arrangement worked well until the early months of 1847, when the family faced tragedy three times over; first, James died suddenly, followed later by two of his young daughters, perhaps taken by the Typhus epidemic ravaging the world at that time.

As a proud and loving patriarch, John did not hesitate to offer a home to his brother's grieving widow, proving himself as a loyal husband and generous father. Despite his reputation in the town for prudence and frugality, he paid for his children's education and indulged them often with gifts and treats. At work John was always genial and welcoming, striving to improve his stock and maintain excellent service. There was a constant stream of customers, and his business acumen and attention to detail were rewarded with increasing profits. The family wanted for nothing. At the start of the 1860s John made a pragmatic decision to purchase the entirety of Crabbe House. Rowley House, still operating as a smaller concern, would have to be sold. On 21 September a property auction was held at the White Lion Hotel, offering:

A well-built Brick and Tiled Lodging House, sash fronted, pleasantly situated near the beach, and commanding an uninterrupted View of the Sea, with ample accommodation for a Genteel Family. Also another Brick and Tile dwelling house with outbuildings and land assigned to its use, adjoining the above, in the occupation of Mrs Beart, with an Old-established GROCER'S AND DRAPER'S SHOP, facing the High Street, wherein a good business has been carried on for many years. There is a small Garden attached.

(The *Suffolk Chronicle*, Saturday, 15 September 1860)

With the proceeds of the sale and a substantial mortgage, John could afford to purchase Crabbe House for £1,300, (£160,000). In the same year, his eldest son Edward left home to seek his own adventure when, financed by his father, he travelled to Hong Kong to work as a Commercial Agent. Second son Henry first became a ship builder, later persuading his father to set him up as the publican of the East Suffolk Hotel in the town. George, still a young man, continued to assist in the shop, happy to play at being the salesman, but shying away from the technicalities of buying stock, negotiating credit or 'mixing the teas'. Although George worked for free, he could always rely on his father for a generous handout when requested.

By 1870, John's daughter Ada was no longer physically able to run her school, closing the doors and the business. Westbourne Lodge became a comfortable home, initially for the two spinster sisters, but as their mother's health deteriorated, a place of peace and relaxation for their aging parents.

At 61, John is still active, happy to travel to other parts of the country to secure business deals. But he knows that in the not so distant future, he might have to be content with helping his community through his self-made wealth, continuing to take an active role in his church and attempt to extend his influence in local politics. His children have made him proud, what more could a man ask for?

# Marianne Elizabeth Murray

Marianne Elizabeth Murray and her attentive gentleman-friend sit as close together in the third-class carriage as etiquette will allow. Marianne is a talented milliner and seamstress who works with her tailor father James Murray, in Mariner's Lane, Norwich. Marianne is a true romantic and it is clear to all where her ambitions lie. While sheltering from the rain on the platform at Yarmouth, Marianne had watched enviously as another young couple mixed with their friends. She overheard much of their animated conversation, envying their high spirits, realising to her delight that Mr Scott and Miss Mileham were married that very morning, celebrating their nuptials at the coast with their closest friends.

Marianne's parents married in Norwich in 1845, moving in to shared accommodation in the deprived area of Globe Lane, where Marianne was born a year later. Her father, James Murray, was already establishing his business as a bespoke tailor in the cramped conditions of Globe Lane. James was skilled at his craft, tempting the aspiring middle classes away from the larger drapers' shops in the city, in their quest to imitate the iconic silhouette of an English Gentleman. Fashion was a means of portraying status and wealth. If an independent tailor could offer quality, speed and customer service at the right price, then there was plenty of work to be had. As business improved, James improved the family's living conditions, achieving a workroom where he could teach his daughter the skills of his trade. From 14 years old Marianne laboured long hours in poor light, perfecting the techniques of pattern cutting, accurate measurement, operating a sewing machine, selecting fabrics and perfecting a consistency when stitching. While her father continued creating frock coats and silk shirts, Marianne began to specialise in creating skirts, dresses and bonnets for fine ladies. Her section of the workroom was scattered with colour from her selection of silks, ribbons, braids, feathers and eye-catching decorations. In time they took on apprentices, the business improving year on year.

But in September 1874, at 27, Marianne feels the social stigma of remaining unmarried. Many of her closest friends have tied the knot, some already have children. But she is now at least 'walking out' with a young man, confident enough to introduce him as her fiancé. Time will tell. But cuddling as close as possible on the train will do very nicely for the moment.

## Reverend Henry Stacey and Mrs Mary Ann Stacey

Reverend Henry Stacey and his wife Mary Ann, have only recently returned to their birth city of Norwich, having lived and served in the Norfolk/Suffolk border town of Beccles for many decades. Their thirty-year marriage had sadly failed to produce children. Instead, Henry devoted himself to his Lord and the Congregational Chapel of Hungate in Beccles. Today the couple have celebrated their significant wedding anniversary with a day out in Yarmouth, sharing the joy with family friend and retired Norwich businessman James Hall. James has declined the offer to travel back with Henry and Mary Ann. James has other plans.

Mary Ann had enjoyed her life in Beccles where she was known as 'The Minister's Wife', demonstrating a mix of piety, generosity and patience. At the popular Friday market she was always stopping to talk with residents and traders. She felt safe in this ancient market town, with its broad, well-lit streets. Her husband Henry not only presided over services at the Congregational Independent Chapel, but also taught at the school and helped with afternoon preaching duties when required. In 1873 the much-loved Reverend John Flower retired after over forty years in the town. Such was his popularity that a subscription fund was established, and donations flooded in from all sections of the local community. At his retirement event, Reverend Flower was overwhelmed to be presented with a purse containing not the usual handful of gold sovereigns, but a stack of notes amounting to £325 (£39,000).

Henry had been considering applying for the now vacant role of Pastor, but a newcomer, Mr John Robinson, was appointed instead. His disappointment triggered a decision to retire, leave Beccles and return to Norwich, where they would join worshippers at the Congregational Church known as Chapel-in-the-Field, with its twin turrets and magnificent rose window. Their Beccles home was offered for sale at auction on 1 July 1874, along with china, glass, 200 volumes of books and a featherbed. Henry secured suitable accommodation in the prestigious Upper St Giles Street, where they would enjoy mixing with respected members of the Norwich professional classes. Today has been a good day taking the sea air, even if they did nearly get blown over on the front. They will sleep soundly tonight.

## Susanna Lincoln

Sitting alone in third class is Susanna Lincoln, a spinster of 35, resident cook at the Thorpe Road residence of Norwich Gentleman, Mr Arthur Coyte and his wife Theophilia. The grand four-storey villa is known as The Cedars, situated just up the hill from Thorpe railway station. Early this morning, Susanna had left instructions for housemaid Sarah Groom, placing her in charge of a stew pan of ox-cheek soup, which had been bubbling on the range from first light. Please God there have been no disasters. Susanna has been in service all of her adult life, first as a general servant for a widowed gentleman in her hometown of Attleborough, where she and her siblings were raised in Leys Lane, a vast area of agricultural land and woodland on the edge of the town.

As the eldest child, Susanna always knew her future would be 'in service', the majority of her wages sent home to help feed younger brothers and sisters. At 21 she worked within a short distance of her family home, but in the early 1860s, an opportunity arose to move into the city and work for the Coytes. Her master was a fair and kind employer, who was conscientious in his role as Overseer of the Poor for Thorpe. Hopefully Sarah has left some cold cuts in the larder. Susanna is feeling distinctly peckish.

# Dr Peter Eade

Towards the engine, sitting in relative comfort inside the first class compartment of the composite carriage, directly behind the laden fish truck, is Dr Peter Eade. He smiles as he spots the slumped figure of Richard Wentworth White, the spirited young dentist, snoring quietly. As Dr Eade settles into his seat, snuggling into his gabardine coat, he reflects on today's consultation with his patient in Yarmouth. It feels good to be back at work, now that the rigours and over indulgences of the BMA Conference are far behind him.

Born on 19 January 1825, in the Norfolk rural parish of Acle, mid-way between Norwich and Yarmouth, Peter has never lost his soft Norfolk accent, or his love of the great outdoors. As the only boy in a household of sisters, his father, a country physician from the nearby village of Blofield, was keen that his son should take up medicine. His schooldays were traumatic; he had been unable to deal with the discipline and cruelty experienced at the Yarmouth Proprietary Grammar School for Boys. He far preferred the time he spent with his father, learning how to dispense drugs, helping with minor surgical procedures, discovering anatomy through the dissection of rabbits and rats. In his free time he embraced country life; riding, boating, fishing, playing cricket in the village team and attending Blofield parish Church.

In 1844 Peter was entered as a medical student into King's College Hospital in London, where he excelled, winning many prizes. His ambition was aroused, knowing he could not be content working in a country practice. In 1856, he settled in the city, working first for the Norwich Dispensary for two years. When a vacancy arose for a Physician to work at the Norfolk and Norwich Hospital, Peter put himself forward as a candidate, securing the role. His lifelong association with the hospital had begun.

This evening, Dr Eade shares his compartment with a Mr Dimmock, the proprietor of the Fine Art Gallery at 66 London Street in the city. Mr Dimmock is looking forward to good news resulting from his recent press advertisement for a well-educated youth to join the gallery. Business is good, especially after the success of this year's Loan Collection of Works of Art, held during late August at St Andrew's Hall, and he could really do with another pair of hands in the workshop.

# Dr Edward Smith

Nearby sits Louisa Stevens, wife of Norwich Solicitor George Alden. Tonight she is travelling with her three children: Edith, 15, Walter, 14 and Alice, 11. She wishes the children would stop squabbling, she finds it difficult to cope. Her husband is detained yet again, at a meeting of the Perseverance Masonic Lodge in the city, where he has been a member for less than a year. George is always busy at something. Louisa recognises one of the gentlemen travelling in her first class carriage as being Dr Edward Smith from Surrey Street. Louisa is intrigued but is determined not to engage with him. In the opinion of many, Dr Smith is most certainly a charlatan or even a Quack. Although many people subscribe to Dr Smith's particular branch of medicine, others are sceptical. Dr Smith takes no notice of the woman's hostile glances.

Dr Edward Mark Smith is indeed a medical botanist and practitioner, known throughout East Anglia and beyond. As a child in the South Norfolk town of Diss, near the Suffolk border, his father was a Medicine Vender, enjoying a status in the town, and listed as the owner of a freehold house and land in Cock Street in 1844, an area in former times notorious for cock fighting. The street became a safer place when the barbaric sport was banned in 1835. As a boy, the colourful lotions and potions in his father's workshop fascinated Edward. He was never happier than when he was observing or assisting his father, or pouring over books written by renowned medical herbalists such as Cullen and Culpepper.

When Edward was 19, despite his father still having eight other mouths to feed, Mark paid for his son to study botany and medicine at the renowned Friedrich Schiller University in Jena, a small town in central Germany. It is probable that Edward was taught by Matthias Jakob Schleiden, a German Botanist, known for developing the ground-breaking concept that all living things are made up of microscopic units called cells. Edward spent four years in Germany before graduating and returning to England in 1846, wasting no time in finding a bride. Sarah Warne was the daughter of a retired cabinetmaker from Diss. The newlyweds moved into the house next door to his family home in Cock Street. There would be no children. In 1849 Mark Smith died and Edward inherited his business, determined to transform it into a more sophisticated and lucrative practice.

Within two years Edward was listed as a 'Medical Botanist practicing', the work paying well enough to keep a cook and two housemaids. He spent the following decade broadening his knowledge, improving his skills and building up his clientele. Consequently, by May 1866, he was ready to upgrade his business and take a city office in Stanley House, Surrey Street. His banner slogan in the classified section of local newspapers, read that Dr Smith could offer 'Hope for the Afflicted', promising 'A cure for the incurable', and advising that 'Dr Smith's system of treatment has proved itself to be the best adapted to those diseases hitherto considered incurable.' Glowing and compelling testimonials changed every week, including one alleged to be from a resident of Illinois in America, claiming that it was Dr Smith's herbal treatments that had 'cured his leg sores, saved his limb from amputation and restored his mobility'.

Edward was conscientious in his quest for success, travelling around the country opening surgeries in pubs and hotels in Cambridge, Ipswich and Bedford Square in London. He was even prepared to undertake special journeys to visit patients at any distance, particularly if they were afflicted by 'Scrofula, abscesses, scurvy, leprosy or diseases of an impure state of the blood.' In October 1866, however, the *London Gazette* exposed Edward as a bankrupt. Shortly afterwards, his case opened at the London Court of Bankruptcy with a long list of debts totalling an astonishing £41,000, (£4 million). Creditors included solicitors, auctioneers, printers, upholsterers and the *Suffolk Chronicle* and *Ipswich Journal*. The case for the prosecution centred upon a considerable sum owed to a city stockbroker, in return for a large number of shares, purchased by a broker on Edward's behalf, but as yet unpaid.

At a further hearing at the end of November, Edward narrowly escaped imprisonment, his solicitor persuading the judge to award his client protection from arrest, pending further investigation. Edward and his wife were under considerable strain for over four months, their future hanging in the balance. However, in February 1867, Edward's position improved considerably. The judge at the final sitting concluded that Edward's failure to pay his creditors had not been his fault. He had been unfairly induced to take shares in certain banks, which had since been wound up, with no opportunity for refunds. Edward's detailed business accounts, voluntarily filed, were agreed by the judge as 'accurate, correct and satisfactory', Edward's solicitor revealing that Edward would be settling out of court for a much lesser amount of £12,752, (£1.5 million) to be paid in quarterly instalments. The judge approved Edward's conduct and granted him an immediate order of discharge. Such was Edward's confidence of a good result that on the very same morning, his regular advertisement had appeared in the *Norfolk News*, complete with timetable of future surgeries. Dr Edward Smith was back in business.

Edward's mother-in-law died exactly a week after his case was dismissed. If he was hoping for a substantial legacy to help pay off his debts, then he was disappointed. However, twelve months later, on 26 February 1870, the *Norfolk News* carried an official statement from the Bank of England concerning an unclaimed dividend. It read:

> Application having been made to the Governors of the Bank of England to direct the payment of One Dividend on the sum of £1,546, 19s, 3d. [£183,000] Consolidated £3 per cent Annuities, heretofore standing in the name of EDWARD SMITH, Esquire, of Diss, Norfolk and which dividend was paid over to the Commissioners for the Reduction of the National Debt, in consequence of its having remained unclaimed since the 5th July 1859. Notice is hereby given

that, on the expiration of Three Months from this date, the said Dividend will be paid to Edward Smith, who has claimed the same, unless some other claimant shall sooner appear and make out his claim thereto.

On the assumption that no such person came forward, by the end of May Edward had come into money from an unexpected source. In view of his dire financial situation, it would have seemed prudent for Edward to sell his substantial mansion-house in fashionable Surrey Street. Instead, stubbornly refusing to give up, his press advertisements continued to promote extravagant claims. On Saturday, 5 September 1874, he listed his next out-of-town surgery as being on the following Tuesday in Ipswich. Unusually, the subsequent date was not until 16 September in London. Did Edward have alternative plans for those missing days, maybe taking a short break? Whatever the reason, on 10 September, having been to either Lowestoft or Great Yarmouth, Edward was returning home on the evening train.

# John Betts

In third class, Stoker John Betts smiled to himself, recalling moments from his half-day out with his family, rare moments of fun with his two small sons. To be truthful it had not proved easy amusing little Charles in the terrible weather. But the bracing sea air had blown away a few cobwebs, the toddler giggling while making footprints in the wet sand. Now, the young parents are exhausted and the train's arrival at Brundall gives them hope – not long now. Of all the passengers on the train that night, John probably knows more than most about the importance of keeping the engine's steam boilers running smoothly. As a fireman, his life revolves around checking the water level, ensuring it always remains above the copper crown-sheet of the firebox, the aim to avoid a boiler explosion. The gradient going through Thorpe often gives him a problem as the level changes constantly. It is also his responsibility to use the fuel efficiently, coke is expensive and a tight rein is kept on the amount available. While his engineman holds the chain of the fire door tightly in his hand, opening it for as short a time as possible, John's job is to throw in shovelfuls of coke, evenly distributing it throughout the fire. This way his driver will always have an adequate supply of steam at his disposal. The heat inside the cab and the hard physical labour makes the job almost unbearable, but it is well paid, with every opportunity to progress, even maybe to become a driver.

But tonight all this is the responsibility of a colleague. John can relax.

# Miss Mary Ann Taylor & Mrs Sarah Gilding

Mary Ann Taylor, 46, is the supervisor at the renowned and much patronised J.W. Caley, Drapers of Norwich. She has found herself a seat in the second-class compartment, near to the engine. A lifelong spinster, she is proud to be one of the longest serving members of staff. Having joined the firm twenty years ago, she had worked hard to progress to become Mr Caley's most valuable employee. The shop sells high quality fashionable clothing and silks, stockings, Norwich shawls, haberdashery and the like. But her domain is the bespoke dressmaking and mantle making departments, responsible as Supervisor, for the talented and hard-working women employed in the enormous workrooms at the rear of the shop. Queen Victoria is known to be an admirer of Caley's bonnets, and has purchased a number of their most exclusive designs, resulting in Caley's receiving the Royal Warrant, setting the store above all others in Norwich, even Mr Womack's establishment.

Mary Ann's early life and influences made her ideally suited to her role. A local girl, she was the third daughter of tailor William Taylor, originally from Wymondham in South Norfolk. Born in 1827, on the day after Christmas, Mary Ann was baptised into the non-conformist Wesleyan Methodist faith at the chapel in Calvert Street. By 1851, the family of five daughters and one son were living in Princes Street, three of the girls recorded as Dress Makers, one as a Milliner and Mary Ann as a Shop Maid. Her twenty-three-year career with Caley's was underway.

Throughout the summer of 1874, Mary Ann worked alongside her colleagues preparing for the first deliveries of early autumn fashions and accessories, helping to source and order items including wool poplins, Shetland and Bolivian serge, a variety of tweeds and other fashionable dress materials. Also expected were the usual stock of fur coats, and this year, a collection of sealskin jackets from Russia.

Mary Ann's married sister Adelaide and her brother-in-law, confectioner John Harboard, live in Great Yarmouth. She adores being the favourite Aunt of their boy and two girls, visiting whenever she can get time off work. To pass the time this evening, Mary Ann nods politely at the well-dressed lady sitting opposite, who appears to be travelling with her young daughter. Once her signals have been acknowledged, Mary Ann quickly ascertains that the woman is Sarah Gilding, 38 years old, born Sarah Smith in the mid-Norfolk village of Tunstead. Sarah introduces her little girl as 4-year-old Laura. Sarah is the wife of a London insurance agent, Charles Gilding. In the early years of their marriage, Sarah had loyally supported her husband through his initial but futile efforts at shoe-making and selling tea. But earlier this year, his brother Richard had been appointed as a director at the Pearl Assurance Company, immediately arranging a position for his struggling little brother. The future looks brighter. The couple also have two young sons, presently at home with their father in the Mile End Road in London. The two women enjoy a harmless gossip, while attempting to keep little Laura entertained. Mary Ann has an empathy with youngsters and today she relishes Laura's company, smiling as the young girl snuggles close to her mother's warm body, while impatiently kicking her plump little legs against the wooden seats.

*****

The service from Lowestoft had departed at 8.20 pm, many passengers having attended the popular Lowestoft Flower Show. The five carriages were hooked up to the mail train at the riverside village station of Reedham. The chatter among the flower lovers is of this final show of the season, held on the South Pier. If the weather had been kinder many would have stayed longer into the evening to listen to the concert from the 7th (Queen's Own) Hussars and enjoy a beer or two. After all, the Railway Company was providing a special excursion train, due to leave Lowestoft at 9.30 pm.

But as the temperature dropped, the winds increased and the waves beneath the pier grew more menacing, many decided to make their way home, be it to Yarmouth, Brundall or Norwich. It has been a great day out, Lowestoft enjoying far better weather than further inland; the standard of dahlias, roses, asters, stocks, carrots and lettuces deemed outstanding.

There had been exhibitors from well beyond the town, including Hemsby, Fritton, Somerleyton, Melton and Ipswich. A particular highlight was Mrs Leathes from Herringfleet Hall near Yarmouth, beating her husband the Colonel into second place, her excellent collection of pot herbs bagging her the trophy.

# Mr William Bransby Francis

Seated in one of these rear carriages is physician Mr William Bransby Francis. It has already been a long, cold ride from Lowestoft, his extremities stiff and numb from prolonged exposure to the damp. He reflects on his increasing age, considering when might be the right time to retire from medical practice. Despite being well respected among his colleagues, at nearly 60, he will soon have to consider his options. He has, however, enjoyed this rare day out with his wife, taking in the scents and the colours of the many flower exhibits displayed on the pier. Retirement could guarantee more days like this. He rather envies his wife staying on at the coast for a few days longer, hoping to benefit from the invigorating sea air.

William was born in the Suffolk village of Beccles in 1815. His father, Robert John Francis, a clergyman, was for forty years the Rector of Rollesby, a village near Yarmouth and the Chaplain to Beccles Gaol. As a young man, William was sent as a pupil to the well known Beccles surgeon William Henchman Crowfoot, whose family had been medical men for five generations. Dr Crowfoot was a keen botanist, passing on his knowledge and enthusiasm to his young student. William completed his medical education at Guy's Hospital in London, his first job after graduation was in Lowestoft. When a partnership opportunity with a general surgeon arose in Norwich, William applied, later succeeding to the practice when his partner passed away.

William never lost his interest in Botany, combining it with a passion for the recent invention known as photography. He is accredited with creating one of the earliest known medical photographs, a salted paper print, taken in 1845, of a human bladder containing fourteen urinary stones. At this time the Norfolk and Norwich Hospital was renowned for its collection of Urinary Calculi, held in its museum containing pathological and morbid parts, within which this pioneering photograph was taken. William was elected Vice-President of the Norwich Photographic Society for the years 1856 and 1857, his photos of Beccles Church, printed from waxed paper negatives, appearing in an exhibition of the society's work.

On Friday, 3 April 1846, William had married Jane Mathias, at Charles The Martyr Church in Plymouth. The groom was 31 and the bride 23. Jane was born in Calcutta, the daughter of Colonel John Mathias of the Indian Staff Corps. Jane looked after their domestic arrangements, while William built up his practice, at the same time contributing to a number of societies, sitting on various management committees. He was a founding member of the Norwich Pathological Society, meetings often held in the medical library of the County Asylum in Thorpe-Next-Norwich. In 1867, the Society was renamed as the Norwich Medico-Chirurgical Society, in which William played a leading part in drawing up the constitution and code of law. His good friend Dr Peter Eade was elected its first president and in the early years the meetings were held only on nights with a full moon, so that members could return home safely by moonlight.

Tonight, all these years later, the moon is lost behind a sky filled with black clouds. As he rests his eyes, William recalls his father enjoying a long retirement, eventually dying in 1869, at the extraordinary age of 94. William fancies that he might even improve on that.

\*\*\*\*\*

Exactly as timetabled at 9.26 pm, the mail train pulls into the riverside station of Brundall, marking the start of the single line into Trowse, eight miles to the east, heralding the approach into Thorpe Station. The new double track is complete, but annoyingly the Government inspector still hasn't arrived to certify the line as operational. Passenger Guard James Chapman, travelling from Lowestoft, stands in the entrance of his van, nine carriages from the engine. He keeps watch as some passengers disembark, while new travellers climb aboard, anxious to be out of the rain.

These new arrivals include a group of three gentlemen, Reverend Charles Morse, William Yaxley and Charles Gilman, anxiously searching for seats together in a first class compartment. The three men have spent the day sailing and fishing on the Yare near Brundall.

# Reverend Charles Morse

For a man fast-approaching 70, the Reverend Charles Morse is in fine fettle, described by his wife as being, 'in excellent health, displaying singular vitality and endowed with great strength' (*Norwich Mercury*, Wednesday, 7 April 1875). He is known to be a man of equable temperament, with a hearty appetite, never failing in his clerical duties. Charles has been the popular Rector of both St Michael's at Plea and St Mary Coslany churches in Norwich for decades. He is regularly invited to preach at other churches, often at a distance from Norwich. Charles is always willing to oblige, never concerned about the journey. He loves to spend time tending his small plot of land in Catton, weeding, pruning and planting. Married twice, he has fathered twelve children, the eldest now 39, his youngest just 20. Many in the city warmly remember his first wife Sophia, mother of seven children within ten years. Sophia had died in 1845, only a year after the birth of little Lucy. The Reverend had been distraught, his depth of feeling at her loss amply illustrated by the inscription on Sophia's stone memorial plaque, set on the inside wall near the vestry at St Michael at Plea Church.

> In a Vault beneath this vestry lie the interred remains of Sophia Susanna, wife of Charles Morse, Rector of this Parish who died March 4 1845, aged 34.
>
> Virtuous, kind and unassuming, she was beloved by all who knew her. The tenderest of mothers, the most affectionate and dutiful of wives. This tablet was erected to her memory by him who best knew her value and most deeply feels her loss, her disconsolate husband.
>
> (Findagrave.com)

With Sophia gone, Charles struggled to cope as a widower. In 1846 he took a second wife, Frances Colls, a young Irish woman originally from County Meath, just north of Dublin. Frances gave Charles a further five children, his home once again filled with young voices. Today he is indulging another of his passions, sailing on the delightful waters near Brundall, pleased when two of his dear friends agreed to accompany him.

# William Yaxley

Despite being thirty years younger than Reverend Morse, Church Warden William always enjoys his company, be it serving alongside him at Sunday morning communion at St Mary Coslany, or when out on one of their trips together, honoured to be counted among the Rector's many friends. William works at Beecheno's grocers shop in London Street, totally responsible for the day-to-day running since the sudden death of the owner in March. The wine and spirits licence was transferred to William's name in May and business is brisk, providing a modest annual income of around £400 (£45,000), enough to comfortably house and feed his wife and six children. The son of a publican, William was born just a year after his father Henry took over the King's Arms, in the busy working-class area of Botolph Street. His parents ran the business together for twenty years until Henry died in 1859, leaving his wife Elizabeth to carry on alone. William was quite used to meeting new people, but today, he will admit to having been a little daunted when told that on this occasion, the Reverend had invited the much-respected solicitor Charles Gilman to join them. William would have to be on his best behaviour.

# Charles Rackham Gilman

William Yaxley had every justification for being a little daunted by Charles Gilman. It was well known that the wealthy Gilman family could trace its Norfolk roots back as far as the sixteenth century, with the great Norfolk hero Nelson counted among their among the maternal ancestors. His father was Charles Suckling Gilman, a prominent Norwich solicitor and member of the Board of Guardians. As the oldest son, Charles had trained in his father's law firm, showing a preference and aptitude for the more risky insurance line of the law. He became fascinated by the success of the Railway Passengers' Assurance Company, the first of its kind in the world, which had opened in 1848. His shrewd mind saw great business potential and in 1856, aged only 23, Charles had the confidence to persuade a number of prominent Norwich citizens to invest in his new venture. Charles appointed his father as Manager, taking the role of Secretary for himself and on 8 September 1856, The Norwich and

London Accident Association issued its first policy to a George Forrester of Cathedral Close, a Land Agent. The reputation and prosperity of the company continues to grow year on year. Charles married in 1858, three children quickly following. William knows very little else about his companion today, but it is clear that Charles Gilman loves to sail.

*****

William Platford has been the stationmaster at Brundall for over eight years, before that he was eighteen months at Somerleyton. Every day, he sees to the safe working of up to twenty trains calling into his small rural station, not forgetting the occasional 'specials'. Brundall is known as a 'Meeting Station', where the double line from Reedham to Brundall meets with the single line on to Norwich. One of his special duties is to detain the mail train from Brundall until the down train from Norwich arrives. The only exception is when the train from London is late into Norwich, but his only happens a few times each month. Tonight Platford's 12-year-old son, William, is helping his father by monitoring the telegraph, something he does quite frequently. He is a good lad, never working the machine unless his father is in the room. On the train, Peter Eade peers out through the gloom, just able to make out the stationmaster approaching the driver's cab, passing up a piece of paper and mouthing a few words, before striding back to speak to the guard. Immediately, the green flag is lowered and the mail train pulls slowly away in a cloud of steam. For a moment Dr Eade wonders at this anomaly; this train is usually held at Brundall for far longer. But knowing the London train's a habit of arriving late into Norwich, he dismisses the thought. Young Mail Guard Ellis, busying himself in the mail van, has the same concern, but has no time to dwell on it. He has a truckload of parcels to sort before reaching Norwich.

Driver John Prior is nearly 50, married for thirty years, with five grown up children to show for it. He has seen two of them married and set up home, now delighting in his first grandchild, a girl named Edith, born in June last year. A Suffolk man, he was working on the land when he married Norfolk girl Sarah Ann Andrews in 1844. Their family began in the following year with baby Mary Ann, followed closely by a further daughter, Sarah Elizabeth, and three sons, William, John Robert and Andrew George in 1854. As soon as the babies began arriving, John knew he needed to improve his prospects. Having joined the railway as a labourer, he worked his way through the ranks with impressive speed; listed as an engine driver by the birth of his third son. Two baby daughters died as infants, both baptised as Emma, before the couple completed their family with Frederick in 1859, followed by Alice Harriet in 1864.

Ten years later and John's older children are adults. William has joined the railway as an engine fitter and another, John, works in the printing business. Their father has been working for the Great Eastern Railway for over twenty years, building a reputation as 'the steadiest and most trusted driver in the district'. John takes a keen interest in the rolling stock, knowing that tonight he is driving No.54, a good example of a W Class Single Outside Cylinder 2-2-2 tender engine, designed by the famous Robert Sinclair. This particular one was built exactly ten years ago and looks grand with its paintwork of GER pea green with shiny black bands, elaborately pierced metal splashers and 7ft 1in driving wheels. But her history is by no means spotless. Back in July 1865, when brand new, she successfully pulled the 5.00 pm out of Bishopsgate, but was then derailed between Hethersett and Trowse. She was subsequently patched up and frankly, looks as good as new.

John's fireman today is James Light, a single man of half John's age. Born in Southampton, James moved up to Norwich with his parents in or around 1849. The family now live in Wilderness Place, a heavily industrialised area of the city. James is the eldest of three boys, his brothers are Richard and George. Their father Isaac, a driver and fitter on the railway, was extremely proud when his two eldest, James and Richard, joined the service.

Ever since the beginning of the railways, it was common for sons to emulate their fathers, with railway dynasties enduring for generation after generation. It was common knowledge that railway companies favoured the children of existing employees who were of good character. But railway servants came from every walk of life. Literacy was no barrier, the improved pay and welfare benefits attracting farmworkers and labourers into the cities.

For Isaac and more recently for his sons, it meant working long and demanding shifts with limited pay, at first given the dirtiest and most dangerous tasks. In the cavernous steam sheds, young boys were taken on as 'divers', crawling into the cooled locomotive boiler with a wire brush, specifically to remove limescale and slime built up inside.

Those who made the grade could then progress to jobs such as engine cleaner, lamp-room boy, shunter, maintenance man, porter, pointsman and signalman. But the dream was to travel on the footplate, in control of a mighty engine, pulling goods or passengers from cities and towns, steaming through the countryside, admiring spectators waving and cheering. James was ambitious, determined that one day he too would be promoted to driver, hopefully ahead of his brother Richard.

On the command of Driver John Prior, James stokes the boiler as the train disappears out of sight, leaving the smell of burnt coal lingering in the air.

# Norwich Thorpe Station

It is 9.00 pm in Thorpe Station on the eastern edge of Norwich. Night Inspector Alfred Cooper arrives for his shift. The five-minute walk along the river from his home in Lollards Terrace, involved rain cascading down the back of his neck, a bombardment of early autumn leaves threatening to spill him over, debris scattered about in the near gale-force wind. Alfred is 45 years old, Suffolk born and bred, and has been working for Great Eastern Railway for fifteen years, most of that working the night shift. By age 23 Alfred was a rural police constable, living in police accommodation next door to the parsonage in the Suffolk hamlet of Hulver, four miles from Beccles. Within a year he had left the force, becoming an Inspector at the Harbour Works in Lowestoft. Here he met Louisa Balls, the daughter of a local stonemason, marrying on 7 September 1852 when his bride was seven months pregnant. Alfred James arrived in November. Looking for better prospects, Alfred senior joined Great Eastern Railways in 1861, and transferred to Norwich as a Night Inspector. The couple have lived in Norwich for thirteen years, and the family has expanded to six, Alfred, 21, now working as a Government Telegraph Clerk; Margaret, 16; Harry, 12; Louisa, 8; William, 6; and little Gustavus, still a 'toddlekins'. Three days ago was Alfred and Louisa's anniversary, the couple have been married for twenty-two years. Although the drudgery of working nights has never fazed Alfred, the life has been hard on his dear wife Louisa.

As Cooper enters the station forecourt, there is no sign of the London express. He grumbles to himself. It's due into the platform right about now, for departure at 9.10, but yet again it appears to be running late. He drops his sodden coat into his office, before walking up the covered platform to check in with his stationmaster, Henry Sproul. He keeps a look out for Inspector William Parker, due to finish his day shift. Parker's final responsibility is always to despatch the 9.10 down express to Yarmouth. Parker is nowhere to be seen. Alfred taps on Mr Sproul's door, entering to see him hurriedly signing pay sheets and letters, intent on getting them off on the mail train tonight.

Cooper collects up the jobs sheet for overnight, enquiring about the express. With no telegram having arrived, alerting them of any prolonged delay, they must assume it will be in very soon. The two men have a decision to make.

Cooper is impatient, only too aware that the mail will shortly be waiting at Brundall.

"What about having the mail up Sir?"

Mr Sproul checks his watch. It is 9.17. "When is the mail due at Brundall?"

"9.25."

Mr Sproul makes his decision.

"We will not have the mail up. Certainly not."

But Cooper is not convinced.

"You do know of the order allowing us to detain the 9.10 down train as late as 9.35?"

Mr Sproul, referring to the incoming London express, snaps back, "Alright, alright, we'll soon get her off."

Cooper, satisfied now that Sproul has conceded his point, leaves the room, turning towards the next-door telegraph office. Even with the deafening wind wailing around the platform, he can hear chatter and laughter inside. Cooper is instantly vexed. Wasn't Robson fined a day's pay only last year for breaking the rules when entertaining his sweetheart at work? He would have to keep an eye on that young man.

At exactly 9.22 Cooper knocks loudly on the telegraph wicket. There is no access from the platform into the Telegraph office, but there is a small window, with an aperture in it, known as the wicket, kept closed by a wooden shutter. It is through this that the public communicate with the telegraph operator when sending messages to friends or businesses. Robson has been on duty for just one hour of his twelve-hour night shift. He is not yet 18, but GER must have thought highly of him, transferring him to Norwich from London only fourteen months earlier. His job is as a General Clerk, but as an experienced telegraph operator the young man also acts as an agent for the Post Office. Cooper cannot help but wonder if it is too much responsibility for one so young. Robson leans over the desk, opening the wicket. Inspector Cooper is peering past him into the office, the scene confirming his suspicions. The compact space within appears to be full of young men, some of whom Alfred recognises, others he does not. The men freeze, aware that their presence is flouting regulations. Alfred is precise with his instruction.

"Tell Brundall to send the mail on to Norwich before the down train leaves."

Following procedure, Robson immediately writes down the message on a piece of paper. Normally, he would then hand the chit to his inspector for signature, before writing it in the 'Single Line Book'. The regulations are clear that a message should not be sent without an inspector's signature. In fact, if an inspector does not sign a message, any self-respecting railway servant would not act upon it. At that moment the sound of the express arriving at the platform alerts Cooper, who turns on his heel and hurries away, muttering something inaudible. Robson, presuming that Cooper intends returning within a few minutes, closes the wicket but does not fasten it. He asks his friend, John Keeble, to give up his chair. He needs to record the instruction in the book. Unable to see the clock, Robson asks Keeble to give him the time. Keeble replies, " 9.23". Robson rounds it up to 9.24. There are eight telegraph instruments in the office. Turning to the one used for single line messages to Brundall, he taps out the message, watching intently as the needles spelt out each letter in turn. Then, almost as an afterthought he added 'A. Cooper', before sending it up to Brundall.

Keeble is impressed by his friend's skill. He has no idea how to operate the delicate instrument. The reply comes back almost immediately.

"I will send the up mail train on to Norwich before the 9.10 pm down passenger train leaves Norwich. Signed W. Platford. Time received 9.25."

Again Keeble watches as his friend writes down the reply, before recording it again in the 'Single Line Book'. During this time the other young men, John Holroyd and Charles Donkin, continue their lively conversation, discussing the state of their lodgings, not at all concerned that they might be distracting Robson from his duties.

\*\*\*\*\*

# George Womack

With the late arrival of the express at Thorpe Station, the platform is filling up with frustrated passengers, desperate to head home on this dreadful night. The London express had been due in at 9.00 pm, with the connecting train to Yarmouth due out at 9.10. George Womack is returning to his lady friend in Yarmouth, after a day dealing with difficult clients at his draper's store in the city. Why did wet weather always make everyone so demanding? He knows that tonight could be trying but he had to remain resolved to dismantle this ill thought-out domestic arrangement and return home to the comfort of his family. He is pleased to see his friend and colleague Joseph Banks, a glass and china merchant, on the platform, saying goodbye to his 12-year-old daughter, Kate. There also appears to be a delightful young woman, introduced as Miss Chapman, who will be accompanying Kate to Yarmouth. George gallantly offers to travel with the two ladies.

# *Job John Hupton*

Harness-Maker Job Hupton, 45, has completed his business in the big city, buying harnesses on behalf of his employer Mr Foreman, a Yarmouth fish carrier, and he wants his supper. Not many would guess that this down-to-earth, practical working man was actually the son of a celebrated Baptist minister. When Job was born, his father, Reverend Job Hupton, at 68, was already an elderly man. He had been widowed twice when he married Frances Pack in 1821, when she was 32. He already had four children by his second wife, and by 1833 there were three more including Job.

The seven Hupton children were raised together in the Norfolk parish of Claxton, a community nestled just south of the River Yare, between Loddon and Rockland St Mary. Their lives were restricted within the confines of the Strict and Particular Baptist faith. Their father was renowned throughout the country as a 'fire and brimstone' preacher, poet, and published writer of theological treatises and composer of uplifting hymns. By the time of his death in 1849, at the splendid age of 87, his ministry in Claxton had lasted fifty-five years. He was buried in the graveyard attached to Claxton Chapel, alongside his first two wives.

Once widowed, Frances moved to Norwich with her schoolteacher daughter, also named Frances, and two sons. Job, having recently completed his apprenticeship as a harness-maker, was now fully qualified and considered competent to find work. Samuel, the younger by five years, was training to be a carpenter. Frances took in boarders at their Lakenham home, enabling her to keep a house servant, Suffolk-born Elizabeth Gerrel. This single woman, then in her early thirties, remained loyal to her mistress and her spinster daughter for over twenty-three years.

In the late 1850s, with his younger brother busy working as a carpenter and raising a family, Job was making fundamental decisions about his life. Moving away from non-conformism, Job offered himself up for baptism into the Anglican church at St Marks in Lakenham in April 1862. Five years later Job was preparing for his own wedding. Ann Eliza Rant, known as Eliza, was the daughter of fellow harness-maker James Rant from Great Yarmouth. The Rant family lived in The Rows, an entangled maze of narrow and often claustrophobic medieval streets, unique to Yarmouth; the streets so narrow, one could touch the walls on each side at the same time. On visiting the home of his sweetheart, Job may have been struck by the overhanging eaves blocking out the natural light, the windows flung open in all weathers to admit much needed fresh air. The smells from the many cooking pots, poor sanitation and fumes from a forest of industrial chimneys made for a heady mix.

Having lived for a short while in Beccles, Job and Eliza made a decision to take their firstborn son to live near Eliza's parents in Yarmouth. They settled into rooms in Row 44, known as Angel Row, just in time for their second son to be born. Close to the nearby pub and to a second beer house, the air was saturated with the smell of hops and the late night voices of revellers. Four years later Job and Eliza welcomed their daughter, Frances Eliza, named after Job's mother.

Frances Hupton barely had time to get to know the most recent of her many grandchildren, passing away at home in Trafalgar Terrace, Lakenham on 16 May 1874. She was 86 years old. Although certainly not wealthy, Frances left a modest legacy for her children, a sum recorded as £600 (£68,000). With his share, Job planned to set up his own leather business, ensuring a more secure future for his three small children. The legalities might take a little time to resolve, but in the meantime, at least he was employed, still doing his master's bidding, as he has been this day in Norwich.

# Stephen Abbott

A group of well-dressed gentlemen bound onto the platform, looking for the first class smoking carriage destined for Lowestoft. Once the new engine is hooked up, these will form the rear of the train. To onlookers the men appear a little merry, for they have come directly from a most satisfactory Masonic dinner at the magnificent Assembly House. The celebration was the opening of the new Walpole Lodge in St Giles Street. The ebullient Lowestoft clergyman, the Reverend F.B. de Chair, heads up this party of Norfolk gentry, landowners and aspiring middle classes. They all agree that had they known the train would be delayed, they would have enjoyed another brandy. One of the Brethren is Mr Stephen Abbott, 60, formerly of Castle Acre in West Norfolk, now living in Yarmouth. Stephen is newly returned to England, having spent two years living on the Continent. It has been a stimulating evening in the company of new friends. Once on board, he will attempt to sleep a little.

Stephen is the son of the late Henry Abbott, a farmer from the Broadland village of Hainford. In 1821, Henry had realised a long-held dream to become a tenant of wealthy landowner Thomas William Coke, later the Earl of Leicester. Following a series of pleading letters, he succeeded in his quest, relocating his family into a farmhouse at Wicken Farm, in the north west Norfolk hilltop community of Castle Acre, north of Swaffham. Their arrival coincided with a particularly harsh period for the farming community. A poor harvest in 1820, increased taxes and onerous Corn Laws meant farmers were cutting back, their previous prosperity a distant memory. The previous tenant at Wicken had been forced to sell every stick of furniture to pay his creditors.

While Henry embarked on making the necessary extensive repairs to their new home, Stephen and his older brother William enjoyed boyhood pursuits, swimming in the River Nare, discovering nesting ducks and swans, exploring the water meadows and climbing through the ruined medieval priory. Henry was determined to succeed in his new venture, soon becoming a churchwarden at the parish church of St James, and indulging his passion for hunting with hounds, his home often surrounded by impatient horses and barking dogs at the start of regular meets.

William, a single man, died unexpectedly aged just 32, within two years of his father. This meant that by 1844, Stephen found himself responsible not only for his wife Fanny, but also his widowed mother and the running of Wicken Farm. Stephen had been married for two years and the couple never dreamt they would take over the land so soon. Happily for Stephen, his young wife came with money, a legacy from her landowner father. The farm and his investments prospered and by 1850 Stephen was employing a coachman, a groom and four house servants at Wicken Farm.

It took six years for Stephen and Fanny to produce a living child. At the age of 34, Fanny finally presented Stephen with a daughter, Fanny Elizabeth. A son followed two years later. Stephen continued to prosper, adding a cook, footman and two nursemaids to his below-stairs staff. Stephen's mother remained close by, living alone at Old Wicken, a cottage on the estate, cared for by a housekeeper and pageboy.

The mid-1860s proved an exceptionally difficult period for farmers. An outbreak of cattle plague was followed by a cholera epidemic and failed harvests leading to commercial panic and bankruptcies. With escalating rumours of a working-class uprising, Stephen decided he had had enough. In September 1867, Stephen advised the local community that he was 'declining farming'. He instructed an auctioneer to sell his paraphernalia, including forty-two carthorses, 800 sheep and lambs, eighty-four head of oxen and heifers, thirty-eight pigs and a vast array of agricultural instruments. The notice of sale helpfully advised that, 'conveyances will be on hand to transfer rail travellers from Swaffham station to the farm'. (*Norfolk Chronicle*, Saturday, 21 September, 1867).

On 3 October, Stephen's household contents also went under the hammer, including his cellar of choice wines, oil paintings, stuffed birds, greenhouse plants, 100 dining room chairs, card tables, velvet carpets, and mahogany four-post beds, complete with blankets and counterpanes. His collection of old and foreign china was described as being one of the most valuable in Norfolk. Fanny must have been broken-hearted. The family left Castle Acre, relocating to a considerably more modest Victorian villa at 16, Nelson Road in Great Yarmouth, where they survived with the aid of just two servants.

Three years later, when a pandemic of scarlet fever swept through Europe, Stephen and Fanny were horrified when their only son Stephen showed signs of the tell-tale red rash. His condition deteriorated and the boy was dead by 29 October 1870. He was just 12 years old. Mercifully, his elder sister Fanny escaped the illness. In March 1872, he once again offered the contents of his home for auction. The family was leaving Yarmouth for Stuttgart in Germany, where his daughter would be educated for the following two years; Stephen presumably recognizing the advanced reforms in schooling for girls taking place on the continent. By 11 October 1873, from a letter published in the Norwich Mercury, it is clear that his close friends were expecting him to soon return home. Mr Thomas Daniel, a member of the landed gentry, wrote to the editor from The Beach House in Caister, a coastal village near Great Yarmouth, thanking those who helped with a recent fire at his farm. In among the copious gratitude is this line:

> Allow also me to state that no plate belonging to my friend, Stephen, was ever placed in my barn; the property belonging to him, which was so happily rescued, consisted of large packages containing china and glass, which I trust soon to have the pleasure of restoring to their rightful owner on his welcome return to old England.

By the summer of 1874, the Abbott family were returned to Great Yarmouth, Stephen anxious to increase his business contacts and resume his status in Norfolk society. The Masonic links could prove most useful. He must be sure to keep in touch.

*****

At precisely 9.23, the express finally runs in under the arcade, filling the space with noxious smoke and deafening noise, coming to a halt on the arrivals platform, just before the buffers. The combined stench of a coal fire and hot oil saturates the air. The crowd surges forward. Those who are now finally at their ultimate destination pour from the carriages, squeezing through the impatient throng, hurrying to be the first in the inevitable queue for cabs. For the station staff, there is much yet to do to get the train away, from replacing the engine to sorting out the pieces of luggage. Porters move fast to lift portmanteaus and packages off one train and on to another, aware that the Inspector will want the delayed connection away quickly.

On arrival in Norwich, Mrs Charlotte Coote, 40, an extraordinarily large lady, struggles to disembark, handing their baggage to her

12-year-old daughter Mary Ann. They have travelled all the way from Shoreditch in East London, but as yet their journey is still not complete. They find space in a third-class carriage and await the departure for Yarmouth. Over the past eighteen years, Charlotte and husband George have raised eight children, including twin girls. Her youngest, Elizabeth, is only 5 years old. Charlotte has her hands full caring for them all, while George works in a distillery as a warehouseman. She is well used to the trade, after all, her father James Brunsden has managed two London pubs over the past thirty years, the most recent being the Red Cow in Richmond.

In August 1855, Charlotte had married George Coote, the son of a cooper, starting their family a year later. As the babies kept coming, her mother helped out. Once her mother was widowed Charlotte welcomed her into their Stepney home, where she would stay for sixteen years. Charlotte had been devastated when her mother died just last year. She missed her company very much. This visit to the coast with young Mary Ann should be a real tonic. The pair cannot help but be excited.

\*\*\*\*\*

# Thomas Clarke

The driver of the express from London this evening is 40-year-old Thomas Clarke, recently transferred from Norwich to Lowestoft where he lives with his wife and family. Thomas is always pleased to drive the Norwich to Yarmouth line. Along with three siblings, he was born and raised in Thorpe-Next-Norwich during the 1830s and 1840s, where his father was an agricultural labourer. Thomas will enjoy once again regaling his fireman with tales of his youth, as they speed across Thorpe Island.

Having reached his twenties, Thomas left home to work for the Great Eastern, promoted to fireman by the 1860s, lodging in Bury St Edmunds with an engine driver and his wife, less than ten minutes' walk from the railway station. It was here that Thomas met his future wife, Rosetta Rose, the daughter of a railway porter. They married in Wisbech, one of the major Cambridgeshire railway towns, on 21 September 1863 when Thomas was 29. A year later their first son, John William, was born there.

By 1865 the family were on the move again, transferred to Norwich, finding a home in Bull Yard where, over the next three years, Rosetta had two further sons and a daughter. It was not a pleasurable place to live; overcrowded, smelly, dark and noisy. This transfer to Lowestoft could only be good for the family. The sea air would really benefit baby Rosetta, born only a few weeks earlier.

Like John Prior, Thomas also has a reputation for being a conscientious and experienced driver, and he is proud of his achievements. And like John, he also knows his engines. The third and final engine to pull tonight's down service from London is No.218, a Y Class with a 2-4-0 wheel formation. Designed by Daniel Gooch, this model is known as the 'Butterfly' and was built for Eastern Counties Railway at Canada Works in Birkenhead in April 1856. She's a little older than some Thomas has driven, but she's relatively light and fast.

Thomas loves his job. Not everyone reaches his prestigious position; promotion to driver can literally mean waiting for 'dead men's shoes'. The company expects their servants to have high levels of fitness and punctuality. The job is dirty, tiring and demanding, but it fosters pride, loyalty and self-discipline. The railway servants, whatever their level, are expected to be always well turned out, to develop a trust with the public, not to drink or swear, and above all, to obey company rules, which they are instructed to memorise from day one. However, if you step out of line, make a mistake or disobey an order, the penalties are harsh. Thomas knows of men being either demoted, or posted to an obscure part of the network, separated from family and friends.

But there are benefits. He now takes home as much as 39 shillings a week, a good deal more than the 21 shillings earned by firemen. There are the welfare benefits too, including paid funeral costs and access to the union, The Amalgamated Society of Railway Servants, only set up in 1871. Whatever demands this job make on him, Thomas is proud to wear the uniform of the Great Eastern Railway.

# Frederick Sewell

Assisting him this evening is Fireman Frederick Sewell, a farmer's son, the fourth of nine children, originally from Oulton in Suffolk. In

1866 Frederick, then a railway labourer, married young widow Emily Cummings, a bricklayer's daughter. The wedding was held at St John's Church in Lowestoft, and in the congregation sat 2-year-old Clara, Emily's child by her late husband. Frederick set up home with his readymade family in New Nelson Street in Lowestoft. Five years later the household had expanded, with the addition of four half-siblings for Clara, namely Ellen, George, Ernest and Harry. At work, Frederick is soon considered to be trustworthy enough to be called in on occasion to act as a fireman on the footplate. Today is one of those days. Frederick enjoys these opportunities, especially when working alongside an experienced driver like Thomas Clarke.

*****

Not wishing to cause any further delay, George Womack encourages his two charges further up the platform. He is surprised to find the four carriages nearest the new engine to be running empty. While he dithers, Kate spots a horsebox behind the tender. She is keen to investigate further, but there is no time and George ushers the two ladies into a first class compartment positioned about halfway up the train. As the three settle in, Kate complains about her seat. Miss Chapman smiles coquettishly, requesting that maybe Mr Womack might be a gentleman and exchange seats with them? Always delighted to please a lady, George readily agrees. Following one more irritating delay as Inspector Parker calls a porter to bring some forgotten luggage from the waiting room, the whistle blows and with the sound of surging steam the driving wheels turn and they are away. George checks his pocket watch. It is precisely 9.31. The so-called express is now running twenty-one minutes late.

*****

From inside the telegraph office, with the wicket door closed, it is not possible to see the comings and goings of the trains in the station. With still no sign of Cooper returning to sign his chit, Robson continues with his work, all the while showing off his skills to his young friends. At precisely 9.30 pm, Railway Police Inspector Edward Trew comes to the wicket, clutching a message intended for the pilgrimage village of

Walsingham. On opening the wicket door, Robson immediately sees through the gap that the express is no longer on the platform. He is startled.

"Where is the down train? Has it left the yard?"

Trew looks perplexed. "Yes".

At that moment, Inspector Cooper rushes up, in a state of great excitement.

"Robson, cancel the single line message, stop the mail."

Robson checks the clock. 9.32. There is no time to write the message in the book. Robson sends the telegraph.

"Stop Mail."

The response from Brundall is immediate.

"Mail left."

Before the consequences of this can even register, Robson approaches Cooper, covertly suggesting that he signs the original messages retrospectively.

Cooper shrugs him away, having none of it, the colour already draining from his face.

"No, I never gave you a message."

Finding his courage, Robson's response is assertive.

"Yes you did, or why, if you did not give me a message, do you now come back to cancel it?"

Having overheard some of this exchange, both Sproul and Parker enter the office. Suddenly aware of the inevitable consequences, Parker breaks the silence.

Speaking slowly and deliberately he says, "This is a very serious thing, the most serious thing that ever occurred."

Robson can scarcely breathe, avoiding looking anyone in the eye. Cooper moves in close to the boy, staring intently.

"Robson, Robson, my God, you have done for me now."

*****

Relieved to be finally on their way, passengers try and settle into the journey. Under normal circumstances, Clarke and Sewell would share stories but tonight the conditions are too extreme. It is critical to maintain concentration when your screen is smeared with rain.

The express crosses the first bridge over the Yare onto Thorpe Island, maintaining a conservative speed of about twenty miles per hour. Convinced that the mail train is waiting impatiently for them at Brundall, Clarke resolves to pick up speed once they have crossed the second bridge, by the Three Tuns pub. From there the single track runs straight and true.

# Chapter 4

# Impact

The mail train approaches the flickering lights of the Norfolk Asylum, the place where regular rail passengers allow themselves a moment of hope. They are nearly at Norwich. Bookseller William Green observes that upon their arrival, walking in this rain will be most unpleasant, so would the ladies like to ride with his wife in their carriage, while he makes his way home on foot, equipped as he is with an umbrella? As the mail reaches the slippery incline from Postwick, it naturally picks up speed. Sarah Booty turns anxiously to her husband. The good Reverend stirs from his slumber, happy to address her fears. She feels unsettled, nervous. While he gently covers their sleeping son with Sarah's woollen shawl, her husband reassures her that they are a mere two minutes from the Three Tuns bridge and the long flat section over the island. All will be well.

Emerging from the blind curve, the mail train driver and fireman become aware of a flickering outline approaching them at speed. A sense of dismay prompts drivers of both trains to attempt shutting off the steam, their firemen struggling to apply the brakes on the tender. Then nothing. Nothing at all. John, James, Thomas and Frederick are crushed to death in an instant.

The impact is catastrophic. The express engine reels to the left, the axles of its leading wheels thrown out of square. Its coal-laden tender crashes down upon its opposite number, forcing it around to face the opposite way. Buffers snap, thick copper and brass tubes wrenched apart. The massive funnel of the mail sheers away, hurtling to the ground below, thick iron plates torn into ribbons. Piston rods displace and bend, massive iron framing folding in, as might thin pewter. An iron cylinder splits into sheets of metal, projected nearly 30 yards into a nearby garden, shattering the roof of an outhouse.

Those seated nearest the engines are stunned, the wooden carriages trembling and oscillating, creaking and cracking apart, disintegrating into match-sized shards, showering the surrounding marshland. Carriages remaining intact are pitched upwards, twisting and turning, one tangled in a telegraph wire, before settling into a ghastly pyramid, some 20ft high. The fish truck is forced skyward, its cargo cascading as locusts on to the rails below, the hapless horse tipped out, its life force extinguished. Scalding steam blows from the boilers at a tremendous rate, adding to the ominous cacophony, black smoke further blackening the already leaden skies. Engine wheels spin, out of control, intent on progressing their journey. Slowly, sluggishly, the mountain of wreckage sinks down into one hideous heap. It is then that the screams begin.

Villagers living nearest the tracks are instantly alarmed as the din reaches them. Some fear their house is falling in, others believe it to be merely an unprecedented clap of thunder. Instinct kicks in and within seconds, doors are flung open. A growing stream of gentlemen, grooms, bakers, shoemakers, needlewomen, widows, cab drivers, coachmen, housemaids, farm labourers, boat builders, schoolteachers, painters and grocers, all holding lighted lanterns, run scared towards the noise, with no notion of what might be ahead, but anxious to find out. Those unable to leave, peer from their windows into the night, attracted to the tiny points of light moving swiftly through the dark, mesmerised by the wreaths of smoke rising above the rooftop of the Three Tuns.

Dr Eade is suddenly shaken by a violent stunning shock, followed immediately by the sound of a sharp metallic concussion. His carriage has come to a sudden standstill and for two or three seconds he is aware of uncertain oscillating movements as his first class compartment seems to diminish, growing smaller, at the same time turning sideways, the roof crumbling apart. Projected through the void, he finds himself lying in the wet grass of a meadow, quite alone and surprisingly conscious. There is little doubt that there has been an accident. He is then struck by the notion that he might be about to die. His quick brain rejects this, instead assessing his situation, aware of the steam roaring from the funnel of an engine, far too close for his liking. Bruised and cut about the head and face, he tries to stand, relieved that he appears not to have broken a leg. Despite his pain, he knows he must help those less fortunate. Wiping away blood from his forehead, he limps towards the carnage on the line. As he comes to his senses, he assesses his own injuries, estimating two blows and cuts upon his head, two bruises on his back, and three bruises and abrasions upon his legs.

If he can walk then he is probably not mortally wounded. He looks around for signs of other survivors. Some remain inside the carriages, others are standing at the side of the small embankment. Many were crying out for help, two or three sitting on the cold wet earth, moaning and nursing their broken limbs. All around them are shattered, heaped-up fragments of the front portion of the mail train, steam roaring and escaping from the funnel of the express. While recognising the scene before him as truly awful, for just one fleeting moment he considers it to be something wonderful and almost grand. His head is bleeding, his face covered with dust and dirt, his cap gone, coat torn and his whole body feeling the influence of nervous shock and excitement. At this moment, a local resident approaches him through the gloom, offering his hospitality, some brandy and maybe a wash. He thankfully accepts. Greatly restored, Dr Eade returns to the fray, doing what little he can for the injured, some of whom are already being lifted to the lower room of the nearby Three Tuns. As Dr Eade makes his way towards the pub, he sees Mr Dimmock emerging blindly from his ruined carriage, emerging against the hot funnel of an engine, striking his arm and badly burning his wrist. He scrambles away before rising to his feet to survey the scene and listen for sounds of life.

Mr William Bransby Francis is a realist. From his many years of studying and practising medicine, he recognises the signs of broken ribs and a fractured thigh. Unable to move and in great discomfort, he decides his best course of action is to stay completely still and wait for help to arrive. At his age, he is dubious about his chances of survival.

As the floor of their third-class carriage collapses below their feet, the militia men are brutally sucked onto the rails below. As the carriage shudders uncontrollably, Mr Green and his party of ladies are knocked senseless and pitched out into the black void. Stirring, Mr Green finds himself at the bottom of the embankment, submersed in a bed of mud and gravel, heavy pieces of debris falling around from all directions. His first thought is to find his wife, but his foot is trapped under a great weight. With supreme effort, he pushes the obstacle aside, ignoring the pain as he crawls and gropes about in the murky darkness. Happily for them, his wife's white frock is a beacon of hope. He grasps her hand, relieved and thankful to find her conscious and seemingly unhurt, albeit dazed and distressed. But what has become of his wife's two sisters? At the rear of the mail, those travellers from Lowestoft are more blessed, most merely thrown forwards in their seats, ears ringing with the almighty metallic crash, left in complete darkness as gas lamps extinguish.

Similarly at the rear of the Norwich express is the first class smoking carriage where the group of Masonic Brothers had been engaged in hearty conversation. As three sudden shocks, one after the other, shake the carriage, the men are scarcely moved from the comfort of their padded seats. The train comes to an abrupt halt over the river. Having no idea of the cause, Reverend de Chair puts forward a theory. That morning, during his journey up from Lowestoft, he witnessed repair works taking place on this very bridge. Maybe a workman left something on the track, causing the engine to run off the line? Their first thoughts are to abandon the carriage, concerned that if another train should come up behind, they might be thrown into the water below. Despite the warning cries of John Hart, stood on the bank outside his pub, urging them to stay put, the group nevertheless struggle to climb down onto the narrow ledge of the bridge, thankful to reach firm ground.

Directly behind them, in the final third-class carriage of the express are three gentlemen from King's Lynn. Mr John Devonshire, 33, and his brother Henry, both fish merchants, are accompanied by their friend Mr Winch, a fruiterer and fish dealer. John, having found enough room to lay full length and take a nap, is woken with a start, hurled against the edge of the opposite seat, the recoil throwing him back to the seat he had left, his nose striking the edge. As the initial shock dissipates, he realises blood is pouring from his nostrils. What about the others? Realising that they too are still alive, John exclaims, "Good God, we are alive. Thank God for that." With no inkling that they have collided with the mail train, and thinking that it must be a derailment, the three men shake hands, congratulating each other on their hairsbreadth escape. As they sit catching their breath, a cry goes up from outside, "The boilers have burst." To their disbelief the men find that their carriage is balanced on a bridge. Keen to reach safety, John steps from the carriage, immediately slipping through the maintenance gaps into the River Yare below. He swims for a few yards before sliding into a bed of mud, almost up to his waist, his instinct to cling to the piles. As he struggles to extricate himself, his cries for help are whipped away in the wind. Once on dry land, the full extent of the horror before him is apparent. He must find the others.

Guard Black, working in the brake van at the very rear of the express, is pitched forward at the impact, landing among packages and pieces of luggage. For one or two moments he is unable to move. His mind clearing, he pulls himself together, picking up his lamp and peering outside, shocked to see the glint of water directly below. Anxious to investigate up ahead, Black steps down onto the bridge, surprised to see a glow of lamplight heading towards him. A young passenger, Frank Ellingham, is easing his way along the bridge. Frank can see that Black is injured. Over the escalating rumbling and hissing, Frank urges Black to return to his van and rest, for his head is badly cut, his face lined with blood. However, although half-insensible, the guard is aware of his duties, his overriding priority is the safety of the passengers. As Frank sets off towards the city to raise the alarm, closely followed by the posse of Masons, Black reaches the end of the bridge. Wading through the gravel, he is shocked to find his path blocked by a wall of debris. Manoeuvring around it as best he can, he is again faced with mounds of shattered wood and glass. From within he can hear pitiful groans and desperate cries for help.

Further up the line, businessman Alfred Page is tipped from his second-class carriage of the mail train, rolling down the embankment into a ditch of filthy water, coming-to feeling dazed and confused. Peering about him, he can just make out the limp figures of brother George and friend Russell Skinner, lying prostate on the rails. He inches over to them, attempting to ignore increasing pain, cradling his dear brother's head in his lap, silently praying that help might come.

A little further back, Mail Guard Ellis is thrown, at considerable speed, through the side of his van, followed by the pile of mail sacks. Although dazed and bleeding, he struggles to stand, gathering up as many of the sacks as he can carry, and without looking back, strides, stumbles and staggers for nearly an hour through the driving rain, intent on delivering his letters and parcels to Norwich Post Office. On his arrival, the Post Master, horrified at the state of the young man, pleads in vain with him to go to the hospital. Ellis is insistent and, courtesy of the Post Office, returns home to Yarmouth in a carriage. James Chapman, the guard at the head of the section from Lowestoft, assuming that the telegraph wires must be damaged, immediately shows initiative and courage by running the six miles along the track back to Brundall Station, with his red danger lamp guiding his way, in order to alert the station master to hold the 9.30 pm special from Lowestoft.

At the front of the express, the horsebox is wrecked, the twisted body of the unfortunate animal lying dead next the track. Young Kate Banks, who so admired the fine steed at Thorpe Station, has been thrown from the train alongside Miss Chapman, their clothes virtually stripped from their backs as they tumble through bushes, brambles and branches, before landing in a sea of mud. A horrified onlooker assists the young woman and her charge to climb over a low fence into the garden of residents Mr and Mrs Herbert Day, who are frantic about the dreadful events taking place directly outside their home. Fortunately, Miss Chapman and Kate appear uninjured and the kindly couple offer them rest, warm drinks and sympathy; Mrs Day scurries to find some appropriate clothing for their return to the city. As the evening progresses, and word gets out, a stream of shaken passengers call upon the Day's hospitality. These include the Boast family from Market Road in Great Yarmouth, father, mother, two of their children and two orphaned nieces, who are grateful to receive 'stimulants and other requisites' as they endeavour to recover their sensibilities. There are more lucky escapes, including Louisa Stevens and her three children. Although violently knocked over, they remain uninjured, crawling through the carriage windows and scrambling to safety. The Reverend Booty, Sarah and young Horace, although shaken, are thankful for their merciful escape, particularly when they later realise the first carriage they entered in Brundall, had been reduced to atoms.

Others continue to suffer. Off duty fireman John Betts lies unconscious with a fractured skull, having been struck on the head by an enormous lump of coal. His wife Elizabeth desperately clings tightly to her baby, reaching out in vain to find little Charles before the world around her melts away forever.

The rescuers start to arrive, stunned to find an almighty heap of wreckage towering above them, boilers spitting and sparking, air full of swirling cinders. The lanterns give a little light, helping to discern if the forlorn figures are dead or alive, but they will need bonfires if they are to make any headway. The call is answered with those who can, setting to work piling splinters into mounds, setting them all around the accident site. One by one, dark figures begin an exodus from the broken carriages, many struggling to put one foot in front of the other, others crawling on hands and knees. While John Hart alerts passengers not to climb onto the bridge, his wife pulls bed sheets, shirts and tablecloths from cabinets, the children tearing them into strips to make bandages. Boat Builder Stephen Field, clears the floor of his nearby boat shed as best he can, only too aware that this covered space will soon be needed to shelter victims, whether they be alive or dead.

Later, a Thorpe resident will describe the scene as witnessed from his window looking down along the old river to the point of the collision:

> It was one of the most unearthly and dreadful, yet wonderfully magnificent and varied in effect of colouring. At first the glare of the Norwich train's red lamps alone broke through the thick darkness, making the night still more hideous. Suddenly small lights, held in the hands of the searchers, glimmered and flittered like 'Will o' the Wisp' around a spot. Soon there appeared the larger stationary light of two fires, whose flames rapidly gathered force, and rose high and bright above the huge wreaths of smoke, which curled and were carried off into space by the wind. These fires became great bonfires, and threw abundant light upon the trees around and in the distance – even the woods of Whitlingham were illuminated. The figures of men were seen gliding about the pile of carriages which was gradually reduced, while the departing flashes of lightening became gradually less brilliant, and except for the light from the fires and lamps, darkness prevailed.
>
> (*Norwich Mercury*, Wednesday, 16 September 1874)

Among those first on the scene is William Birkbeck, successful banker, landowner and self-styled Lord of the Manor in Thorpe-Next-Norwich. On hearing the horrendous crash, he leaves his wife Susan and the comforts of his elegant drawing room at The High House, Thunder Lane, calling out instructions to his parlour maids, grooms, footmen and gardeners, leading them into the darkness. His house is sited almost directly opposite the embankment and the group can see the rising plumes of black smoke as they clamber across the marshland. Mr Birkbeck is later described as, 'behaving like a gentleman while working like a Navvy'.

William's neighbour, Captain Henry L'estrange Herring, is no stranger to challenging situations. As a former soldier, serving in the 30th Foot (59th) East Lancashire Regiment in 1852, and the son of a former rector in Thorpe, Henry is well prepared to face the unexpected. Two more retired military men are among the first to arrive. Captain John Douglas, 43, retired officer from the Royal Berkshire Militia, living conveniently close in 'The White House' at the foot of Thunder Lane, and Captain Charles Foster, 45, a solicitor and Clerk of the Peace for Norfolk, his home directly west of the Three Tuns. Captain Foster is much admired in the village for his swimming, sculling and riding skills, seen out often on the River Yare or astride his horse high above the city on Mousehold Heath. All of these successful men are a similar age, some are friends, sharing similar experiences and values. Tonight will test them sorely.

A short time later, Dr Hills and Dr Owens reach the scene by carriage from the asylum, accompanied by loyal staff members in horse-drawn ambulances. Physically strong and capable carers, they willingly add their weight and skills to the rescue effort. Furthermore, the asylum horse-drawn ambulances are readily available to transport victims to hospital. There will be plenty of trips to make.

It is Captain Douglas who leads the way into the forest of broken timbers, armed with nothing but a flask of brandy and a lamp. Female arms are visible above the debris. Captain Douglas, his strength enhanced by adrenaline, first pulls at the limp figure of Miss Ellen Ramsdale, discovering that her right foot has been torn off and she is bleeding heavily. Calling for volunteers to carry this young woman into the safety of the pub, he turns to find dressmaker Elizabeth Smith, still conscious, but with her body pinned down by a heavy weight, her thigh fractured, and clearly in great danger. Captain Douglas despairs as to how best to release her. Elizabeth appeals, "Sir, go to those who require more assistance than I do". Impressed by her courage, he gently replies, "You are a plucky woman." (*East Anglian Handbook 1875*)

Charles Gilman is ejected through the splintered roof, becoming entangled in telegraph wires, before crashing back, landing on top of the carriage, where he clings on for dear life. William Yaxley lies unconscious beneath his carriage. Reverend Morse knows nothing until he wakes to find himself prostate on the ground, something crushing down upon him, rendering him unable to move. As another piece of wreckage ricochets towards him, colliding with his body, he again passes out, only opening his eyes as the weight is lifted and helping hands raise him to his feet. Blood is seeping from the back of his head, and on attempting to walk he can only do so slowly, suffering from acute pain in his legs. His hat is gone, his clothes rent and torn. Shadowy faces plead with him to take shelter in the pub, where a kindly soul offers him a glass of water and wraps a handkerchief around his head to stem the blood. But Charles refuses to rest; he has to get home, his only option to walk. Despite his confusion he finds the Rectory on Thorpe Road, knocking loudly on the door. Reverend Patteson is not at home, the Rector's wife horrified to see the respected clergyman in such a dreadful state. But he won't wait. Morse continues on his way into the city, oblivious to the walking wounded all around him, anxious to reach the safety of his home in St George's.

Inside the skittle alley on the ground floor of The Three Tuns pub, Dr Eade is distressed to find most of the victims there to be beyond human aid, either dead, the life crushed out of them, or cold, collapsed, and dying. With no appliances, save broken sticks or chairs for splints, and only torn up towels and sheets for bandages, Dr Eade can do very little for the sufferers, apart from straighten bent and fractured limbs, or fashion the broken limb to the sound one, administering brandy to relieve the cold and numb their pain.

*****

At Thorpe Station, as soon as the telegraphic response from Brundall is read out, everyone knows there is no way to stop the inevitable collision of the two trains. With Inspector Cooper pale and paralysed with shock, Mr Sproul immediately takes charge, sending staff out to the station yard to implore cab drivers to drive their horses as fast as possible, one to the hospital, others to the homes of the city physicians and surgeons. Once found, the cabs should bring them back to the station with all urgency. Another is sent to nearby hotels and inns to secure a good supply of brandy. Meantime, the breakdown van is brought from the yard, already prepared and equipped with all kinds of mechanical appliances, including a large hand-powered accident crane, screw jacks, chains, hoists and large baulks of wood for packing. This is linked to a spare locomotive, along with one or two passenger carriages. The gas lights are fired up, the firebox lit.

The breakdown crew is quickly assembled, every man willing to face whatever might await him down the line. Sproul refuses to allow Cooper or Robson to join the team, standing them down for the evening, pending investigation. Everyone is aware of an incident about seventeen years earlier, when the then stationmaster, Thomas Stevenson, had ordered up a 'special' for Yarmouth. A shunter, with no authority to start the train, had inexplicitly given an order for it to leave the station. Just as on this evening, the two trains unknowingly approached each other on the same single track. But unlike tonight, that event had taken place in daylight with good visibility, and both drivers had seen each other in time to pull up, albeit within only a few yards of each other. There was no such certainty on a filthy night such as this.

Throughout the city, and particularly in the St Giles area, door knockers slam loudly, terrified housemaids conveying the pleas of the cab drivers to their masters. Each one gallantly gathers up their surgical bags, making their way with much speed to Thorpe Station. Wives left behind worry for the safety of their husbands, having to decide whether to wait at home for news or to make their own way to the station to await the eventual outcome. The doctors climb aboard the waiting train, anxious but ready. The team is assembled, steam is up, and the rescue trucks pull out of Thorpe Station, accompanied by much shouting and hullaballoo.

As they arrive at the bridge over the Yare, railway workers and surgeons move quickly, each with a purpose in mind, a task to perform. They are welcomed by those already engaged in digging through mud and wreckage, desperate to locate those still alive, their cries of pain and terror spurring them on, others offering brandy to the wounded lying on the embankment or inside the pub. Dr Beverley is shocked to find his old friend William Francis lying alone inside the Three Tuns, pale and semi-conscious. Working together, Dr Beverley and Dr Hills fight to alleviate Williams' suffering, offering sips of brandy before ensuring his safe conveyance to his home in Colegate, where a team of doctors set his fractures.

It is imperative to lift the wreckage. There might still be victims buried deep beneath the carnage. But the enormous fractured metal parts of engines are far too heavy to lift without help, so the arrival of the accident crew and screw-jacks immediately has an impact on progress. Critically, the rescue train becomes an ambulance, travelling the short distance up and down the track, time and time again, ferrying its fragile cargo. The worst of the injured need onward transportation to the hospital with all haste. Among these are George Womack, George Page, Job Hupton, John Betts, Charlotte Coote, John Beart, and Jane Ann Faulkner.

As the long evening progresses, excitement centres on the ruined pyramid of wreckage, as it becomes clear there are victims trapped inside a carriage raised on its end and stood on top of several others. Wooden ladders are brought to the scene, workmen taking at least an hour to carefully manoeuvre them into position. Waiting to be rescued are Mr Hills, a bookseller from Ely, nursing his lacerated hand; nearby, dentist Richard White, suffering from far greater injuries, lies trapped 'upside down like a man in a coffin' (*Eastern Daily Press*, 14 September 1874), with a brass rod pressing heavily against his body, the same rod that is holding the weight of the carriage above, preventing both men from being crushed to death. It takes several hours for the team to reach them, cutting their way through the wreckage, under the determined supervision of railway officials. Throughout the long laborious effort, Captain Douglas, Dr Pitt and Captain Foster contrive to sustain Richard, using a brandy soaked handkerchief, placed on the end of a long stick, carefully sliding it up into the young man's mouth.

As the track is slowly cleared to the side, the awful extent of injury and death is exposed. The railway workers arriving from Thorpe Station quite naturally keep a close watch for their unfortunate friends and colleagues to emerge. Groups of men stand together, dazed and dismayed, speaking in hushed voices, hoping for the best, but fearing the worst, their faces displaying grief and sympathy. One young man from the Goods Department, James Allthorpe, is given the grim task of heading up an operation, lasting most of the night, to retrieve items of property strewn across the scene, before the inevitable pilfering begins. A vast collection of assorted shoes, hats, so many hats, suitcases, spectacles, and a pipe with its bowl carved into a death's head, are gathered together. A Yarmouth jeweller was later grateful to be reunited with a package of valuable gold watches, intended for a customer in London.

Parish constable Mr Hardy is working hard to coordinate the rescue effort, assessing priority cases, instructing volunteers to keep the fires burning and to fetch more brandy from the pub. The dead and the injured are carried into Stephen Field's boatyard or into the pub, where, in the half-light of the skittle alley, helped by local women, medical men are desperately attending to the wounds. Outside, the condition of Marianne Murray gives cause for concern. She is discovered jammed in the wreck of one of the engines, suffering from internal injuries and rambling incoherently, pleading for her lover to come to her, unaware that he has already been taken away, suffering with little more than a fractured leg. As rescuers battle to extricate her, she becomes progressively weaker, her voice fading. Another passenger, found to be confused and distressed, is standing alone in front of the debris, his face cut and his hat in ribbons. On being asked why he has not yet made his way home, he points at the wreckage, saying, "Do you see that hole? That's where I came from. There's someone else in there, and I must see him, dead or alive." (*East Anglian Handbook 1875*). He is offered some brandy, at first refusing anything, but then changing his mind and requesting a pipe of tobacco to help calm his nerves.

*****

As word gets out throughout the city and the nearby countryside, concerned relatives make their way to Thorpe Station or directly to the site of the accident, anxious to learn the fate of their loved ones. One man rushes about, frantic for news of his wife. A rescuer lights his way with a lantern, searching through the dead and wounded without success. He is eventually persuaded to return home in case his wife has arrived before him. She is not there, but he does find a telegram, informing him that she plans to stay in Yarmouth for a further day. A baker from Yarmouth has a similar experience. Expecting his wife and child to return from a visit to Norwich on the 9.10 express, he is horrified at around midnight to receive news of the accident. He saddles his horse and rides to the city, a journey of about two hours, to find the pair at the home of her relations, safely tucked up in bed having decided to stay another night. Once satisfied for their well-being, the baker selflessly rides to Thorpe to assist with the sufferers.

All evening much needed transport arrives from all directions; cabs from the city, horse-drawn ambulances from the asylum, carts and carriages belonging to local farmers and gentry. Once the injured are brought to a safe distance from the wreck, depending on the severity of their condition, they are driven through wind and rain, over cobbles and mud either directly to the hospital, the Royal Hotel or to their homes. Included among these are Susan Browne, Elizabeth Smith and gallery owner Mr Dimmock, who is greatly shaken and nursing his burnt wrist. Mr Hills also takes a cab, feeling grateful that, having been rescued after several hours spent encouraging fellow victim Richard White to remain conscious, he is feeling surprisingly well and is sure he can make his way home.

As the midnight hour passes, there are seventeen bodies inside the skittle alley, laid out on tables or on the floor. Within the space of a few hours the room has changed from a place of fun to a scene of horror; both a hospital ward and temporary mortuary. Relatives and friends are brought to the pub, along with local newspaper correspondents, to witness the scene and confirm, unofficially at this stage, the identity of the dead. Fathers, sisters, nephews and neighbours nervously file into the half-light, ill-prepared for what they find. Straw strewn on the ground is sodden with blood, bodies displaying rigid and contorted limbs and features, skin pallid or black with soot, corpses mutilated beyond recognition. The remains of the drivers and firemen leave friends and relatives deeply distressed. Heads driven into their bodies, flesh scalded and hung in shreds.

There is a slim hope for Ellen Ramsdale. Once she is taken inside the pub, it quickly becomes apparent that without immediate surgery, Ellen will not survive the night. Hospital surgeons Messrs Goodwin and Robinson, arrive, equipped with saws and bandages, amputating Ellen's crushed leg, first just below the knee, followed immediately by a second cut just above. Witnesses said later that Ellen bore the experience with wonderful fortitude, sustained only by sips of brandy. There was nothing now to do but pray.

Throughout the night, the road from Thorpe to the city is one long procession of those able to make their own way back, be it on foot, by cart, cab or carriage. Among them are Mr and Mrs Scott, the newlyweds so envied by Marianne Murray. They both have injuries to their legs and back, but are grateful to have survived, determined to start their married lives together at home in Gas Hill, in sore need of a nourishing bowl of hot broth. In Exchange Street, Mr Smith unlocks his chemist shop, willing to stay open throughout the night, supplying remedies for countless cuts and bruises, or simply offering a place of refuge from the incessant rain.

The special train, laid on to transport late-night revellers from the Lowestoft Flower Show, pulls into Brundall at the advertised time of 10.10 pm, the passengers oblivious to any issues and not expecting any delay. For fifty minutes the train for Norwich sits at the platform, with no explanation forthcoming from driver, guard or porters. This is irritating in the extreme, but when travellers venture to make enquiries, they are faced with a blanket, "Don't know Sir." The stationmaster is said to be in bed, but it is obvious he is hiding in his office. At midnight one of the porters finally gives in to pressure, admitting the true reason for the delay. The response from passengers is shock and anger; if they'd only been told the truth on arrival at Brundall, the more fit among them could have walked to Norwich, probably arriving home before midnight. As it is, it will be a further two hours before the special is cleared to leave, and then only as far as Whitlingham Lane, just before the crash site, whereupon everyone has to disembark and make their own way into the city.

# Chapter 5

# The Days Following

## Friday, 11 September 1874

The rescuers finally made it home to their beds at around 2.30 am. Those who were able to sleep did so fitfully, tormented by nightmares. By dawn, the more seriously injured had either been registered as in-patients at the hospital, were resting at city hotels or lying in their own beds at home. Two victims remained in the waiting room at Thorpe Station, deemed too weak for onward transport to the Norfolk and Norwich. During the early hours of Friday morning, both gave up the fight for life, the law dictating that their corpses remain at the railway station until the afternoon, when an initial city inquest would take place. The mood at the station was despondent. Rumours were rife.

From first light, with the weather much improved and news spreading among the early risers, an invasion of the morbid, the curious and the respectful, arrived in Thorpe-Next-Norwich, determined to gaze upon the wreckage. Over the following hours, tens turned into hundreds, increasing to thousands, a moving wave of people invading the village, some even arriving by boat. Most were disappointed. The crash site was hardly visible from the road and railway officials and police were guarding the scene. Their instructions were clear, prevent the public from obstructing the dredging and clear-up operations, while keeping a look-out for anyone attempting to pilfer a macabre relic or souvenir. The river was being dredged for bodies, thankfully with no results, and by early afternoon the embankment beyond the railway bridge appeared to be unscathed, apart from blood stained patches of ground, a few bent rails and nine slightly dented wooden sleepers.

The rolling stock was a very different matter. The heavier engine, No.51, from Yarmouth, was so completely wrecked that it had to be trucked away in pieces. Taken to the maintenance shed at Thorpe to await assessment, engineers feared she was only fit for spare parts. It was a similar story for No.218, deemed to be totally beyond repair. Of the two trains, five out of twenty-seven carriages were completely smashed, six so badly damaged that they would need extensive repairs to make them fit for the rails. Only nine carriages remained intact.

In readiness for the influx of curious spectators to Thorpe-Next-Norwich, the Reverend John Patteson had prepared an address. On arrival home from his evening engagement he was distraught to think of his parishioners experiencing such an appalling event. And he had not even been there to help. He instructed his warden to place more candles inside the church. People may wish to light one as a prayer for the dead and the dying. Once a crowd had assembled at the riverside, the Rector stood aloft on the church wall, leading the prayers and requesting that the peace of the village be respected. Later that day, much to everyone's surprise, the Queen's son, the Duke of Connaught, currently stationed at Norwich with his regiment, the 7th Hussars, rode into the village on his horse, speaking at length with police and officials. His Royal Highness seemed anxious to elicit all the information he could, offering sympathy and compassionate words.

Outside the front door of the Three Tuns, undertakers and carpenters unloaded simple temporary caskets, described as 'shells'. Volunteers cleaned the bodies as best they could, wiping away mud and blood, rearranging broken limbs, adjusting torn and mangled clothing and even brushing beards and heads of hair. The final act was to respectfully lift each body into its shell. Tomorrow, Saturday, there was to be an inquest. The victims deserved to been seen at their best.

*****

That same Friday morning, the city of Norwich was a miserable place. Customers in coffee shops, traders at market stalls, drivers at cabstands and those frequenting public houses, speculated about the railway accident. How many were dead? Who was to blame? What happens next? The first newspaper to break the news was the *Eastern Daily Press*, the local correspondent up all night questioning witnesses at Thorpe Station. Instead of the usual 2,000 copies sold each day, circulation that morning rose to a massive 20,500. (*Eastern Daily Press*, 10 October 2020)

At Womack's Draper's store, staff members were sombre, the mood lifting a little when reading in the *Eastern Daily Press* that George Womack was not yet dead, despite appearing mortally injured. Staff knew George had been 'in good health and the full vigour of manhood', although he had seemed depressed lately. It was unthinkable that he might be now close to death. As details of the incident emerged, members of the Press Association and scores of Norfolk journalists scurried to send telegrams to newspaper editors in all parts of the country. A handful of the more resourceful were able to run a skeleton story in their Friday second editions, including *Manchester Evening News*, *Evening Mail* in London and the *Daily Gazette* for Middleborough, where a tiny paragraph appeared on page eight.

Great Eastern Railway prepared a special train to bring officials and lawyers from London to Norwich. On arriving at 10.00 am, the group headed straight to the crash site. Although too late to view the worst of the carnage, they began their investigation in earnest. This was going to prove expensive. By 2.00 pm that day, the line through Thorpe was reopened, with a train for Yarmouth leaving almost immediately. Some of the more informed passengers may have felt strangely unsettled, as the train rattled cautiously over the bridge by the Three Tuns, knowing that down there, somewhere inside the building, lay the mortal remains of the dead.

On the Friday afternoon, a collection of gentlemen assembled in the waiting room at Norwich Thorpe station. Mr Edward Bignold, Coroner for the City of Norwich welcomed the jury of fifteen men, reminding them that this was just a preliminary inquiry, held solely for the purpose of identification. He then introduced Mr Robertson, superintendent of the line and Mr Taylor, lawyer, both representing Great Eastern.

# George Womack

The first witness to give evidence was Edward Blackburn, a Norwich tailor.

> I was foreman at the late Mr Womack's shop. I have seen a
> body, which I identify as that of George Robert Womack.
> (*Eastern Daily Press*, Saturday, 12 September 1874)

George's gallantry in exchanging seats with Miss Chapman and young Kate had cost him his life. Later in the week, a letter from George's friend Joseph Banks was published in the local press, informing readers that his daughter Kate had survived unscathed, and that Miss Chapman, was now resting at his city home, 'much bruised, shaken and extremely ill, under the care of Dr Williams'. George was found among the wreckage, unconscious, head hanging down, his body slumped over that of a lifeless woman. Rescuers had dragged him to safety, setting him down in the rescue train. On arrival at the station, his broken body was clinging to life. Volunteers watched over him until dawn when George finally succumbed to his injuries. George's estranged wife Emma was now his widow. She immediately instructed a solicitor to represent her at the inquest. It was George's right-hand man from his shop who identified his master's body.

George's funeral took place on the following Tuesday, 15 September, in The Rosary, the first non-denominational cemetery in the country, which was becoming a fashionable final resting place. George's body was interred inside the Womack family vault, a stone obelisk with ornate carving, alongside his parents George and Ann, his brother and sister Henry and Elizabeth, who had both died in childhood, and others of his ancestors. His own infant daughter Maude had also been placed there twelve years earlier. George's funeral attracted a great number of mourners and onlookers but it is doubtful that George's lady-friend put in an appearance.


# George Page

Next to give evidence was a Mr Page, confectioner from Norwich:

> Deceased was a relation to me by marriage and I identify the body as that of George Page. I married his cousin and have known him well for over thirty years. Deceased was not a married man.
> (*Eastern Daily Press*, Saturday, 12 September 1874)

If he had not been in the hospital, still being treated for a serious scalp wound, George's younger brother Alfred would doubtless have been there in person to identify his sibling. Alfred was too weak even to attend George's funeral at Norwich Cemetery, held the following Monday in Earlham. As he lay in his sickbed, Alfred was only too aware that with George's premature demise, he was now solely responsible for the ongoing care of his cantankerous elderly father, the old man inconsolable at the sudden death of his eldest son.

The formal procedures now complete, Mr Bignold adjourned the City Inquest until the following Friday morning at the Guildhall.

# Saturday, 12 September 1874
# The County Inquest begins

By Saturday morning, tens of thousands of newspaper readers throughout Great Britain became aware of the riverside village of Thorpe-Next-Norwich. A vast and varied list of publications began weeks of coverage, with running updates, editorial pieces and special supplements. Readers had insatiable appetites and every possible detail, factual and sensational, theories of blame and suggestions for helping the suffering were published day after day. Correspondents flooded into Thorpe and into the city, interviewing relatives, eyewitnesses and railway servants, in fact, anyone who would speak to them. Thousands of words were telegraphed to impatient editors. Some simply plagiarised copy, others made quick money by syndicating reports. Publications as the *Bradford Observer*, *London Times*, *Illustrated London News*, *Whitby Times*, *The Scotsman*, *Cardiff Times*, *Exmouth Journal* and even the *Shipping and Mercantile Gazette*, scrutinised news from the city of Norwich, hungry for more revelations, the more dramatic the better. On that Saturday, Queen Victoria was staying at her Highland castle of Balmoral, expecting the arrival of Prime Minister Benjamin Disraeli as her dinner guest. With the tragedy in Norfolk plastered all over the newspapers, including an explicit artists' impression of the scene on the front cover of the *Illustrated London News*, it is probable that at the royal dining table that evening, the collision was on everyone's lips. (*Queen Victoria's Diary* at Royal Collection Trust)

*****

On Saturday afternoon the skittle alley of the Three Tuns fell silent, relatives and friends of the dead watching vigil over their loved ones, waiting for the identifications to begin. The grief was palpable. A huge crowd had gathered outside, whispering in hushed tones at the arrival of Edward Press Esq, County Coroner. Greeted by John Hart, the grand gentleman was brought into the makeshift morgue, where he respectfully removed his hat. Mr Press was no stranger to the stench of death. It overpowered everything. But as members of the jury arrived, some found it impossible not to splutter and cough as bile rose in their throats. The seventeen shells were laid in a neat row. Each corpse was different, those who died of suffocation or dislocation of the neck appeared peaceful, unscathed, as if they were simply sleeping. Others were frightfully maimed, limbs missing, crushed faces barely recognisable. The next hour would be most unpleasant.

If the collision had taken place within the city boundaries, there would be no need to hold two inquests. But with both George Womack and George Page breathing their last in the waiting room of Thorpe Station, it meant two coroners, two juries, and two inquests. The complications were just beginning. City Coroner Edward Bignold, along with the chairman of his jury, were also at the Three Tuns, observing proceedings. A number of Norwich lawyers had been instructed, watching and taking notes on behalf of the families of the deceased.

The jury were sworn in; twelve men, including a number of the rescuers who had rushed to the scene, among them William Birkbeck, Captain Herring and Captain Douglas. Mr Press outlined the task ahead.

> Your first duty is to see the bodies of those unfortunate persons who have been killed, not I am afraid by a railway 'accident', for I must not use that word, but by a railway collision. The object to which you will have to draw your attention is the question, 'How did this collision take place?' You will have to inquire whether it occurred through carelessness, negligence, or reckless inattention to duty.
>
> (*Eastern Daily Press*, Monday, 14 September 1874)

For those identifying the remains of the drivers and firemen, the experience was particularly harrowing, for, as reported in the *Norfolk Chronicle* that afternoon, the four men were,

> horribly mutilated, heads driven into the trunk of the body, with flesh hung in shreds, apparently from the action of boiling water upon it.
>
> (*Norfolk Chronicle* Saturday, 12 September 1874)

# Thomas Henry Clarke

My name is Elizabeth Brazier. My husband's name is Edward Brazier and he lives in Thorpe St Andrew. He is an engine driver. I am a sister of the deceased Thomas Clarke, and I have seen his body. He was forty years of age I think and he lived at Lowestoft. He was in the employ of the Great Eastern Railway Company. He leaves a wife and five children.

(Eastern Daily Press, Monday, 14 September 1874)

Rosetta was too grief stricken to identify her husband's body, instead she asked her sister-in-law Elizabeth, a resident of Thorpe Road since childhood, to attend the inquest on her behalf. Rosetta had given birth only two months earlier, still nursing her baby daughter, so travelling from Lowestoft was impossible. With four other children to care for, the eldest just 10, Rosetta's future looked bleak. Elizabeth was also married to an engine driver, Edward Brazier, known as Ted; the wedding had taken place in the local parish church eleven years earlier. Ted was a Suffolk boy, born in Bury-St-Edmunds and a second-generation railway man. Wives of railway workers were always aware of the risks, but seeing her brother meet his end in such a horrible and violent manner, while doing the job he loved, could only make Elizabeth fear for her husband's safety even more than before.

Two days later Rosetta travelled to Thorpe to attend her husband's funeral. The mourners gathered in the small chapel at Thorpe Cemetery, at the eastern edge of the village, set adjacent to the railway track. The widow was surprised and touched by the number of railway staff who arrived to offer their condolences and say goodbye to a respected colleague. With emotions running high Reverend John Patteson preached the eulogy. As he spoke, the unmistakable sound of a passing train broke through the solemnity. Rosetta became instantly hysterical; inconsolable, she was gently helped from the building. The Rector attempted to bring the service to a close, but found himself overcome, quite unable to proceed.

# John Prior

My name is Andrew George Prior. I live at 3, Synagogue Street, Norwich. I am a clothier's assistant. I am the son

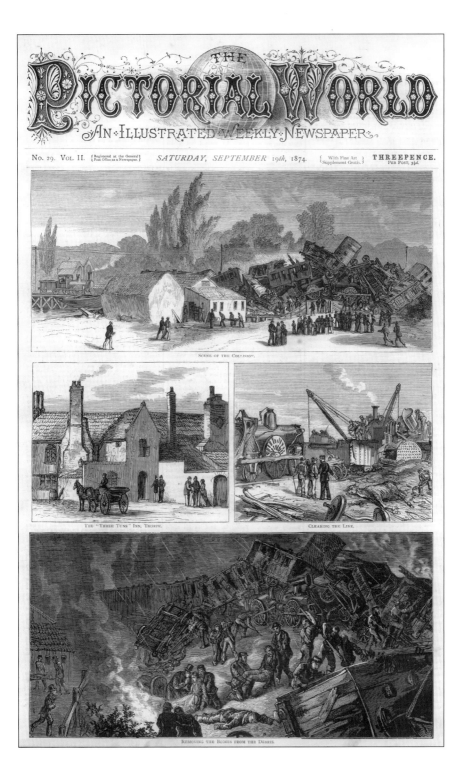

*The Pictorial World*, 19 September 1874. With permission from Vintagedition.com

Queen Victoria, 1875, © National
Portrait Gallery, London.

Arthur Duke of
Connaught, 1879.

The construction of Thorpe Station, 1843 © Norfolk Museums Service (Norwich Castle Museum & Art Gallery).

The Foundry Bridge and Railway Station Norwich © Norfolk Museums Service (Norwich Castle Museum and Art Gallery).

Norwich Thorpe Station, 1845, *Illustrated London News* © Mary Evans Picture Library.

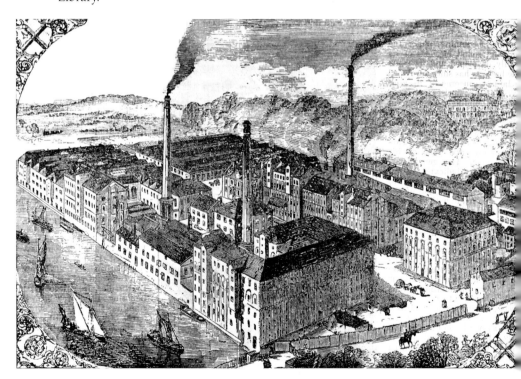

Industries on the River Wensum © Norfolk Industrial Archaeology Society.

YARMOUTH.

Engraving showing a view of Great Yarmouth, 1878 © istock by Getty Images.

VAUXHALL STATION

An artist's impression of Vauxhall Station in Great Yarmouth, in the form of a mural on the station wall today © Phyllida Scrivens 2020.

*Above*: South Quay at Yarmouth © Norfolk Industrial Archaeology Society.

*Below*: Passengers on a train, 1870s © istock by Getty.

SOLDIER, PRIEST, AND PEASANT

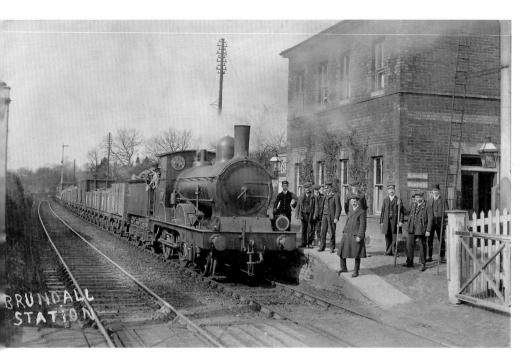

Brundall Station, c.1915 © Brundall Local History Group Archive *(www. brundallvillagehistory.org.uk)*.

Thorpe, [THE NORFOLK COUNTY LUNATIC ASYLUM.]

Thorpe-Next-Norwich, County Lunatic Asylum with passing train by G.F. Sargent © Norfolk County Council.

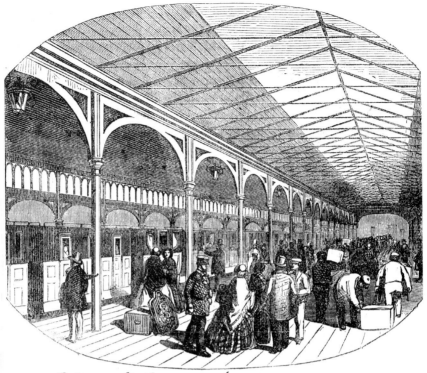

*Railway Station, Norwich. 1863.*

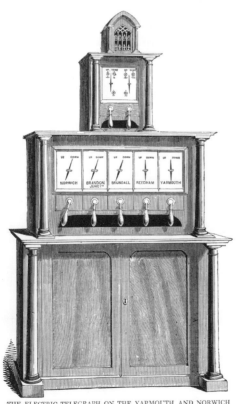

THE ELECTRIC TELEGRAPH ON THE YARMOUTH AND NORWICH
RAILWAY.

*Above*: Norwich Thorpe Station interior, 1863, © Norfolk County Council.

*Left*: Cooke & Wheatstone needle telegraph as used on the Yarmouth and Norwich Railway, 1845 © World History Archive/Alamy Stock Photo.

*Above*: The Crash
Site, *Illustrated London
News*, 19 September
1874 © The Victorian
Picture Library.

*Right*: The Rescue
Mission, *Illustrated
London News* © The
Victorian Picture
Library.

An accident truck arrives to raise wreckage (generic) © The Victorian Picture Library.

THORPE GARDENS, WITH THE FATAL RAILWAY BRIDGE AND FIELD'S BOAT-HOUSE IN THE DISTANCE.

The Three Tuns on the River Yare, next to the railway bridge © Norfolk County Council.

Mail train from Lowestoft to Norwich. Model similar to No. 54. Robert Sinclair outside cylinder 2-2-2 design locomotive for express passenger work, built between 1862 and 1867 © Science Museum Picture Library.

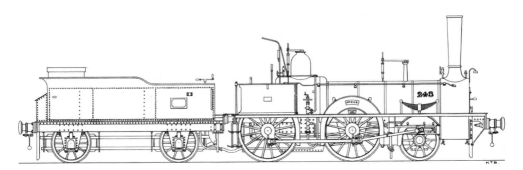

Express from Norwich to Lowestoft. Model similar to No. 218. Y Class. Gooch design 'Butterfly', 2-4-0, built in April 1856 for Eastern Counties © Science Museum Picture Library.

*Above*: Consultant Medical Staff, Norfolk &
Norwich Hospital, c.1871. Top row left to right:
Sir Frederick Bateman, William Cadge, Thomas
Crosse, Peter Eade. Bottom left to right: Edward
Copeman, W.P. Nichols, G. Firth © Norfolk and
Norwich Hospital

*Left*: Ellen Eugenie Ramsdale and her
fiancé, Dr Alex Mitchell, taken at Miller
Photographic Studio, King Street, Great
Yarmouth. By permission of Kathleen Irwin,
OldPhotosFound.blogspot.com.

Charles Rackham Gilman
Esq. Norwich businessman,
politician and philanthropist
© Norfolk Industrial
Archaeology Society.

St Andrew's
Church, Thorpe-
Next-Norwich,
built behind the
old church in
1866 © Norfolk
Museums Service
(Norwich Castle
Museum and Art
Gallery).

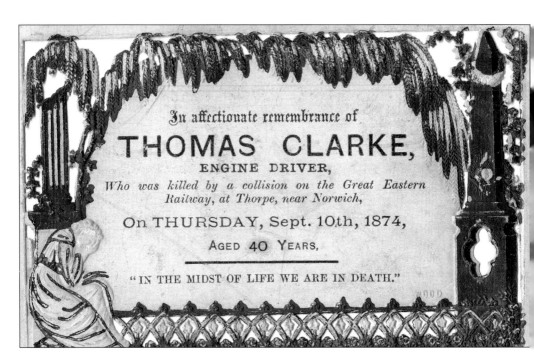

*Above*: Mourning card for driver Thomas Clarke © Norfolk County Council.

*Left*: Mourning card for fireman James Light © Norfolk County Council.

Mr Justice Grove, Judge at the Manslaughter Trial © National Portrait Gallery.

Walking stick believed to be made from sections of carriage taken from the collision site © John Bolle, 2020.

*Above*: The Rushcutters (formerly Three Tuns) in 2020. Photo taken from Thorpe Railway Bridge © Phyllida Scrivens.

*Below*: Crash site in 2020 looking west towards the city with the bridge up ahead © Phyllida Scrivens.

of the deceased John Prior, and have seen his body lying here. He was forty-nine years of age and lived in Synagogue Street in the same house I live in. He was an engine driver in the employ of Great Eastern Railway Company.

(*Eastern Daily Press*, Monday, 14 September 1874)

It fell to John's third son, Andrew George, 19, a tailor and draper's clerk, to identify his father's disfigured body. There was very little said. John's distraught widow Sarah Ann remained at their home in Synagogue Street for the next seventeen years, as one by one her children left home to make their own way in the world. Her son William achieved his ambition to become an engine driver, like his father. Towards the end of Sarah Ann's life, she moved to Orchard Street on the Dereham Road, dying in May 1894, having outlived John by nearly twenty years. The family arranged that her body be buried at Rosary Cemetery, in the same plot as her husband, their names linked forever on the shared carved headstone.

# James Light

My name is Richard Light. I live in Wilderness Place, King Street and I am a fireman. The deceased James Light was my brother. I have identified his body lying here. My brother was a fireman in the employ of the Great Eastern Railway Company. He was twenty-five years of age and lived in Wilderness Place, King Street.

(*Eastern Daily Press*, Monday, 14 September 1874)

The faint photograph on James' marble tribute, shows a tidy young man with slicked black hair, combed with a straight side parting, wearing a pristine velvet collared jacket and an enigmatic smile. His career had been progressing well, James learning from the best, taking decent money home to help put food on the table, enjoying the life of a single man with a bright future.

On the following Tuesday, 15 September, there was a joint funeral at the Rosary Cemetery, paid for by Great Eastern Railway. The bodies of both John Prior and James Light were carried aloft by railway colleagues and buried side by side, while the accumulated ranks of the Great Eastern Railway looked on.

His brother Richard, who so bravely identified the remains of his older brother, now had the sole responsibility to achieve his promotion to Driver. But it was not to be; less than three years later, on 19 June 1877, Richard drowned in the River Wensum, swimming in contaminated water. He was 24 years old, buried in the Rosary alongside his brother.

## Frederick Sewell

Richard Light was recalled stating:

> I know Frederick Sewell. He was not related to me. I have seen a body and identify it as that of Frederick Sewell. He was about thirty-five years of age and lived at Lowestoft. He was occasionally employed as a fireman on the railway, but generally worked at Lowestoft as a cleaner.
>
> (*Eastern Daily Press*, Monday, 14 September 1874)

Frederick had one more train journey to complete before he was laid to rest. His body was returned to Lowestoft, to be interred at the parish church of St Margaret's, also on the following Tuesday. Emily had been widowed for a second time. At the funeral, she was supported by many of Frederick's colleagues from Lowestoft station. One week before Christmas, Emily honoured Frederick's memory by taking her eldest daughter, the child of her first husband, to be baptised with the name Clara Louisa Sewell.

## Marianne Murray

> My name is James Murray. I live in Mariner's Lane in the city of Norwich and I am a tailor. The deceased Marian Elizabeth Murray was my daughter. She resided with me. I have seen her body. She was twenty-seven years of age and was a spinster.
>
> (*Eastern Daily Press*, Monday, 14 September 1874)

Marianne's final words to her rescuers, as she lay among the mound of timbers and broken metal were said to be, "Now my friends, for a great effort" (*East Anglian Handbook*, 1875), spoken seconds before the young milliner breathed her last. It took several hours to retrieve her body, finally bringing her into the pub, her left arm raised in the air, as if protecting herself from some danger. With rigor mortis already set in, it had proved impossible to lay the arm by her side. Marianne had been well known in the city, and a week later photographic artist Edwin Cunningham placed an advertisement in the Eastern Daily Press: 'Portraits of the late lamented Miss Marianne Murray may be had at Cunningham's, St Benedict's Norwich. By post 6d each.'

On the Wednesday following the inquest, the *Eastern Daily Press* claimed that the couple had been due to be married on 11 September, setting off a very public rumour that upset Marianne's alleged fiancé. He immediately complained, requesting total anonymity and a retraction in the following day's edition:

> We have been informed that the paragraph relating to Miss Murray was in some particulars inaccurate. We find that the young man who was riding with her is not suffering from a broken leg, but from fractured ribs, and there is no grounds for the statement that they were upon the eve of their marriage, no time having been set for that event.
>
> (*Eastern Daily Press*, Monday, 12 September 1874)

In the same newspaper, Marianne's parents, James and Mary Ann, placed a notice announcing the death of their only, and much-loved, child. She would be much missed.

## Sergeant Ward and Sergeant-Major Cassell

My name is Frederick Mills. I live at the Militia Barracks in the city of Norwich. I am quartermaster sergeant in the West Norfolk Militia. I knew Robert Ward well and I identify his body. He was colour-sergeant in West Norfolk Militia, and I should think he was about 50. He was not on duty when in the train but was on a fishing excursion. The deceased lived in Cherry Street, Lakenham, in the city of Norwich. I also identify Frederick Cassell, who was a sergeant major in the West Norfolk Militia. He was about forty-six years of age. He lived at the Militia Barracks.

(*Eastern Daily Press*, Monday, 14 September 1874)

In death, as in life, the two old soldiers were linked together at the inquest, identified not by a relative, but by a colleague from the Barracks. On the following Monday both men were buried with full military honours, the ceremonies held at separate churches, the timings calculated so that the drum and fife band of the West Norfolk Militia could make an appearance at both. Robert Ward was interred at his local church of St Mark's in Lakenham, Frederick Cassell at Norwich Cemetery at Earlham. Large crowds gathered to watch the proceedings, intrigued to be mixing with high-ranking officers from the British Army and the local Militia.

Sympathy was high and the Army set about raising money to support the two grieving families. On 7 November 1874, the *Norfolk News* published a joint message from Eleanor and Eliza:

> Mrs Cassell and Mrs Ward, widows of the two sergeants in the West Norfolk Militia, whose husbands were killed in the late terrible Thorpe collision, desire return their sincere and grateful thanks to the pensioners in Colonel Cockburn's district for their kind and handsome present to them from their last quarterly payments.

In the meantime, both widows worked together to instruct lawyers to represent them in a compensation claim against GER. Uncertain how long they could feed their children on charity alone, for Eleanor and Eliza the hearing could not come soon enough.

## Sarah Ann Gilding and daughter Laura

My name is Charles Chaplin. I live in Stephen's Street, Norwich and am a boot and shoe manufacturer. I knew Sarah Gilding well, but she was not a relative of mine.

I identify her body. She was a married woman living at 40, Grafton Street, Mile-end-Road, London. Her husband is an insurance agent. I should think the deceased's age was about 38. I can also identify the body of Laura Harriet Caroline, daughter of the deceased Sarah Gilding. The age of the child, I think, was about four years and she resided with her father at 40 Grafton-Street, Mile-end-Road, London. They were here on a visit. I do not know Mr Gilding's Christian name.

(Eastern Daily Press, Monday, 14 September 1874)

Mr Chaplin was not quite correct. Sarah Ann was in fact only 31 when she died along with little Laura. It is to be hoped that they had enjoyed a happy day together, for the circumstances of their death was reported as being particularly horrific. *The Scotsman* newspaper wrote that Laura's lifeless figure was 'black', her body cut nearly in two, while her mother was also cut into several pieces. On receiving the unexpected and devastating news, Sarah Ann's husband Charles was faced with the reality of single-handedly caring for his two baby sons, the youngest only 5 months old.

# Russell William Skinner

My name is John Downing Farrer. I live at Ivy Gates, Mount Pleasant, Eaton, Norwich. I am of no business or profession. The deceased William was a personal friend of mine. He was a retired farmer or tradesman. I cannot say which. I saw his body yesterday, and recognise it as his. He lived on Newmarket Road. He was a gentleman, and think his age was about 40.

(Eastern Daily Press, Monday, 14 September 1874)

Russell's body was taken to childhood home of Swaffling, for burial in the ancient, remote and tranquil churchyard of St Mary the Virgin, alongside his sister Lucy. Seven days following his inquest, mourners came together on the hillside overlooking the Suffolk village, comforted to learn that Russell's death would have almost certainly been instantaneous. Rumours passed from family to friends were that in death, his face was perfectly calm and placid. One leg was broken, but it was internal injuries that had proved fatal. The family were upset to hear that Russell's gold watch was missing from his wrist, allegedly pilfered at the scene of the crash.

At Russell's graveside, Annie grieved for her husband while Russell's elderly parents lamented the loss of a second child. The officiating parson spoke candidly.

'It was not an ordinary death. It was violent, painful and awfully sudden, and such as might happen to ourselves.' (*Ipswich Journal*, 19 September 1874) After the interment, the mourners lingered for some time, the enormity of Russell's premature death difficult to comprehend. As the newspaper reported later, 'there were few eyes that were not bedimmed with tears on this mournful day'. (*Ipswich Journal*, 19 September 1874)

In the knowledge that she could not simply rely on her in-laws to help her out financially, Annie knew she had the winter months to prepare a case for a compensation claim against GER. There was a lot of money at stake.

# Susanna Lincoln

> My name is Arthur Coyte. I am a gentleman, living at Thorpe. I knew Susanna Lincoln well. She was in my service for about thirteen years as cook. I have seen her body and identify it. Her age was about 35 as near as I can tell. She resided with me.
>
> (*Eastern Daily Press*, Monday, 14 September 1874)

On the late evening of 10 September, the Coyte household were concerned by Susanna's continuing absence from home. They knew she'd been on a visit to Great Yarmouth, but she was expected back that night. The son of a Suffolk Rector, Arthur was a beer merchant, married to his cousin Theophilia Reynolds. They made their home in Thorpe Hamlet, Norwich, quickly becoming well known in the best social circles. They loved to entertain and so employing a good cook was essential. For thirteen years Susanna had proved herself an excellent cook. At around

9.40 pm, the couple might have become aware of a commotion outside their door in Thorpe Road. A procession of carriages, cabs and carts was hurrying past heading towards Thorpe-Next-Norwich. Raised excitable voices called to each other, struggling to be heard over the relentless storm.

Arthur and Theophilia had no inkling that their cook was in trouble until, some hours later, there was a loud banging on the front door. One of those attending the wreck had recognised the fatally injured Susanna as his niece, immediately sending word to her employer. On Saturday morning it was Arthur Coyle who identified her broken body. Susanna's life's savings, modest as they were, passed to her heartbroken father.

# Reverend Henry and Mrs Stacey

My name is James Hall. I reside at No.7, Park-lane. Norwich. I am retired from business. I knew the deceased Henry Stacey perfectly well. I have seen his body, and identify it. His age was about 56, as near as I can tell. He lived at No.12, Upper St Giles. He was an Independent minister. He and Mrs Stacey came over to Yarmouth on Thursday to spend the day with me. I can also identify the body of Mary Ann Stacey. She was the wife of Rev. Henry Stacey. Her age was about 52.

(*Eastern Daily Press*, Monday, 14 September 1874)

James Hall had enjoyed his day with the Staceys, helping to celebrate thirty years of marriage. He was horrified to be summoned by the Coroner, arriving at the Three Tuns in time for the inquest. On Sunday morning, the Reverend Philip Colbourne addressed his congregation at the Chapel-in-the-Field, lamenting the loss of their new Brother Stacey, and assuring the shocked worshippers that Henry was as much under his Lord's protection when he met his death, as he was when engaged in preaching to them on the previous Sunday. The couple's joint funeral was arranged for the following Tuesday at Norwich Cemetery in Earlham, the same date as those of Miss Murray, Mrs Gilding and her daughter. It was said that the interment of Henry and Mary Ann was delayed, as the grave had been initially dug too small to take both coffins.

# Mary Ann Taylor

My name is William Joseph Nightingale of Elm Hill, merchant's clerk. The deceased Mary Ann Taylor was my Aunt. I have seen her body and I identify it as hers. She was forty-six years of age. She resided at Mr Caley's, London Street, Norwich and was what is called a Silk Mercher's Assistant. She had been there twenty-three years.

(*Eastern Daily Press*, Monday, 14 September 1874)

Initially the local press described Mary Ann's body as being 'shapeless and horribly disfigured', but in a later edition of the *Eastern Daily Press* on 14 September, the editor apologised, retracting the distressing comment;

> We regret to learn that in our first edition of this morning, one of the horribly disfigured corpses was wrongly identified as Miss Taylor, Mr Caley's Forewoman. A correspondent informs us that she looked most calm and peaceful.

William Joseph was the son of the late William Royal Nightingale, a well-known Norwich grocer and tea dealer, who had died in 1867. Mary Ann was, in fact, only distantly related to them through marriage, but she was much loved throughout the extended family. Her body was laid to rest on the non-conformist side of Norwich Cemetery, the ceremony attended by loyal customers, gathering to say goodbye to this popular and respected employee at the famous Caley's Draper's store. Her coffin was almost hidden by the mountain of flowers thrown into her grave. On the following Friday, 18 September, a disturbing letter appeared in the *Eastern Daily Press*, signed by her nephew William:

> Sir – it has become known to the relatives of the late Miss Taylor that a person is going about the city with a brief purporting to be from friends of the deceased, soliciting contributions towards defraying the expenses of her funeral. I beg to state that such a person is acting without any instructions or authority whatsoever, and I wish to warn the public against giving anything. If any person can give me any information, which might lead to the identity of

the person, I shall be gratefully obliged. She is described to me as a smartly dressed young woman. Yours truly, W.J. Nightingale, Elm Hill.

A memorial service for Mary Ann was held two weeks later at the Calvert Street Chapel, every seat taken, many unable to gain admittance. During his sermon, the Reverend Ogden spoke of how Mary Ann had been a loyal member of the congregation for nineteen years, continuing to attend services right up to her death. He added, 'She was very kind to the poor and more than one aged and infirm person will mourn for the friend they have lost.' (*Norfolk News*, 3 October 1874). The final two hymns were said to be particular favourites of Mary Ann. During the renditions of 'Safe in the Arms of Jesus' and 'Home Sweet Home', there was much weeping among the congregation.

Three weeks later William Nightingale was feeling stressed. Not only had his beloved Aunt died under the direst of circumstances, but he had been planning his wedding for the 20 October, only five weeks after her death. Despite everything, the wedding went ahead. Mary Ann's nephew married his fiancée, Emily Elizabeth Ringer, daughter of Robert Ringer, a Norfolk gunmaker. The wedding took place in the same Calvert Street Chapel where Mary Ann's memorial service was held. The absence of the groom's Aunt at his nuptials would be much lamented.

## Elizabeth Betts and infant William Betts

Cordwainer William Gibbs of Cherry Street in Lakenham, spoke up in front of the County Coroner Edward Press and the members of the jury.

> The deceased Elizabeth Betts was my daughter. I have seen the body and identify it as hers. She was 29 years old. Her husband's name was John Betts of Cherry Street, Lakenham. He was a fireman in the employ of the G.E.R.
> (*Eastern Daily Press*, Monday, 14 September 1874)

Mercifully, Elizabeth's suffering had been brief. As their carriage disintegrated around them, she and her infant son were killed instantly, as the child lay cradled in her arms. Her husband John lay unconscious beside her, oblivious to Elizabeth's fate. As rescuers dragged young Charles from the wreckage, they were elated to discover the 3-year-old was still breathing, the only sign of injury being a slight scalp wound. He was taken along with his father to the hospital, his mother and baby brother left behind on the floor of the Three Tuns. Eliza and her infant son were buried together on the following Wednesday, a day of widespread mourning in Norwich and beyond. Family, neighbours and railway workers from the GER arrived at St Marks Church in Lakenham, to pay their respects. The only person missing was her husband John.

# The Man Unknown

> William Hardy, bricklayer, Thorpe, said—l am parish constable. There the body of a man lying dead here whose name is unknown. We have tried, but have been unable ascertain his name. I should say he is about 40 years of age.
>
> (*Eastern Daily Press*, Monday, 14 September 1874)

This information was disturbing. The Foreman asked whether the witness had examined the linen to see whether there are any marks upon it. The Coroner intervened.

> I am afraid that would not help us. There are some marks on the shirt being 'S.R.S.' If the body is identified before the time for burial, we will take care to enter his name upon the proceedings.
>
> (*Eastern Daily Press*, Monday, 14 September 1874)

The Chief Constable stepped in:

> The police have searched the body thoroughly, they find only some initials on the linen. There are no papers to lead us to the identity of the body. A photograph of the deceased has been taken.
>
> (*Eastern Daily Press*, Monday, 14 September 1874)

Without identification, the body could not be removed from the pub. John Hart reluctantly agreed that he could remain there, as long as it wasn't for *too* long. Something like this could kill his trade.

With all the bodies, bar one, accounted for, the Coroner officially released them for burial. The jury was bound over to meet again at the Shirehall on the following Thursday. As the witnesses gasped for fresh air on the forecourt of the pub, the shells were brought out one by one, loaded onto carts to be delivered into the care of undertakers. As the slow solemn procession trundled along Thorpe Road towards the city, villagers respectfully drew their curtains, stood in doorways or lined the streets. Men doffed their hats, heads hung low, as they bade farewell to their unfortunate temporary guests.

\*\*\*\*\*

The detective work to identify the unknown corpse continued. That very day, on reading details of the accident in the local press, George Colk from the Bath Hotel in Yarmouth, contacted his local police station, alerting officers that a male guest was missing. Superintendent Tewsley did not hesitate to travel to the coast, where Mr Colk produced his guest book, showing the superintendent the entry for Richard Slade of Regent Street in London.

Mr Colk unlocked the door to the man's bedroom, where the detective respectfully searched the guest's portmanteau, relieved to find a number of expensive neatly steamed shirts, each marked with initials S.R.S. A letter addressed to Slade, care of the hotel, was found to be from the victim's brother, a Mr James Slade, London auctioneer and land agent. James was summoned, arriving in Norwich on the following Tuesday, where he met with William Hardy, parish constable in Thorpe-Next-Norwich. The two men visited the Three Tuns to view the body of the man who had been lying alone, inside its temporary shell, for nearly five days. James knew immediately that this was his younger brother, Standley Richard Slade, of 41 Elliott Road, Brixton, aged 25, an architect and surveyor with Ackerman, Slade and Co., of Regent Street in London. He was born in Poole in Dorset in 1849 and was an unmarried man. Formalities over, James arranged for an undertaker to place his brother into a solid oak coffin, to be taken to London, most probably by rail. Standley's funeral was held on 19 September, at Norwood Cemetery, only two miles from his home.

Not many in attendance that day would be aware that the deceased and his three surviving siblings, Robert, James, and Emma, were born illegitimate, to the same father; his identity remained a family secret. Standley's mother Amelia, now 51, was herself born 'out of wedlock' to Charlotte Ballams, in the Dorset village of Winterbourne, eighteen miles inland from Poole. Three years later Charlotte married mariner John Ford, most likely Amelia's father, a man who spent much of his time away from home, travelling the Atlantic on merchant ships belonging to his employer, Robert Slade of Poole. Robert Slade was from a celebrated dynasty of successful merchants who, during the mid-eighteenth century, were responsible for opening up territory in Newfoundland, developing a profitable trade with Europe, importing cod, salmon and animal furs. Year on year the family business expanded, with sons and nephews building fleets of swift, small square-rigged merchant ships known as brigs, often operating in competition with each other.

In March 1817, as a young man of 22, Robert Slade married Sarah Gardiner, the 17-year-old daughter of a local brewer. Within ten months Sarah produced the all-important male heir, naming him John. Over the following twenty years, Sarah, despite five miscarriages, bore three further sons and a daughter. She had married into one of the wealthiest and influential families in Dorset, her husband was ambitious, hard working and in time, both a magistrate and Sheriff of Poole, when only 30 years old. The social expectations on Sarah would have been enormous.

Early in 1830, a criminal case at the Dorchester Assizes stunned the county of Dorset, every word transcribed in the *Sherbourne Mercury* of 22 March. Robert Slade, now 35, was seeking compensation from a Mr Henry Furnell, Timber Merchant and married man. Robert accused Furnell of 'having criminal conversation with his wife Sarah' and by doing so, not only deprived Robert of the 'affections of his wife and of the comfort and enjoyment of her society', but he had also robbed Robert's five children of their mother.

Robert was furious at being seen as a cuckolded husband, and sought a colossal £3,000 in damages (£345,000). The opening remarks by counsel for the prosecution set the tone:

> I will call witnesses to prove that the wife of the plaintiff
> is a most abandoned and profligate woman and that the

defendant had conferred a blessing upon her children by causing her being removed from them.

*(Sherbourne Mercury*, 22 March 1830)

In a session that lasted for over ten hours, closing finally at half-past midnight, the intrigued public gallery learnt that Robert and Sarah had been living apart since Christmas with Sarah denied access to her children. As each witness stepped into the dock, Sarah's reputation as a devoted wife and mother was steadily demolished.

It was claimed that for five years Sarah had been actively flirtatious with random army officers, the family gardener, and latterly had publicly demonstrated signs of over familiarity with the defendant, Mr Furnell, a colleague and so-called friend of the plaintiff. In turn Furnell denied that anything improper ever took place.

Whether Sarah was guilty or not, her gender was against her. The jury of twelve men found for the plaintiff, also showing sympathy for Mr Furnell, who had clearly been seduced by the temptress. Damages were set at only £400 (£46,000) considerably less than Robert had requested. Furnell claimed he was bankrupt, virtually destitute. But Robert refused to show leniency, refusing to drop the debt. Furnell was imprisoned for ten months. But Robert had not finished yet.

In the *Dorset County Chronicle* of Thursday, 18 November 1830, tucked away among the official notices, was a legal announcement:

> Slade v. Slade. This was a suit instituted by Robert Slade, Junior, of Poole, Esq., against Mrs Slade, his wife, in the Ecclesiastical Court of the Royal Peculiar of Great Canford and Poole, for a divorce a mensa et thoro. The evidence in the suit on the part of the husband arose out of a cause 'Slade v. Furnell' which it will be recollected was tried at the last Lent Assizes at Dorchester.

It was the first divorce case in Dorset, in which sentence was pronounced in a public court. However, it is important to note that the wording of the decree meant that Robert and Sarah were simply no longer legally obliged to live together as man and wife. The marriage was not actually dissolved, meaning that neither party could remarry. Sarah's disgrace was complete. She disappears without trace.

It is about now that Robert finds himself attracted to the much younger Amelia Ford. When she was 22 Amelia gave birth to a son, his baptism recorded in the family church of St James, Poole in 1835, as 'Robert Slade, born of Amelia Ford, Spinster'. Six years later Amelia has three children, and is living with her mother Charlotte in West Street in Poole. The census records Amelia as being 'independent', suggesting that Robert is financially supporting his growing 'second family'.

Over the next fourteen years Amelia gave birth to four more of Robert's children. However, during this period, tragedy was never far away. In 1847, in the space of two months, Robert lost his eldest son to illness and his second son was drowned in the sea off the coast of Newfoundland. The Slade business empire was going through a bad time.

Two years later, Amelia had a fourth child, named Standley Richard Slade, Standley being a traditional Slade family name. When he was just 2, his two older brothers left home for boarding school in Christchurch, Hampshire. Robert moved Amelia into a fashionable merchant's house in the West Street area of Poole, next door to Robert's legitimate son, Thomas. It seems likely that over the years, the two families were building a discreet understanding. However, by 1861 Robert Slade and Company had dissolved, Robert is 65 years old, sharing a home with David, his youngest surviving son, bitter and increasingly intolerant, withdrawing from many of his civic and community responsibilities. Just three years later in January 1864, Robert Slade died unexpectedly one Sunday evening after supper, having suffered for some time from acute indigestion. His body was consigned to the family tomb, his funeral attracting a great many people from the town and beyond. The newspaper report named his sons Thomas and David as chief mourners, but there was no mention of Amelia, Robert, James or Standley. Social mores of the time determined that it was unacceptable for them to attend. However, Amelia was well provided for and continued to live on a modest income provided by her late lover.

Amelia's three sons were destined to lead very different lives. The eldest trained in medicine in Bermondsey, becoming a member of the Royal College of Surgeons and working as a country doctor. James found respectable work as a Land Agent, and Standley, after a difficult start, gained employment at a large auction house. If he had not travelled to Great Yarmouth when he did, his future could have been successful, perhaps taking a wife, having children, making his mother proud. Instead, in death Standley became the subject of unwelcome and public speculation, his final journey home inside an oak coffin, accompanied by his elder brother James.

*****

During Saturday, the Bishop of Norwich issued a circular to his clergy, urging them to amend their planned Sunday services to include prayers for those involved in or bereaved by the late sad accident. Sunday became a day of mourning in the city, ministers and priests of all denominations referring to the recent calamity in Thorpe, offering up prayers and preaching on the subject of resurrection. Donations were collected for the families, including one at St Stephen's Church, raising money for the widows of John Ward and Frederick Cassell, the congregation shocked that two fine men who had worshipped with them only the previous Sunday were now no more. At Norwich Cathedral, the Reverend Canon Ormesby appealed to his congregation not to allow such a tragedy shake their faith in the Lord. During that afternoon the 'Dead March' was played on the cathedral organ before and after the service while hundreds of candles were lit.

# Chapter 6

# The Norfolk and Norwich Hospital

Despite the severity of the collision, the majority of the passengers were able to make their own way home, shaken, aching and confused, but thankful to be alive. Those with live-in servants, attentive spouses or able to pay for medical help, were sent home to rest. Mark Smith, Peter Eade, Richard White, William Francis and Charles Gilman all slept in their own beds that first night, with doctors regularly attending to them for as long as was required.

From about 10.00 pm, a bedraggled group of walking wounded began arriving at the Norfolk and Norwich Hospital demanding help, some accompanied by anxious, agitated and often unruly family members. The outpatients department was very soon overrun. A message went out to off-duty, retired and trainee surgeons, physicians and nurses, urging them to come in and help. Additional nursing staff were requested from St John's House in London, a training institution for nurses founded in 1848 and a reliable source of extra staff if needed. Reinforcements were promised by the morning train. Many of the passengers had relatively minor injuries, mainly cuts and bruises. They were examined, patched up, offered wooden crutches if required and dismissed with a bottle of purgative. This mixture of iron, sulphate of magnesia and cod liver oil was traditionally dispensed from a large brown jug. The importance of good bowel movements in recovery could never be over-estimated.

However, twenty-seven of the injured gave real cause for concern, some in need of immediate surgery. This included the normally ebullient John Beart from Aldburgh, whose arm was beyond saving. Patients were distributed among the different wards and next of kin informed. Copious mugs of hot tea eased the patients' incessant thirst, thought to be a result of smoke inhalation. Nursing staff noted how calm the patients appeared, facing painful examination of broken limbs without complaint, as if resigned to their fate. But as the hours passed, the initial effects of shock began to ease. Inevitable aches and soreness, fever and raised pulse rates, caused patients to become restless, crying out in distress. Pain relief and sleep came courtesy of a dose of opium.

Among many others, three members of the surgical staff stood out for their role in the unfolding events over the weeks that followed. Senior surgeon Thomas William Crosse, 48, known to his friends as Tom, was also the Chief of Medical Staff, responsible for admissions. He had attended the crash site, fighting to save lives under the most extreme circumstances, later heard to admit his relief on returning to the 'comparative calm, systematic and orderly condition of the hospital'. It was Thomas who diligently submitted daily progress reports to the newspapers.

Assistant surgeon Michael Beverley, 33, was rarely away from his patients, constantly assessing signs of improvement or deterioration. Live-in house surgeon Richard Baumgartner, the youngest at 28, had organised the initial processing and registration during the chaos of the first night, assisted with surgical procedures and was responsible for monitoring procedures on the wards. Sadly, the staff did not have long to wait for the first death.

In the collision, harness-maker Job Hupton's jaw and skull had been fractured and he suffered internal injuries. In the early hours of Friday morning he was taken straight from Thorpe to the hospital, supported by Constable John Smith. One look at Job and medical staff feared the worse. Samuel Hupton arrived during the evening, anxiously searching for his older brother, sitting at his bedside until Job succumbed to his wounds at 10.00 pm that evening. Samuel returned home to spend the weekend sharing his grief with the family, promising to return on Tuesday next for the inquest.

At 9.00 pm on Saturday evening, Thomas Crosse finally found a moment to sit at his desk. Despite feeling drained, sleep-deprived, and demoralised, he had to prepare his first progress report for Monday's newspapers, a duty that continued for some weeks, the public craving detail after detail. He wrote:

> Most of the patients are going on well and there have been
> no further deaths. Several of the female sufferers are very

ill, and manifest signs of internal injuries in addition to their broken limbs and wounds. The man Betts remains in very nearly the same condition as yesterday; he has been a little less restless today. Mr Beart, whose arm was amputated, is going on remarkably well, and so is Mr Page. The latter gentleman will probably be removed home in a day or two.

(*Eastern Daily Press*, Monday, 14 September 1874)

For three nights the hospital had been inundated with enquiries from anxious friends and relatives. In addition, an army of well wishers continued to arrive at all hours, many offering generous donations and bringing gifts for the sick. The halls were piled high with boxes of linen, bags of flour, books, volumes of illustrated newspapers, bed jackets, patchwork quilts, grapes, splints, home brewed ale, game and floral tributes. As he completed his report, Thomas had something else to say:

Much trouble and inconvenience has been occasioned at the Hospital by numerous enquiries and visits that are made by friends and acquaintances of the inmates, which not only entail great additional labour upon the executive but are also calculated to prejudice the recovery of the patients. (Signed) T.W. Crosse.

(*Eastern Daily Press*, 14 September 1874)

As he wrote the report, Tom made the decision not yet to mention the death of Job Hupton. Best to wait for the inquest.

# Inquest of Job John Hupton
# Died Friday night, 11 September 1874

Samuel Barnard Hupton stepped up saying,

I am carpenter and joiner living in Norwich. The body, which has been shown the jury, is that of my brother, Job John Hupton, who lived at Yarmouth, and was a harness maker. He was 45 years of age.

John Smith said, 'I am a constable in the Norwich Police Force. On Thursday night last I was on duty at Thorpe Station, and shortly after twelve o'clock I heard of the collision at Thorpe. About a quarter to one I saw the train come in. It was composed of engine, tender, and a goods train. I saw a man taken out who was then unknown, and who was very seriously wounded. He was put upon a stretcher and taken to the Hospital, to which place I accompanied him. I have seen the body now lying in the dead-house, and which has just been shown to the jury; it is the body of the man whom I accompanied to the Hospital on Friday morning.'

Mr Baumgartner added, 'I was there on Friday morning last when the deceased was brought in. He was suffering from a fracture of the skull, and I considered at the time that the wounds were of fatal nature.'

(*Norwich Mercury*, Wednesday, 16 September 1874)

At the appointed time, City Coroner Mr Bignold arrived at the hospital mortuary, his intention, as before, to identify the body and establish cause of death. Gathered together were Mr Baumgartner, Police Constable John Smith and Samuel Hupton. At the conclusion of the formalities there was nothing left to say. Samuel arranged for Job's body to be taken to Great Yarmouth, where he was buried at the Parish Church of St Nicholas on 18 September. The Hupton family had experienced the deaths of two close family members within four months. Job's wife Eliza was now a single mother at 29 years old, her youngest just 6 months old. She had little choice but to find the money to pay for a lawyer. She must fight for compensation from GER. She would have to wait until the following February for her day in court.

At the hospital, the days immediately following Job's death were relatively uneventful. The erratic behaviour of railway fireman John Betts continued to be a concern. He was becoming increasingly deranged, ranting that he'd been riding in the cab of his engine at the time of the accident, insisting he'd been struck on the head by a stone, thrown by an unknown mischievous boy.

On the following Tuesday, Mr Baumgartner faced his next summons from the Coroner.

# Inquest of Susan Browne
# Died Tuesday, 15 September 1874

My name is Edward Robinson and I am a cab-driver in the employ of Mr Meadows of the White Hart. On Thursday evening last I was at Thorpe Station. From what I heard that night I went to Thorpe to render what assistance I could. I brought two wounded females from the Tuns public house to this Hospital. The body lying here is that of one of the females whom I brought here. I knew her in her lifetime, and I identify the body that of Susan Browne. I do not think that she was a married woman.

Mr Baumgartner added, 'I remember Susan Browne being brought here the same morning. She had a compound dislocation of the ankle joint and severe internal injuries. The internal injuries have since been ascertained by post-mortem examination. She died from inflammation resulting from those internal injuries. She was, I believe, conscious during the whole of the time she was here.'

(*Eastern Daily Press*, Friday, 18 September 1874)

Susan was 33, an unmarried seamstress and the daughter of Thomas Browne, a shoemaker. Born in the Broadland village of Salhouse, in 1841, the family later moved into the city to find work. Her trade took her to the south bank of the River Wensum, where the textile industry had flourished since the Middle Ages. With an increasing demand for inexpensive ready-made garments, such as breeches, shirts, waistcoats, shifts and petticoats, work as a seamstress could mean working eighteen-hour shifts alongside dozens of others, often working through the night in a poorly lit workshop, cold in winter, too hot in summer. Susan may have suffered bleeding fingers, puffy strained eyes, constant pain in the back and ribs and continual hunger pangs. Opening a window for ventilation meant allowing the overwhelming putrid smells of the river below to infiltrate the air. Rotting fish, vermin, domestic rubbish and sewage accumulated with the stinking tannins, oils and arsenic spewing into the river from the dyeing works in the Maddermarket area. Susan took lodgings in Mary's Yard, where her living conditions were equally as squalid as her workplace. What little she did earn was used to support her family. Losing her life in the Thorpe accident meant even further hardship for those left behind. Susan was most probably laid to rest at a pauper's funeral, buried without ceremony or headstone to mark the spot.

\*\*\*\*\*

Over the night of 14/15 September, John Betts' life hung in the balance. Consumed by grief and suffering interminable agony from the deep cut in the centre of his head, John died on Wednesday morning from inflammation of the brain. The Coroner made his way once again to the hospital.

## Inquest of John Willis Betts
## Died Wednesday, 15 September 1874

My name is John Smith and I am a constable in the Norwich Police Force. I have seen the body just shown to the jury, and it is that of John Betts. I knew him in his lifetime. I saw him about a quarter to one on Friday morning last, when I was at Thorpe Railway Station. I saw a brake or a van arrive from the scene of the accident at Thorpe. The deceased was in an unconscious state. I assisted in taking him out of the van, and accompanied him to the Hospital. I identify him as the body lying there.

Mr J.R. Baumgartner stepped forward. 'I was here on Friday morning last when the deceased John Betts was brought here. He was suffering from a large wound on the forehead and a fractured skull. I considered at the time that he was fatally wounded.'

(*Eastern Daily Press*, Friday, 18 September 1874)

Everyone attending the inquest was painfully aware of the family tragedy unfolding in front of them. Over the past few days, newspapers had published numerous bulletins about John's progress, the public fascinated by his story. The prime concern now was for 3-year-old orphan Charles. The bulletin issued by Thomas Crosse on 19 September read: 'Betts' little orphan child, who was admitted with concussion of the brain, is nearly well.' This good news broke on the same day that John Betts was buried alongside his wife and baby son, in St Mark's Churchyard in Lakenham, witnessed by colleagues from the Great Eastern Railway.

With both Charles' parents now gone, decisions had to be made. The boy's maternal grandparents, William and Mary Gibbs, offered to raise the boy in Lakenham, where they lived next door to the boy's uncle, their surviving son Frederick, who supported the family as a skilled cordwainer, making fine leather shoes and boots. It was a busy household with little Charles fussed over by five uncles and aunts, including Aunt Sarah, a domestic nurse. As the years passed, any memories of John, Elizabeth and baby brother William, would fade away, becoming the stuff of family legend.

# Inquest of Charlotte Coote
# Died Tuesday, 29 September 1874

I am Mr George Coote. warehouseman, in the employ of Mr C. Larke, distiller, Mile End. London, and I identify the body of this female as my wife. I was not with the deceased at the time of the collision.

(*Eastern Daily Press*, 1 October 1874)

Mr Baumgartner recalled Charlotte being admitted to the hospital suffering from a compound fracture of her left leg and severe bruising all over her body. Her left knee was set in a temporary splint when she passed into the care of the ward nursing staff. Despite being classified as a grave case with little chance of recovery, for eighteen days she fought for life, even showing signs of improvement, sustained by the knowledge that her daughter was safe. But in the early hours of the morning on Tuesday 29 September, Charlotte quietly slipped away. A post mortem, carried out by Dr Beverley, with Mr Baumgartner observing, revealed severe internal injuries and evidence of blood poisoning. Anxious not to raise alarm, Mr Baumgartner testified that in his opinion it was

Charlotte's injuries that ultimately killed her. Nonetheless, real concern was growing among the hospital staff about a potential outbreak of the dreaded Pyaemia (a form of Septicaemia) arising among an increasing number of patients.

Charlotte was 40 years old when she died. On the night of the accident, as her mother was placed in a carriage and taken to hospital, the shocked and bruised Mary Ann was cared for in the King's Head pub until a family member could be found to take her home. While his wife and daughter were away, Charlotte's husband George was visiting Liverpool. He wrote Charlotte a letter, sending it to her Yarmouth lodgings, a letter she never received. Concerned when he did not hear from her, George made some inquiries, horrified to learn that his wife was a victim of the well-publicised railway incident. He rushed to her bedside before collecting Mary Ann from the Thorpe pub, grateful for the kindness shown to her. At the inquest, George explained that Charlotte had always been so robust, never suffering any ill health. This had come as a dreadful blow.

George arranged for his wife's body to be transported back to London, hastily arranging a funeral for the afternoon of Saturday, 3 October, at Bow Cemetery. The local newspaper reported that, 'a great number of persons attended.' Eight of those mourners were Charlotte's grieving children.

*****

During the next six days, there was some respite from the much-publicised deaths, with everyone praying that the genial John Beart would pull through. On arriving in Norwich, following a tedious journey from Aldeburgh, George Beart found his father to be missing his right arm. The limb had been so severely crushed, that on arrival at the hospital, the surgeons immediately amputated just above the elbow. Over the following days John appeared to be doing well, members of his family visiting on a number of occasions, reassured by medical staff that John would recover. But his right leg, badly swollen and covered with bruises, developed an abscess that refused to heal. He weakened over a matter of days and eventually died, surrounded by family, during the night of Wednesday, 30 September. He was 61 years old.

# Inquest of John Beart
# Died Wednesday, 30 September 1874

I am George Hunt Beart, grocer and draper living at Aldburgh, Suffolk. I can confirm that the male body the jury had just seen is that of my father, who carried on business at Aldburgh. I last saw my father the morning of the 10th of September, when he left home for the purpose of visiting Yarmouth, and afterwards proceeding to Norwich.

(*Eastern Daily Press*, Thursday, 1 October 1874)

Much to the relief of the hospital, there was no sign of infection in John's case, so no need for a post-mortem. His inquest took but a few minutes, the verdict recorded simply that John Beart had come by his death from injuries received at Thorpe.

The *Ipswich Journal* of 3 October reported on John Beart's sudden demise. The editor reassured his shocked readers that John had been 'perfectly resigned and very happy, passing away with little or no pain', reflecting the view of many when he wrote, 'Aldeburgh will miss a genial friend, good neighbour and worthy tradesman and we are of the opinion that his loss will be much felt.' John's broken body was returned to Suffolk on the Thursday night, his funeral set for Saturday, 3 October. Although Saturday was always a busy trading day in the town, a good many of his colleagues either closed their stores out of respect, or at the very least stood at their doorways as the funeral procession passed through the streets on its way to St Peter and St Paul's church, with its magnificent view over the North Sea. During the funeral tea the family discussed the possibility of bringing a compensation claim against GER. They would be contacting their family solicitor.

*****

At the same time as Charlotte and John were losing their lives, another patient was still fighting for hers at the Three Tuns in Thorpe. On 29 September the *Eastern Daily Press* reported on the current state to Miss Ellen Ramsdale:

We regret to state that Miss Ramsdale still lies in a critical condition. A second abscess to the amputated limb is forming. It is now ascertained that she also suffers from an injured spine but it is impossible to state to what extent, as until her leg is sufficient healed, no proper examination can be made. It is greatly to be feared, from the distressing symptoms, that there are other injuries.

*The Morning Post* on 1 October reported:

Miss Ramsdale is still lying in a very unsatisfactory state at the Three Tuns Tavern at Thorpe. She shows excitement as she hears the frequent trains roll by on the railway and it would be very desirable if she could be removed, but at present this cannot be attempted.

The city held its breath. The young heiress was becoming quite the sweetheart. On 10 October there appeared more information from the *Norfolk News*.

It will be, we are sure, gratifying to friends of this young lady to learn from the best authority that she is going on most favourably, and that from the beginning has borne her misfortune with exemplary patience. Her own reconciliation to the sad loss of her leg has been the cause of much comfort to her immediate relatives and attendants.

At the end of the month readers were reassured that Ellen was feeling much improved, had requested to be lifted up so that she might see the passing trains and that fears about her spinal injury were proving groundless. Ellen's recovery was a long and steady journey, but finally, on Sunday, 17 January 1875, Ellen was helped into St Andrew's Church to attend the morning service. She could now safely return to Essex Street and pass into the loving care of her mother. However, it was clear that Ellen would be a cripple for life and her mother began legal proceedings against Great Eastern Railways, claiming compensation.

*****

During October 1874, the majority of the victims recovering in hospital were finally discharged. But after six weeks, housemaid Jane Faulkner was still there, weak and poorly, despite her broken legs appearing to heal. Towards the end of October, her condition swiftly deteriorated, her wounds infected, with doctors forced to admit she was suffering from the highly contagious Pyaemia. This was despite recent efforts made to improve hygiene in the wards by increasing ventilation, closing and cleaning wards by rotation, banning the practice of multi-use sponges and reducing the number of beds to allow more space between them. But progress proved too slow for Jane. Her destiny was to be the final recorded hospital death directly resulting from the Thorpe collision. Her inquest was held on the day of her death, her Aunt Elizabeth called as a witness.

## Inquest of Jane Ann Faulkner
## Died Wednesday, 27 October 1874

> Elizabeth Faulkner said 'I have been a nurse at the Hospital for 25 years. The deceased, Jane Ann Faulkner was my niece. She was brought to the hospital on the night of the collision, and I have nursed her all the time she has been here. She was a general servant, in the employ of Mr Rust, of 31 Prince Wales' Road.'
>
> (*Eastern Daily Press*, Friday, 30 October 1874)

Mr Baumgartner was once again quick to point out that in all probability Jane would have died, even had the infection not made an appearance. The jury, carefully avoiding using the word Pyaemia, cautiously recorded the cause of death as injuries received in the railway collision on the night of 10 September.

With Jane's body released for burial, the hospital was finally free of victims from the Thorpe Disaster. It had been a tough ride, especially with every move recorded and released for public scrutiny. Letters to newspaper editors revealed the sympathy and admiration felt by many for the doctors, nurses and others working at the hospital, resulting in donations flooding in from grateful patients, families and the public.

\*\*\*\*\*

Throughout the country, surgeons and physicians had been following the progress of the patients. There was much still to learn about symptoms of shock, treatment of trauma, avoidance of infection. Dr Peter Eade, writing both from his personal perspective as a survivor and as a physician privileged to attend the victims, promptly sent a detailed report to *The British Medical Journal*. His letter was published on 19 September. Having first outlined his own experience of the collision, he offered some insightful observations of the outcomes:

1. The cold collapsed state of all the injured, indicated by the feeble fluttering pulse, the cold and corpse-like feel of the skin, and the craving for brandy, and especially for extra covering, in several cases almost to the temporary ignoring of the fractures and other injuries they had sustained.
2. The undoubted fact that brandy administered to them in this collapsed state was of great comfort and support, and helped to restore warmth and cardiac steadiness.
3. The absence of bleeding to any serious extent from the scalp or other wounds.
4. The fact that the fractures of the lower extremities were nearly all at or just below the lower third of the limb – a result probably due either to the driving of the seat in front over them, or to the jerking forward of the legs beneath the seat in front; and Mr Crosse, the surgeon of the week at the hospital, and who consequently had the chief charge of those who were delivered thither, tells me that, very curiously where the fracture is single, it is in nearly all instances the left leg.

Dr Eade added;

Further, as has been before observed in railway accidents, the class of carriage seemed to bear a strict relation to the amount and seriousness of the injuries inflicted. And in this case of direct collision – the nearer they were to the engines, the more complete was the destruction of the carriages, and consequently the greater the danger which had been incurred by their occupants; the culminating point of nearness being reached in the case of the driver and the stoker, both of whom on each train were at once and almost necessarily destroyed.

# Chapter 7

# The Doctors

## Mr Thomas William Crosse (1825–1892)

Thomas Crosse was the eldest son of the celebrated surgeon, the late John Green Crosse, who had studied medicine in London, Dublin and Paris. In 1816, he married Dorothy Anne Bayley, the daughter of the Stowmarket Surgeon-Apothecary to whom he was apprenticed. By 1822, John had joined the staff at the Norfolk and Norwich hospital. Thomas was the youngest of five children. Their father's energy, intellect and outstanding surgical abilities led to him becoming a revered figure, described by his peers as 'Crosse of Norwich'. It was inevitable that at least one of his sons would follow him into medicine.

When his older brother, John Mcartney Crosse, entered a legal practice as an articled clerk, Thomas had little choice but to become his father's assistant at the hospital. As a youth of 16 he was given the most basic and challenging role of 'dresser'; one of his more daunting tasks to hold down struggling and screaming patients, watching on nervously as his father wielded the knife. It would be a further five years before Professor Robert Liston of University Hospital in London, famously performed the first operation using ether, an early form of modern anaesthesia.

Thomas was an apprentice for three years, before entering professional training at St Bartholomew's Hospital, qualifying in 1847. When his father died four years later, Thomas took over his practice in Norwich. Initially, as the son of a medical legend, he struggled to live up to people's expectations of him, at times distrusted and criticised by colleagues. Despite this, he was determined to establish himself as a talented and respected surgeon in his own right. In 1857, he was promoted to Assistant-Surgeon at the hospital. His skills proved to be sound, rather than brilliant, but as so many other Norwich surgeons, including his father, he excelled in the field of Lithotomy, the removal of calculi – stones formed inside organs such as the bladder, gallbladder and urinary tract. Norfolk had long held the reputation for having the highest incidence of this condition in the country. Since its foundation in 1771 as an early Stone Hospital, the Norfolk and Norwich Hospital established itself as a centre for excellent in this field. This led directly to the Hospital Pathological Museum, opened in 1845, the first museum at a provincial non-University hospital. At its height the glass cabinets contained over 3,000 specimens, with Thomas curating the collection for many years.

During 1872, increasingly loud voices complained about the deteriorating state of public sanitation and correlating health problems in the city. Councillors voted to appoint a Medical Officer for Health. Thomas Crosse was honoured to be the first to take on the pioneering role. By the time of the railway collision, Thomas had been married for twenty-seven years to Mary Jane Taylor, ten years his junior and daughter of a lawyer, living in an affluent home at 45 St Giles Street. He and Mary had five children, two girls, followed by three boys.

His courage, sense of justice and sense of humour must have helped Thomas get through that difficult period following the accident. But his efforts did not go unnoticed. On 26 September, an editorial piece appeared in the *Eastern Daily Press*, echoing the thoughts of so many:

> It well known that more than twenty of the sufferers were taken to the Norfolk Hospital, some very seriously hurt and others in various degrees injured. It was Mr Crosse's week at the Hospital, and he has had the management of all the wounded admitted at that time. We know, on the best of authority, that his attention to them has been unremitting and to an extraordinary extent personal, having spent hours daily in dressing their wounds with his own hands, and contributing in every way to increase the chances of their recovery. Surely this amount of gratuitous exertion, suddenly called for, and so willingly performed, deserves public expression of thankfulness as much as any other kind of assistance afforded, for it has been continuously employed and will yet, we fear, for many months to come more or less required.

Throughout his adult life, Thomas was plagued with recurring and disabling episodes of painful gout. He bore it cheerfully, never complaining, refusing to allow it to interfere with his commitments to the hospital and to the city. By the time of his retirement through ill health in 1888, after thirty-five years of service, he had sat on Norwich City Council, been Chairman of the Hospital Board of Management, President of the East Anglian Branch of the British Medical Association, Consulting Surgeon for both the Jenny Lind Children's Hospital and the Norwich Lying-in Charity. He lived to see his two eldest sons settled in their chosen professions, Arthur as Vicar of Hickling and Reginald as a house surgeon. His youngest son Herbert also followed his father's example, becoming a physician in Norwich. During 1892, at the age of 65, Thomas died suddenly at home on 26 October, his death attributed to a slow and distressing form of pleuropneumonia.

The funeral attracted an enormous number of mourners, family, friends, colleagues, patients, civic dignitaries and representatives from every association featuring in his life. The horse-drawn hearse left St Giles in the early afternoon, and by the time the procession reached the hospital, so many private carriages had joined it that it extended a quarter of a mile in length.

# Dr Michael Beverley (1841–1930)

During August 1874, Dr Beverley had addressed the Public Medicine Section of the Norwich Conference of the British Medical Association. His presentation proved controversial, triggering a protracted, public and often venomous exchange of views, chiefly between the progressive Dr Beverley and his older, more senior and conservative colleague, Dr Edward Copeman. Other correspondents soon became involved, many writing anonymously, the argument continuing for several weeks following the Thorpe accident. In his speech, Dr Beverley had denounced the Norfolk and Norwich Hospital for its worsening standards of hygiene, claiming increasing numbers of fatal bacterial infections among surgical patients. To a packed audience of his peers, Dr Beverley spoke about how the original design of the building, over one hundred years earlier, had given the hospital a reputation of being a 'relatively safe' place; its 'H' shape single-storey block, allowed 'free circulation of air', as recommended by physicians of the day. The ceilings were 15ft high, beds spaced apart and there was a ban on the admission of infectious cases.

However, over the decades, the hospital board had responded to growing patient numbers by adding new rooms and corridors, including residential rooms for nurses, administration offices, a board room, museum, chapel and two large accident wards, which quickly became overcrowded. There were raised eyebrows when Dr Beverley added: 'All these it would be necessary to sweep away, should any attempt be made to restore the present building to its former hygienic condition.' (*Norwich Mercury*, Saturday, 22 August 1874)

Dr Beverley continued his radical argument, quoting shocking statistics and telling how the hospital had, in the last six months, been forced to commandeer operating space at the City Workhouse hospital, known locally as the Iron Hospital, for twenty-two operations and the care of thirty-two surgical cases. None of these patients were subject to infection, whereas at the Norfolk and Norwich, there had been a fatal case of Pyaemia in recent weeks. His words prompted a number of dissenting comments, but undaunted, Dr Beverley upheld his view that the only way forward was to demolish the current hospital and build a new one. Many in the audience left the room that afternoon impressed and intrigued by the enthusiasm of this impassioned young doctor.

Born in the Norfolk village of Brooke in 1841, Michael's family came from generations of gentlemen farmers from nearby Poringland. On leaving school he was indentured to physician William Francis of Norwich. William kept the young man busy maintaining the surgery, making pills and medicines, learning first-hand about the symptoms of smallpox and typhoid, and accompanying his mentor on visits to poor patients in the city slums, as well as to the gentry in their large houses. When work pressures allowed, William introduced Michael to his personal passion for botany, insects and wild flowers. Michael would later introduce his own pupils to early morning forays for wild flowers and fungi, becoming a founder member of the Norfolk and Norwich Naturalists' Society.

Like Thomas Crosse, Michael also entered the Norfolk and Norwich Hospital as a dresser and clinical clerk, quickly endearing himself to nurses and patients, so establishing an association with the hospital which would endure for forty-eight years. Following his graduation from King's College Hospital in London, he spent a year in Paris, returning to Norwich at the end of 1864, with a promotion to House Surgeon. After seven years Michael resigned his post, studying midwifery in Dublin to before joining his Norwich friend and colleague, Surgeon William Cadge, on a trip to Edinburgh. Here they met the eminent Joseph Lister, pioneer of antiseptic surgery, observing experimental operations and involved in the subsequent treatment of surgical cases. A year later in 1872, Michael returned to Norwich, full of enthusiasm for the new 'Listerian system' of antiseptics. Now an Assistant Surgeon, he embarked on a personal crusade to rid the hospital of fatal bacterial diseases. He and Dr Cadge were the first to use the carbolic spray in an operation in Norwich, a technique that initially left surgeons and patient suffering painful irritation.

Dr Beverley was well respected throughout the city, known to be kind and sympathetic, willing to advise others and blessed with many friends. In August 1873, the city's most eligible bachelor was married to Marion Hotblack, eldest daughter of John Hotblack, a prosperous Norwich shoe- and bootmaker. Dr Beverley's best man was John Baumgartner. The bride, wearing an antique silk dress, was attended by seven bridesmaids, three of whom where her sisters. The splendid wedding breakfast catered for fifty guests, including Mr Francis and his wife. While the newlyweds made their way to London, en route for Switzerland, the bride's parents hosted a ball at the Hotblack family home, St Faith's House, a splendid, eighteenth-century, four-storey red-brick villa, set adjacent to the family shoe factory.

During 1875, Dr Beverley was appointed as a magistrate for the city, a role he undertook alongside his work with the British Medical Association. In 1883, he saw his dream fulfilled with the opening of the new Norfolk and Norwich Hospital. It had taken years of fundraising and four years to build. The former hospital, now demolished, had covered an area of about three acres, this new site was much larger at about seven-and-a-half. With a wide road to the front, landscaped gardens and the outpatients and isolation wards housed in separate buildings, the site was applauded for the improved sanitary conditions incorporated throughout. Here Dr Beverley was promoted to Surgeon, engaged in working closely with pupils, and later to Consulting Surgeon, where he served on the Board of Management.

He was an active member of many committees in the city, relishing a good debate. The family increased to six, with their final child, Russell, born in 1890. In addition to their grand city residence, the family owned a picturesque cottage in Overstrand, a coastal village just east of Cromer. Marion disliked public life, escaping the city whenever she could. In Overstrand her young children would enjoy the freedom and health benefits of the seaside. But even here, her status meant she required a live-in housekeeper and two nursemaids.

In 1881, indulging his love of nature and botany, Dr Beverley purchased seventy-six acres of woodland in the Norfolk village of Brundall, five miles east of Thorpe. Known locally as 'Little Switzerland', he spent the next six years developing Brundall Gardens, planting rare shrubs and trees, adding ponds and rockeries, from where water flowed down to the natural lake, introducing a collection of exotic birds and building a luxury log cabin as a weekend retreat for family and friends.

In April 1883, Marion's beloved mother died. Eighteen months later her father was made Mayor of Norwich, but now being a widower he turned to his daughter for support. Much against her nature, Marion stepped in graciously. As Mayoress, Marion presided over the largest children's fancy dress ball ever given in Norwich, held in St Andrew's Hall on 8 January 1885, when over 700 children arrived in a colourful array of costumes, to a party that would be spoken of for many a year.

It was during the late 1880s that the Beverley family left St Giles Street for the relative privacy of an elegant four-storey residence at 54 Prince of Wales Road, next door to Marion's older brother George Hotblack and his family. This would be their city residence for the next twenty years. In 1892, eldest son Michael, at 18 left England for Australia, perhaps seeking adventure, where he worked as a stockman. His sister Edith became Mrs Frank Jewson in 1909, at a service in St Peter Mancroft Church, Norwich. Her husband was a Norwich solicitor, the son of successful Timber Merchant John Wilson Jewson and brother of Richard Jewson, who successfully developed the family firm, becoming Lord Mayor of Norwich in November 1917.

In March 1913, now living in semi-retirement, Dr Beverley noticed a newspaper advertisement placed by an Auctioneer in Diss. A small Georgian residential estate known as 'The Shrubbery' was going under the hammer in the well-to-do village of Scole on the Norfolk/Suffolk border. It was a well-known property in the vicinity, for many years the location of the annual Flower Show held in the extensive woodland garden. By Christmas 1913 it was the new home of the Beverley family, when Michael, Marion and their two unmarried daughters moved in, immediately becoming involved with village life and the local church.

Sadly, Marion was only able to enjoy her new countryside home for four years, all of them dominated by the events of the Great War. Her youngest child Russell joined the British Army in 1914, at 23 promoted to captain and sent out to India. Michael volunteered for the Australian Infantry AIF 9th Battalion as a private. Marion missed her sons very much. Dr Beverley spoke at many public meetings in the early years of the conflict, encouraging local youth to heed Lord Kitchener's appeal, while his wife and daughters actively helped to raise funds for the Red Cross. During 1917, Marion fell ill. In June she would be cheered to hear of Russell's marriage in Madras, his bride was the daughter of a Public Works Engineer with the East India Company. Six months later the newlyweds made the long journey to England to attend a family funeral.

Marion died on 14 December 1917 at home in Scole. Her funeral was held at St Peter Mancroft Church, with many wishing to pay last respects, Michael also travelled home meaning that the entire family was together to say goodbye. Marion was buried on the edge of the Rosary Cemetery, with a decorated stone sundial marking the spot. Within three months, in March 1918, Dr Beverley received the telegram no parent wants to see. Michael was fighting in Belgium, when, while helping a wounded man, he was hit by a machine gun bullet in the stomach. Although his comrades tried to bring him to safety, they were surrounded by enemy fire and Michael died in No Man's Land. He was 44 years old. He was buried in the Bedford House Cemetery in Ypres and awarded the Military Medal for bravery in the field.

Dr Beverley and his daughters continued to live in Scole until 1920, when they returned to their beloved Overstrand on the Norfolk coast. The town had been much developed since they last lived there, with the addition of palatial villas, some designed by the fashionable architect Edward Lutyens. The village was now referred to locally as 'the village of millionaires', known for summer visitors including national figures such as Winston Churchill, Arthur Conan Doyle and Henry Royce. Dr Beverley bought 'The Gables' and enjoyed ten years there, dying on 31 August 1930, in his 89th year. Such was the affection and esteem in which he was held, that his funeral service took place in the medieval grandeur and beauty of Norwich Cathedral. He was buried beneath the sundial in the Rosary Cemetery, alongside his much-missed wife.

# Dr John Richard Baumgartner (1836–1920)

John was a direct descendent of Jacob Julian Baumgartner, a wealthy Huguenot merchant from Geneva in Switzerland, who emigrated to England in the early 1800s. Jacob established his 'family seat' at Island Hall, an elegant riverside mansion in the small Cambridgeshire agricultural town of Godmanchester. The house, dating from the 1740s, was admired for its walled garden and Chinese-style bridge linking the garden to an island in the River Great Ouse. The house and land would pass down through six generations. Although he never lived full-time at the Hall, young John and his siblings often visited relatives there. Medicine was in the family; his grandfather John Thomas Baumgartner had been the physician in Godmanchester for many decades, and it was he who most likely encouraged his grandson to follow in his footsteps.

John studied medicine at King's College Hospital in London, graduating in 1871 with his Certificates to Practice. Before leaving London, he worked as a male midwife while he considered his future. A vacancy was advertised for a Resident House Surgeon at the acclaimed Norfolk and Norwich Hospital, arising from the resignation of the popular Dr Michael Beverley, after his seven years in the role. This was an excellent opportunity for John to work in a city only twenty miles from his parents' home in Gorleston, near Great Yarmouth, where his father, John Percy Baumgartner, had become involved in local politics while raising seven children. John's application was successful.

John's involvement in the aftermath of the Thorpe accident increased the young man's confidence, improving his knowledge and raising his profile. At the end of 1875, John was in the news again, this time being lauded for his heroism during a disturbing and shocking incident at the hospital. On Saturday, 13 December, weaver John Edwards, 42, was admitted as a patient, suffering from a 'bodily ailment of a dyspeptic nature'. (*Norfolk News*, Saturday, 14 December 1875) The man was slight and pale, despite being a labouring man, with short light moustache and whiskers. John examined him and on finding the patient to be restless and irritable, openly admitting to episodes of confusion and loss of control, he was prescribed a sleeping draught. In the early hours of Monday morning, with the night nurse absent from his ward, Edwards left the room, a fellow patient alerting the nurse on her return. Being unable to find him, she woke Mr Baumgartner who continued the search. Meantime, in the West Wing, Edwards had entered the Boy's Ward of the children's section, two rooms divided by a passage, where in the first room four lads were sleeping. In what was probably a psychotic episode, Edwards armed himself with a set of tongs from the fireplace, and set about attacking each boy in turn, beating them about the head with cruel ferocity. The thud of the blows attracted the attention of a nurse sleeping in an adjacent room, who opened the door to the ward, shocked by the scene of slaughter. Startled, Edwards moved towards her, to find the door closed and locked in his face. Undeterred, he entered another part of the ward looking for further victims. Fortunately, a boy in this section had the presence of mind, on hearing the assaults, to leave the room and find Mr Baumgartner, leading him to the scene.

Taking up the poker from the fireplace, the doctor and patient began a deadly bout of fencing, culminating in Mr Baumgartner seizing him by the throat, throwing him down and holding him securely until the porter came to his aid. Edwards was handed over to the police, to be charged with 'feloniously killing the three deceased, namely William Martin and Joseph Colman, both 11 and John Lacey, 10.' The inquest and the subsequent murder trial took up much of Mr Baumgartner's time over the following days, with him being called as a witness on several occasions. After much discussion as to the long-term mental state of the accused, the jury found Edwards to be guilty of 'Wilful Murder'. Mr Baumgartner was singled out for praise, the jury stating that 'had he been a little less resolute, or even slightly nervous, probably even he himself might have been murdered'. The prisoner was committed to the Broadmoor Criminal Lunatic Asylum.

The incident and proceedings following may have contributed to John's subsequent decision to leave Norwich. Twelve months later he tendered his resignation, intent on setting up his own medical practice in Newcastle-Upon-Tyne. He would be sorely missed. John was much in demand in Newcastle, for many years acting as police surgeon, alongside senior roles at Newcastle Children's Hospital and Newcastle Lying-in Hospital. In August 1887, at 41, he married Augusta Mary Richardson, 27, second daughter of James Richardson, a well-known

Quaker and major employer in Newcastle. The simple ceremony took place at the Friends Meeting House. As befitting such an illustrious couple, they set up home in fashionable Eldon Square, a collection of elegant townhouses. There the couple welcomed four daughters in six years, Tryce, Cecily, Augusta and Verena. When not working, John was an active member of the Newcastle Society of Antiquaries, the oldest of its kind in England, established in 1813. Here he could escape his all female household and indulge his passion for history, archaeology and ancient music.

John resigned from his position of police surgeon in 1918. He was 72 and it was time to retire to the relative obscurity of Rothay Holme in Ambleside, within a few minutes' walk of the scenic Lake Windermere. He died only two years later, on 9 November 1920, after a long and fulfilling life. Whether or not he embraced the Quaker family traditions is uncertain, but he was buried in the Society of Friends Burial Ground, outside the scenic Lakeland town of Hawkshead.

# Chapter 8

# The Final Four Victims

In addition to those who died at the crash scene, Thorpe Station or while in hospital, there were four other deaths directly connected with the accident. The first, although not unexpected, came as a great shock to many in the city.

## William Bransby Francis
## Died 22 September 1874

At William's inquest, held at William's home on Tuesday, 22 September, it was fitting that Michael Beverley, his former pupil, was the first to give evidence before the City Deputy Coroner.

> I saw the deceased at Thorpe on the night of the collision, and assisted in attending to his injuries at the Tuns Inn, and also in subsequently removing him to his own home. I assisted in setting the fracture his thigh and ribs. I have since seen the deceased daily up to his death, which took place on Sunday evening last.
>
> (*Norfolk News*, Saturday, 26 September 1874)

The proceedings were carried out in a respectful hush and took but only a few minutes to establish that he had died from internal injuries aggravated by the fracture of his ribs.

William had hung on to life for ten nights. The servants tiptoed about, noise kept to a minimum, just the occasional sound of a housemaid quietly weeping. His wife kept vigil, delighting at any signs of improvement, despairing at any deterioration. Every day callers would appear at the door, friends, neighbours, local clergymen, medical colleagues all seeking an update on the patient's progress.

Among these were Doctors Peter Eade, still recovering from his own injuries, and Michael Beverley, each offering company and medical opinion. Diversionary tactics included light conversation or reading aloud from the British Medical Journal or Norwich newspapers. Within these pages, the public were kept abreast of the good doctor's condition. Eight days after the collision, readers' hopes were raised when it was reported that Mr Francis was feeling distinctly better. However, as the second week progressed, word got out that he was fading fast. A large crowd of well-wishers gathered outside his home, left distraught when the death notice was attached to his front door. William's funeral was held at Costessey Cemetery on Thursday, 24 September. As the cortege set out from Colegate, the same neighbours, patients and friends who had held vigil, gathered in the street to pay their respects.

Jane was left well provided for. William had taken out life insurance with the Norwich and London Accident Insurance Association, from which Jane received a sum of £1,000 (£116,000). In addition, being childless, she was left everything in his will. At 51, Jane was a wealthy widow. She was never tempted to remarry. Instead, following the sale of her husband's medical practice, she moved to a comfortable home in St Giles, close to so many of her husband's medical colleagues, enjoying twenty years in the company of other like-minded widows and wives.

# Edward Delevigne
# Died 27 September 1874

An inquest was held on Tuesday 28th September at the Star Inn, Quay Side, Norwich, before the Deputy Coroner, Mr Arthur J. Codling, a schoolmaster from St Clements stepped forward, identifying the body as that of Edward Delevigne, a French national who lived in Bloomsbury Place, Rose Lane. Mr Codling had known the deceased for about three years and had last seen him alive on the previous evening.

(*Norwich Mercury*, Saturday, 3 October 1874)

By the end of September, with readers still fascinated by the recent rail disaster, journalists from local newspapers attended this new inquest, aware that this might be something quite extraordinary. A Frenchman, named Edward Delevingne, around 30, had apparently committed suicide in a public place during the early evening of Monday, 27 September. Witnesses testified to seeing the deceased and his 12-year-old son walking across Fye Bridge School in Colegate Street. There they stopped, the man handing his stick to the boy before climbing over the parapet, sitting on the wall momentarily, before lowering himself, with no noise or struggle, into the Wensum below. Passers-by were shocked and taken aback at this disturbing event, rushing to calm the boy while calling loudly for help. Charles Dawes, a local engine driver from Elm Hill, leapt into his boat and searched the river, finding the body floating about 100 yards from the bridge. Tragically, despite the swift arrival of two surgeons and their desperate attempts to revive him, Edward was already dead when he was taken out of the water.

The inquest revealed that Edward was born in Paris in 1846, fleeing France in July 1870, with his 8-year-old son Charles, in an attempt to escape the outbreak of the Franco-Prussian War. They settled in Norwich, where Edward enrolled young Charles as a boarder at Opie House School in Colegate Street. Charles was called to the stand. Showing great courage, the boy told of how his father had seemed unwell for the last two weeks, since the time of the railway accident in Thorpe. On Monday morning, his father requested that instead of returning to school, Charles should accompany him on a stout walk to Plumstead and back, a distance of about four miles. That same evening, after eating their tea together, his father had gone out for a pint of beer. On return Edward said to his son, 'The sooner I die the better.' (*Norwich Mercury*, Saturday, 3 October 1874) Charles was concerned and decided not to return to school for the night, instead accompanying his father on a short walk into the city. It was then that his father stopped on top of Fye Bridge.

Earlier rumours suggested that the deceased had been a passenger on the ill-fated trains, but the inquest confirmed that Edward had in fact joined others from the city, rushing to Thorpe to help where they could. Charles's schoolmaster confirmed that Edward had indeed been subject to fits of 'excitement' since the railway accident, surmising that Edward had sustained such mental shock from the horrific sights and sounds experienced that evening, that it was his unsound state of mind that led him to drown himself. Edward's death may not have occurred as a direct result of being in the accident, but it appeared to have been indirectly responsible. A verdict of 'Temporary insanity' was returned.

# Stephen Abbott
# Died 29 September 1874

On the evening of 10 September, Stephen Abbott had been among the party of Masonic Brothers travelling home from the inauguration of Walpole Lodge. After his escape from the train he appeared unscathed, one of the lucky ones. However, whether it be from an undiagnosed internal injury, or simply delayed shock, Stephen, an experienced horseman, fell heavily from his mount in Great Yarmouth about two weeks following the accident. He was taken home to recover, but over the following days his condition worsened and he died on 29 September at 60 years old. He was buried in the family vault alongside his son.

Fanny inherited £1,000 (£116,000), a sum which made her consider her future. She left Great Yarmouth with her 14-year-old daughter to live in lodgings in Prince of Wales Road in Norwich, renting rooms from a teacher of music. Nine years later her daughter married surgeon Francis Sydney Smyth, the son of a Yarmouth physician. Their future was in Lewisham, but sadly Stephen's widow did not live to enjoy the brood of grandchildren yet to be born, for she died in Norfolk in 1882, aged 59.

# Dr Edward Mark Smith
# Died 25 January 1875

Late on the afternoon of Monday, 25 January 1875, citizens strolling near to the market in Norwich watched as a middle-aged, well-dressed gentleman fell to the ground, just outside the cloth warehouse of G.L. Coleman, close to the Guildhall. As the man appeared to be seized by an epileptic fit, bystanders moved forward to help him into the shop, sending a boy to fetch a surgeon. Arriving at the scene, the doctor identified him as the medical botanist, Dr Edward Smith, recommending that the man be helped to his residence in nearby Surrey Street. Dr Smith's wife Sarah settled him into their bedroom and sent for medical assistance from Dr Copeman at the hospital. Despite tending to him overnight, their efforts were to no avail and Edward Smith died in his bed at 4.45 am on Tuesday. As Dr Copeman questioned the wife about her husband's recent medical history, he would no doubt have discovered that the sick man had been a passenger on the 9.10 from Yarmouth to Norwich, nearly four months previously. Dr Copeman was well acquainted with the events of that night, and the state of the victims afterwards. He could well have concluded that the gentleman's demise was due to the tremendous shock suffered by his nervous system on that September evening.

At the collision, Edward had suffered severe cuts to his face and hands as the glass of the gas lamp inside his carriage smashed into atoms around him. He had crawled out alive and conscious and was transferred back to his home in Surrey Street to enjoy the gentle administrations of Sarah and his four domestic servants, nourished by soothing broths and jellies provided by his cook Susannah. Despite his injuries, Edward returned to work as soon as he was able, his advertisements reappearing in the newspapers within weeks. The final one was published on Monday, 23 January 1875 – the date of his death. Any patients planning to visit him in Ipswich during the following day were bound to be disappointed. Edward's death certificate recorded the cause as 'Paralysis'. Sarah buried her husband in the Rosary Cemetery on 2 February.

It was imperative that Sarah clear her husband's crippling ongoing debts before she could move on with her life. Sarah received probate of her husband's will on 19 March, inheriting around £5,000 (£590,000). But with his outstanding debts still standing at many thousands of pounds, even this was not going to be of much help. The house had to go. A preliminary notice of sale was posted announcing the sale of Stanley House in early June. It was certainly a grand property.

> For Sale Monday next. Surrey Street, Norwich. Valuable Freehold FAMILY MANSION, with upwards of Two Acres and a Half of LAND in Lawn, Pleasure Grounds, and Gardens, Conservatory, Stabling, and Offices, with several dwelling houses and cottages.
>
> (*Norfolk Chronicle*, Saturday, 5 June 1875)

It appears that Sarah found a buyer because on 12 June, an announcement in the *Norfolk News* informed patients and the public that Sarah had arranged for an eminent Medical Man with thirty years experience, to continue her late husband's practice upon exactly the same botanical principles. Weekly consultations were to be held at Stanley House every Saturday.

It is not known what happened to Sarah. Tragically, for widows in her situation, the poorhouse or debtors' prison were often the only options.

# Chapter 9

# Inquests, Board of Trade Inquiry and Manslaughter Trial

From the resumption of the very first inquests, only days after the dead were identified and released for burial, Alfred Cooper and John Robson found themselves in the centre of a legal storm that would not end until mid-April the following year. Some victims had died in the city, including those at the hospital, thus coming under the City Coroner's jurisdiction. But those who died at the scene in Thorpe-Next-Norwich, were designated as being the responsibility of the county. Consequently the County Coroner, Mr Edward Press, and the City Coroner, Mr Edward Bignold, were obliged to conduct their own independent proceedings, each with its own jury.

On Thursday, 17 September, the County Inquest was resumed, with the same gentlemen of the jury who had filed nervously into the Three Tuns, taking their places inside the Grand Jury Room of the castellated and daunting Shirehall, immediately to the east of Castle Mound and centre of legal proceedings in Norwich since 1822. Suspended from their jobs since the night of the catastrophe, Cooper and Robson had later been given one week's pay and dismissed, on the instructions of senior officers at GER. Now they found themselves surrounded by people determined to get to the truth, including court officials, lawyers, and representatives from both GER and the Amalgamated Society of Railway Servants. Seated in the gallery were witnesses, journalists and correspondents, family and friends of victims and curious onlookers.

Mr Press opened the proceedings by reporting he had lost no time in requesting that the Board of Trade send someone down from London to help with the inquiry. Unfortunately, Captain Henry Tyler, Inspecting Officer for Railways since 1853, a prominent figure on the railway scene and old hand at these inquiries, was unable to arrive in Norwich until

Monday 21. Mr Press had agreed that the official investigation, to be conducted under Section 7 of the Regulations of Railways Act, would open on that Monday. Until then they would have to manage without him.

It was not long before it became patently clear that a bitter difference of opinion existed between Cooper and Robson. Under oath, both men gave conflicting reports of the sequence of events that night at Thorpe Station. Robson was first to be called to the stand, to be questioned by the Coroner.

"Did you on that night receive any instructions as regards the down express train from London and the mail from Yarmouth?"

"Yes Sir."

"Were those instructions in writing?"

"No Sir."

"Who gave you those instructions?"

"Mr Alfred Cooper."

"And you wrote down what he told you?"

"Yes, Sir."

"Did you hand to him what you had written for his signature?"

"I did not."

"You did not?"

"No Sir, not until some minutes afterwards."

Sensing a problem ahead, Mr Press warned Robson that he need answer no question that he thought might tend to incriminate himself.

Robson nodded, going on to explain how Inspector Cooper had not waited to sign the message as was usual, but instead had turned and left the wicket. Robson, admitting that he knew it was against regulations to send up a message unsigned, could not explain why he had, in fact, signed it himself with Cooper's name, before sending the message to Brundall.

"And did you receive a reply?"

"Yes sir. I took the reply. It was received at 9.25 and read, 'I will send up the mail train on to Norwich before the 9.10 pm train leaves Norwich – W. Platford.'"

"So, what occurred next?"

"The book was put on one side for the inspector to see the reply, but he did not come until 9.32, when he rushed to the wicket in a state of agitation and great excitement and said, 'Tell Brundall to cancel my single line message and stop the up mail.'"

"So what did you do?"

"I immediately called Brundall saying 'Stop the Mail'. Brundall then replied, 'Mail left'."

A collective intake of breath sucked the air from the room, as the public digested the horror of that moment. The Coroner spoke again.

"Did anything transpire after that between you and Cooper?"

"Yes, I afterwards saw Cooper and asked him then to sign the first message. He said, 'No, I never gave you the message.'"

Robson was stood down, replaced at the stand by Inspector Cooper. No one dared breathe as Cooper reached the moment when he went to the wicket to first instruct Robson.

The Coroner asked, "In what way did you give that order?"

"I said, 'Have the mail up before the down train leaves Norwich.' As it is awkward writing outside the wicket, Robson writes the message for me and I wait to sign it. I did not see him writing, but turned my back for a minute and saw that the express train was running from the ticket platform into the station. I turned to the wicket and said to Robson, who was standing at the table in the office facing me, 'Don't order the mail up, the express is now running in, and I will get her away first.' They were the words I said to him and at that time he had not written the order in the book. I will not swear to his exact reply, but I believe he said, 'All right Captain', that being the way he usually addresses me."

Robson listened intently to this testimony, fully aware that the inspector's words could be construed as a direct contradiction to his own version of events. The Coroner continued.

"After the train was despatched was anything done by you then?"

"Yes sir. I went across to the telegraph wicket to tell Robson to send an advice to Reedham of the time the train had started. Before I could fairly get the words out Robson said, 'I have ordered the Mail up.' I said, 'Good God, Robson, how dare you order the mail up after my telling you distinctly not to do so?' Robson denied it directly to my face saying, 'You did not tell me anything of the kind. You did not tell me not to order the mail up.' I believe I said, 'How dare you say such a thing or assert such a lie?' I was paralysed, dead very near, on the spot. Inspector Parker then came up. That was all the conversation I had with Robson to the best of my belief.'"

After seven hours of evidence from a list of witnesses, the Coroner called for an adjournment. Everyone was drained and exhausted. There was clearly a case of negligence to answer. Had Cooper really misunderstood his stationmaster's instructions? Why had Cooper not signed the message immediately? Why did Robson send the unsigned message when he knew the regulations? Why did Cooper tell Parker that he had *not* sent an instruction to Brundall? Why had Robson not rung the bell to alert Cooper that a message was awaiting his signature? So many questions. So many conflicting testimonies. Mr Press ordered everyone to return the following day, when further evidence would be given.

So began the chaos. On Friday morning, 18 September, the County Inquest was reassembled at the Shirehall, when it was agreed that there was a problem. Six minutes' walk away at the Guildhall, the City Coroner, Mr Bignold, was welcoming the same witnesses and lawyers. They could not be in two places at once. Much to the delight of the hacks in the Guildhall gallery, Mr Bignold did not hide his anger, proclaiming that Mr Press had agreed some days ago that the County Inquest would be completed by the end of Thursday, leaving Friday for the turn of the city. Back at Shirehall, Mr Press had no option but to adjourn until a week on Monday, when the Board of Trade Inquiry should be finished. Meanwhile, he suggested that the County Jury visit the Telegraph Office at Thorpe Station, to see the instrument in practice.

At the Guildhall, the City Inquest commenced, covering much the same ground as the County on the previous day. However, as Stationmaster Sproul was giving evidence, Cooper's mental health was called into question. Where had Cooper actually spent the two months away from work, about five years earlier, when he was off sick due to alleged 'worry about family matters?' Had Cooper ever been in confinement? The implications were strenuously denied.

During the morning, both Cooper and Robson took to the stand, repeating much the same recollections as before, Cooper maintaining that he had told Robson not to send the message, Robson in turn rebutting Cooper's testimony. Before Mr Bignold adjourned for the day he announced some welcome news just received from GER. The Company stated that it had 'no intention whatever of disputing any claim that might legally arise against them for compensation for any parties who were injured or aggrieved by this accident.' (*Norwich Mercury*, Saturday, 19 September 1874) Good news indeed.

Four days later, Captain Henry Tyler and his entourage from the Board of Trade swept into the Guildhall, fully prepared to undertake the required formal public inquiry. His report and recommendations would eventually be presented to both Houses of Parliament. This was getting serious. The seats were filled with much the same people who had attended the inquests, but with additional expert witnesses and representatives from the Travellers' Protection Association. Captain Tyler, sitting at the elevated and intimidating bench, alongside Legal Assessor Mr Ravenhill, began proceedings, explaining the crucial difference between the on-going Coroner's inquiries and his own on behalf of the Board of Trade.

> The object of the Coroner and his jury is to ascertain cause
> of death, and to ascertain further whether there may be any
> evidence of a criminal nature on the part of any person, or
> any department in reference to such death. The object of the
> Board of Trade enquiry more particularly is to ascertain the
> cause of the accident, and all the circumstances attending it,
> and further to consider what remedies may be applied with
> a view to prevent all such accidents in future.
> (*Norwich Mercury*, 23 September 1874)

One by one, the specialist witnesses were called to the stand, including senior figures such as James Robertson, Superintendent for the GER network, Mr Thomas Stevenson, District Superintendent, and Henry Draper, District Superintendent of Telegraphs. As the local witnesses followed on, the testimonies repeated much of what had come before, especially when it came to individuals such as William Sproul, Inspector Parker and Police Inspector Drew. Sproul, when asked who he thought was to blame, replied: 'I should blame the inspector for giving in an unsigned message, more than the telegraph clerk for receiving it, especially considering the difference of age and experience between Robson and Cooper.' (*Norwich Mercury*, 23 September 1874)

With the Board of Trade inquiry still ongoing, by the morning of Friday, 25 September, City Coroner Mr Bignold was becoming impatient. He'd heard enough. He wanted a verdict from his city jury. Ignoring warning voices from his peers, including that of County Coroner Edward Press, urging him to delay until after final pronouncements from Captain Tyler, Mr Bignold instructed his jury to retire and return with their findings.

They had heard the words of Henry Draper, the District Superintendent of Telegraphs say that there had been a dereliction of duty on the part of both, quite frankly the gist of the whole inquiry. So was Cooper guilty of negligence for not signing the message, or was Robson guilty for sending an unsigned message?

The City jury retired at 10.50 am, returning to court at 11.15 am.

> The jury have come to an unanimous decision. The collision was caused by the negligence of Alfred Cooper and John Robson. But the jury wish to state that they do not attribute the same amount of culpability to John Robson that they do to Alfred Cooper.
>
> (*Norfolk News*, Saturday, 26 September 1874)

From both the dock and the public gallery came a combination of shock, despair, disappointment and relief. For those representing the dead and injured, this was the result they had been waiting for. Mr Bignold, finally satisfied, immediately signed warrants for the apprehension of Robson and Cooper. The Chief Constable took both men into custody. Bail for fixed at £50 (£5,000) for each defendant and the jury gave their fees, amounting to £5 7s (£500) to the Norfolk and Norwich Hospital.

This was just the beginning. The Board of Trade Inquiry was on-going, Robson and Cooper required to attend every day. By the start of the second week, Robson, now resigned to his probable fate, appeared to be bored with the whole thing. On Tuesday morning, 29 September, Captain Tyler completed his questioning and, having dismissed the witnesses, handed back responsibility to the County Coroner, who was impatiently waiting to resume his own inquest. Having finally dismissed his inquiry, Captain Tyler crossed over to Shirehall, his all-important draft report safe inside his bag.

With everyone once again ready to resume, and hopefully conclude, the County Inquest, Robson watched as the group of young men who were in his office that night, took their turn in the witness box. It was during the examination of John Holroyd, that jury member Captain Douglas, suddenly stood to his feet, angrily addressing the court.

> I think it is disgusting and disgraceful that the man Robson should be laughing all the time, or sketching his friends. I don't know whether anyone noticed the like conduct

on his part yesterday. I think in an important matter like this, he ought at all events to have a serious countenance, or else leave the room. It is perfectly disgusting to see a man conducting himself the whole time as if it were a comedy.

(*Eastern Daily Press*, Wednesday, 30 September 1874)

Robson's defence lawyer, Mr Sparrow, leapt to his client's defence, remarking that Captain Douglas might want to reconsider requesting that Robson leave the room, adding, 'I am sorry any person I represent in this solemn inquiry should misconduct himself. I have not noticed anything, and it is with great regret I now hear those remarks made.'

(*Eastern Daily Press*, Wednesday, 30 September 1874)

However, the Coroner sided with Captain Douglas and Robson was asked to leave the courtroom.

Cooper was recalled, and taking advantage of this unexpected turn of events, implied that on the evening of 10 September, Robson may not, in fact, have heard his clear instruction *not* to send up the mail, as he had been more occupied with those in the office, rather than with his duties.

After the summing up, the Coroner asked if Captain Tyler might wish to give a summary of his inquiry findings, before the County Jury was sent to consider its verdict. Getting to his feet and reading from his report, Tyler suggested that he would be concentrating on the key issues of punctuality, the signalling methods, misunderstandings and complacency, before concluding with a most sobering opinion.

This is the most serious collision between trains meeting one another on a single line of rails, if not the most serious railway catastrophe as regards the numbers of lives lost and serious injuries, that has yet been experienced in this country.

(*Eastern Daily Press*, Wednesday, 30 September 1874)

Having taken in the implications of this statement, the County Jury retired to consider its verdict. It was two hours before they returned. For Cooper and Robson, it must have seemed far longer.

The jury are of the opinion that the deaths of several persons, the subject of this inquiry, were caused by a collision between two trains on the single line of railway in the parish of Thorpe-next-Norwich on 10th September, and that such collision was caused by carelessness and neglect on the part of John Robson and Alfred Cooper; and the jury are of the opinion that John Robson is guilty of manslaughter and that Alfred Cooper, although guilty of gross carelessness and neglect, is not in our unanimous opinion, under the conflicting evidence before us guilty of carelessness and neglect sufficient to constitute criminality.

(*Eastern Daily Press*, Wednesday, 30 September 1874)

On the following morning, newspapers throughout the country were denouncing the legal shambles that had just taken in place in Norwich. The editor of the *London Globe* on 30 September summarised the view of many when he wrote:

The County Jury returned a verdict worthy to be ranked among the most extraordinary ever pronounced, even by a Coroner's jury. It will be received with nothing short of astonishment by the general public. ... The verdict given yesterday is almost as diametrically opposite to that given before the City Coroner last week as it could be. ... But whereas the Norwich verdict imputed the guilt of manslaughter to both men, and ascribed the heavier blame to Cooper, the Norfolk jury, reversing this view of the matter, have visited Robson with almost the whole load of blame, and recorded against him verdict of manslaughter, while they allow Cooper to escape, if not scot free, at least with a censure carrying no legal weight.

Once again, the city could talk of nothing else.

For Cooper and Robson, there was one more visit to the courtroom before being committed for trial. County Coroner Edward Press recalled his jury on Saturday afternoon, 3 October. Before the two defendants could hear the verdict read out in its proper legal form, Mr Press had another matter to report. The jury listened astonished, as he read aloud a letter received from Robson's lawyer, Mr Sparrow, claiming that his client had *not* been laughing at the recent Board of Trade inquiry, nor was he sketching his friends.

> He had written upon a piece of paper a question which he wished me to put to the witness then under examination. ... As he handed it to a friend to take the note across the room to me, it is quite possible that in doing so, a smile may have passed across his features. To prevent an unseemly squabble, I acquiesced in the request that Robson should leave the room. The attack made upon Robson exhibited an animus, which to my mind was, to say the least of it, in exceeding bad taste. I am, Sir, yours obediently, John W. Sparrow.
> (*Norfolk News*, Saturday, 3 October 1874)

The County Coroner was not in the least sympathetic to Sparrow's view, declaring that he thought the defence was mistaken, objecting that his jurors were being 'taken to task'. If Sparrow thought this missive would result in mercy, he was wrong. Having pronounced the verdicts, Mr Press turned directly to Robson. 'The calamity which has befallen, must for the rest of your life, whatever the consequences of the trial may be, rest heavily upon you, and will be more than any punishment you can receive.' (*Norfolk News*, Saturday 3 October 1874)

With the trial date set for April 1875, and the futures of both Cooper and Robson still in jeopardy, it would be a long winter ahead.

*****

The winter months of 1874–75 in the East of England proved exceptionally challenging, the weather unusually severe, with more deaths in Norwich than would normally be expected. Two long periods of low temperatures, one before and one immediately after Christmas, meant those living at the edges of society, poverty stricken, hungry, elderly and weak, were particularly vulnerable. Bulletins concerning the September railway accident continued to appear regularly in the press, attention in the city now turning to the compensation cases and forthcoming manslaughter trial.

On Tuesday, 31 March 1875, two gentlemen stepped down from the 12.50 pm train from Ipswich. These two senior judges were to open the Norfolk and Norwich Lent Assizes. Their caseloads included one attempt to poison, one violent assault and robbery, one concealment of birth, two of stealing post letters, one attempted rape and two manslaughter cases, including one arising from the Thorpe Collision of the previous September. This particular bundle of notes included the official public report from the Board of Trade, dated 30 September 1874, giving a detailed and invaluable account of events, statistics and recommendations.

Of the two, it would be Sir William Robert Grove, renowned physical scientist and High Court Judge sent from the Court of Common Pleas, who would in charge of the Thorpe case. The learned men were formally welcomed to Norwich at Thorpe Station by an entourage of dignitaries, including The High Sheriff of the County, the City Sheriff and the Mayor of Norwich. Also there was the Reverend John Patteson, now the High Sheriff's Chaplain, who had stood on his church wall on the morning following the collision, addressing the assembled crowd of onlookers.

The sight of the two handsome State coaches, taking the judges to the cathedral for a special service that afternoon was enough to prick the conscience of the guilty. Both painted deep blue, with coats of arms emblazoned on the door panels, the High Sheriff's coach was pulled by a set of four horses, whereas the City Sheriff had to make do with a pair. Twice a year, a massive crowd would gather in the city hoping to catch a glimpse of this colourful spectacle. There was a strict etiquette for these occasions with the City Sheriff conveying a judge in his carriage when His Lordship was attending to City business, and the County Sheriff in his carriage when County business was being transacted, or on private occasions.

Even before the two former railway servants were once again escorted into a courtroom, an important procedural matter had to be completed. Initially, the county calendar only recorded the name of John Robson, as the County Coroner's jury had not committed Alfred Cooper. However, on the afternoon of 3 April, after much deliberation, the County Grand Jury applied to the Court for an indictment against Cooper. The paperwork had been prepared in advance, and later that day 'true bills' containing the charge of manslaughter, were presented against both men. If Cooper had spent the winter praying for leniency, his pleas had not been answered.

On 6 April, the two former colleagues were led down the spiral staircase from the holding cells in the Gaol, along the tunnel under castle mound and into Shirehall, then placed under guard in a small room, adjacent to the Grand Jury Room. Once everyone was assembled, Cooper and Robson were taken to the dock where, from their elevated position, they were able to see above the ocean of white horse-hair perukes, each adorned with horizontal curls, powdered with scented ground starch, each wig demonstrating the importance and wisdom of its learned wearer. Cooper and Robson had been here before, but had never seen it like this. The white painted room was a scene of activity and excitement, a sea of gowned lawyers and clerks shaking hands, holding earnest conversations, dip pens moving swiftly across parchment as last minute notes were recorded. Journalists from every local newspaper, and some from further afield, were poised to record every word.

Directly opposite the dock stood the high backed chair for the presiding judge, framed by a triangular portico and upholstered in the same deep shade of red as were the entire collection of seat cushions. As the court was called to order, everyone stood to watch the Welshman, Honourable Mr Justice Grove, enter through the panelled wooden door, taking up his position, his full-length periwig and scarlet hooded robe signifying his all-powerful status. With the Grand Jury sworn in, Cooper and Robson were officially charged with feloniously killing and slaying George Robert Womack (his name representative of the total deceased), on 10 September last. Both defendants pleaded not guilty.

For two full days the minutia of the events of that evening were dissected and debated. The personalities, reputations, strengths and weaknesses of the men in the dock called into question, witnesses and defendants cross-examined time and time again. With no fresh evidence, it was very much a repeat of the earlier inquiries. No one was really any the wiser about who should take responsibility for the deaths. Sir William summarised the evidence to the jury, concluding that if they thought either or both the prisoners had been guilty of culpable negligence, they could find both or only one of them guilty.

For forty-five minutes the jury considered the findings, returning to a hushed court, faced with the Clerk of the Court first asking, "Do you find Alfred Cooper guilty or not guilty?" The Foreman responded, "Guilty of common negligence of duty." His Lordship was dumbfounded. This was most unusual. An increasingly heated exchange erupted between him and the Foreman. His Lordship objected.

"That is not guilty. It must be culpable negligence if you mean to find him guilty of manslaughter. A common negligence of duty would virtually be a verdict of not guilty."

"We don't mean not guilty, my Lord." The Foreman explained.

"This is not guilty of manslaughter. It must be something more than ordinary or casual neglect to make him responsible for manslaughter. It must be culpable negligence, which is highly blameable."

At this juncture, Cooper's defence lawyer Mr Bulwer saw a chink of light. He stepped in boldly.

"My Lord, I think the jury meant it was only *ordinary* negligence."

His Lordship was not appeased. "Gentlemen, it is to be your verdict, not mine. He is indicted for manslaughter, not for negligence or breach of duty."

Suitably and very publicly admonished, the jury again stepped outside. After a few moments they returned, to be asked the same question as before. This time the Foreman said loudly and clearly, "Guilty".

"Do you find John Robson guilty or not guilty?" The Clerk spoke again.

"Not guilty." The Foreman replied,

At this a cry of delight from Robson's friends arose from the public gallery, quickly quashed by the Clerk. As the noise died down, the Foreman added, "But we recommend Cooper to mercy."

With Robson hardly able to believe his luck, to everyone's incredulity, Mr Bulwer stepped in once again, dismayed to witness his client's chance of freedom slipping away.

"I submit that the first verdict was the right and correct one. The jury, after consideration, found that he was guilty of common negligence, which was a verdict of not guilty. Having delivered the verdict they are not at liberty to reconsider it, and I think they have given a verdict of manslaughter under a misapprehension of the law."

His Lordship was not about to be censored by a Norfolk defence lawyer, whatever his reputation. He came back.

"My only object is to ascertain the real meaning of the jury, whether they mistook the word culpable to be common I cannot tell. Each juryman might have different views as to the language."

Not wishing to be found in contempt, the Foreman responded with caution.

"We find him guilty of culpable negligence. We put it the other way so that it might recommend him to mercy. We put it as mild as possible."

His Lordship lifted his pince-nez to his eyes, and staring directly at him, concluded, "That is what I thought you intended by your verdict."

The judge now turned to Cooper, who was standing and stock still in the dock.

"I have taken your case and the recommendation into consideration and shall pass upon you a less sentence than I should otherwise have done. I am sorry that a man of respectable character, who had no evil intention, and who was doubtless as shocked as anyone at the result of his negligence, should be placed in such a position. The sentence is that you will be imprisoned and kept to hard labour for eight calendar months."

Alfred Cooper burst into tears.

It was over. The prisoner was returned to the County Gaol to face eight months separated from his wife and children, barely existing as he suffered noise, squalor, damp, darkness, poor rations, a hard-plank bed, and cohabiting with felons of all types. If Alfred had been younger and fitter, he would probably have spent his sentence derigging ships at Yarmouth or breaking up local stone and flint for construction sites. It is, however, more likely that he spent his time oakum picking, untwisting sections of old rope into many corkscrew strands. His hands would be torn to ribbons by the action of rolling the strands on his knees, until the mesh became loose. For part of the day he might be sent to pointlessly walk the treadmill for hour after hour, or turn the crank, a large handle fixed up inside a cell, thousands of times a day.

Conversely, John Robson left Shirehall a free man, surrounded by celebrating family and friends. Throughout the appalling experience, the youth's character, integrity and honesty had been publicly called into question. Throughout the trial, Justice Grove had seemed to give Robson the benefit of the doubt, alluding more than once to his youth and inexperience. This may conceivably have tipped the balance with the jury, leaving his former superior Alfred Cooper to bear all the blame.

From that moment on, John Robson simply disappears from record. It is likely that the inevitable shame and guilt meant he could see no future for himself in Norwich; maybe he changed his name, moved away. He could have returned to the seething mass of humanity in London, seeking anonymity and a fresh start. He would certainly never work for the railways or the post office again. Or he may have arranged to board one of the many steamships heading overseas. It was an era of mass migration from Europe to the New World, the majority of emigrants heading for the United States, Canada, Australia and New Zealand, in search of a better life. John's youth and skills would be attractive to those emerging nations, perhaps offering him an assisted passage, his fare subsidised by the destination government. Wherever he lived his life, there is no doubt that the mistakes made by him and others that night in Norwich will have gone with him to the grave.

On 8 April, Norwich solicitor Isaac Bugg Coaks penned a letter to the *Norfolk Chronicle* from his home in Thorpe Hamlet, in support of Alfred's family, now left with nothing. He wrote:

> I learn on enquiry that the little money Cooper has saved has, through his enforced idleness, all been spent since the sad catastrophe, and the wife and children are now entirely without means of support. There are six children, the eldest, who is about 20, is in the Post office service, but the five at home are all under 13, the younger only two years old. Unless timely help is given their home will be broken up, and the wife and children driven to seek parochial relief. Feeling strongly that some steps should be taken to prevent this, I called upon the Mayor and Sheriff and placed before them the above facts. Both approved a fund being raised for the benefit of the wife and children, and each generously offered to subscribe.

Mr Coaks offered the sum of £5 (£500), with the Mayor and Sheriff matching his generosity. One month later the 'Fund for the Relief of the Wife and Children of Inspector Cooper', had reached £120 (£14,000), with Mr Coaks once again writing to the newspaper, suggesting that further contributions would be welcomed, so that once Alfred Cooper was released from prison, there would be something substantial left to enable him to make a fresh start in life.

On 11 December 1875, a further letter on the subject appeared in the *Norfolk Chronicle*, this time from a different correspondent. It read:

> Dear Sir – will you permit me, through the medium of your valuable paper, to express my feelings of greatest gratitude

to those ladies and gentlemen who so kindly and liberally subscribed to the fund raised for my wife and family. It was a source of great comfort to me, while away from them, to know that they were being so well cared for, and I beg to tender my most sincere and grateful thanks for the sympathy and help which has been given to us, and also for the great pecuniary assistance which the residue will afford us. Yours faithfully, Alfred Cooper, Late Night Inspector Great Eastern Railway.

It was time for the Cooper family to move on. Five years later, the family was living in the small town of Cheetham in the Borough of Manchester. Alfred established a business working as a fish and game salesman, a shop he ran for over ten years. Initially Harry helped his father in the shop, while his younger brothers attended school. His boys grew into men, taking jobs as warehouse clerks and selling furniture. By 1891, at 63, with three lots of wages coming into the house, Alfred was employing a general servant, 18-year-old local girl Elizabeth, to help Louisa keep house for four grown men. Three years later, on 24 March 1894, Alfred died, buried in the Southern municipal cemetery at Chorlton-Cum-Hardy, three miles south of Manchester city centre. He had survived an ordeal that might have ruined a lesser man.

# Chapter 10

# Compensation Cases Spring 1875

At the end of January 1875, the half-yearly general meeting of the Great Eastern Railway Company was held at the City Terminus Hotel, Cannon Street, London. Mr Charles Henry Parkes, the Chairman since 1872, presided over a difficult meeting of shareholders. He had much to report. When he came to his piece concerning the events in Thorpe, he recalled how he had never suffered so much misery and pain as he did in respect of the late accident. It had been a most unexpected calamity and happened at a time when the Directors were doing all they could to double the line between Thorpe and Brundall. The line had been in operation for over thirty years with no accident happening upon it. He had attended the ensuing Board of Trade Inquiry and the damning report, coupled with the manslaughter charges against GER employees Cooper and Robson, meant that Great Eastern had no choice but to accept culpability on the grounds of staff negligence. He reassured his audience that the injury claims would be met as far as possible out of the receipts for the half year. Parkes reported that to date there had been 107 claims for damages, some from survivors, others on behalf of widows and families of the dead. Of those, seventy-one had been settled out of court, the results not publicly announced, with the remainder to be decided in court cases set for the following few months. It was a sobering thought.

It was during February that the hearings began, the full and explicit details reported in newspapers throughout the land. Readers delighted in discovering new names, as yet untold stories of 'that night', enthralled to learn just how much money each claimant was awarded. The majority of the cases were heard in the Sheriffs Court in the ancient Guildhall, or at the Shirehall, where groups of learned lawyers and legal assessors gathered to battle it out in the public arena. For the plaintiffs it could be a humiliating ordeal, with opposing lawyers picking over their personal finances like chicken bones, their integrity questioned, intimate details about their injuries and state of health exposed for all to see.

Throughout the hearings, GER instructed a team of senior defence lawyers, most frequently Mr Bulwer and Mr Marriott, to ensure that the Company paid out as little as possible, without it appearing unsympathetic or parsimonious. Working alongside them were two physicians, Dr Fagge and Mr Erichsen. Having already physically examined the claimants shortly after the accident, their brief was now to examine the claimants again, this time immediately before the hearings, with the plan to undermine the diagnosis of the prosecution doctors. These professional teams were to prove both formidable and effective.

# Tuesday, 23 February 1875
# Sergeant-Major Frederick Cassell v The Great Eastern Railway Company

Handouts and army pensions were not going to keep the two former militia families housed and fed for long. It was imperative that widows Eleanor and Eliza won appropriate damages. The first compensation case to be heard on 17 February was that of Sergeant Major Cassell. Presiding over proceedings was gentleman brewer and Sheriff of Norwich, John Youngs Esq. The jury was composed of Norwich tradesmen and professionals. The Cassell claim was set for £2,500 (£300,000). Mr Metcalfe, QC, acting on behalf of Mrs Cassell, spoke first, explaining to the jury that:

> It is unnecessary for us to discuss under what circumstances the accident was caused, or make any reflection upon the conduct of any person, because it has been legally admitted that the Company or their servants negligently caused the death of these people.
>
> (*Norfolk Chronicle*, 27 February 1875)

Mr Metcalfe, QC, acting on behalf of Mrs Cassell, reminded the jury that Eleanor Cassell and her four children, three under 15, were facing destitution. He detailed the family annual income before the accident as being about £160 (£19,000).

Eleanor was called to the stand to take the oath. Unaccustomed to speaking in public, she was nervous and possibly a little afraid. When questioned, she listed her husband's pensions, allowances and payments received for occasional work such as recruiting and training young soldiers. She estimated that his weekly income had been around £3 5s and 4d (£350). Mr Metcalfe pointed out to the jury that although Cassell had been a healthy and active man, expected to live a further twenty-five years at least, his client was only asking for a fair amount, equal to about fifteen or sixteen years income. The jury took fifteen minutes to consider their verdict. The award was a total of £1,253 (£145,667), representing half of the claim, to be split between family members according to their age and needs. For Eleanor and her legal team this was a disappointing outcome.

## Sergeant Robert Ward v The Great Eastern Railway Company

After a short break, the jury reassembled for the second case of the day. The claim was for the same amount, £2,500 (£300,000), despite Ward's weekly income being substantially less than that of Cassell. Mr Metcalfe told how Mrs Ward had been left destitute with four children to support, the youngest only 9. Her eldest son, Robert, had been working as an errand boy for a baker, but he was a 'delicate' boy and after Christmas was let go, unable to obtain employment ever since. Once again, the jury left the room, returning with a verdict of £1,050 (£122,000), again considerably less than the claim.

As future claimants read every detail of the hearings, they must have heard warning bells loud and clear.

## Thursday, 25 February 1875
## Russell Walton Skinner v The Great Eastern Railway Company

On 25 February, both Russell's widow Annie and his elderly father Reverend Skinner were in the courtroom, although it is unlikely that they were seated together. Once again Mr Metcalfe appeared for the plaintiff, with Mr Bulwer and Mr Marriott defending the Company.

Annie was now a single mother of two small children, the youngest not yet 2. Prior to their marriage, Russell and Annie had signed a marriage settlement, whereby income from their joint properties would pass to her in the event of his death. Annie still retained that income and as such was by no means destitute. However, there was also the small matter of a house in Notting Square, Kensington, part of Russell's inheritance. Six years earlier Russell's father had handed responsibility for the house to the couple, bringing them £175 (£20,000) per annum in rent. Unfortunately for Annie, when Russell was killed the previous year, his father had immediately transferred the house and the income to his 40-year-old spinster daughter Violetta, his only remaining child. There were further complications too, as Russell's father had now changed his will to exclude her. Annie was facing an uncertain future.

It was suggested that the Reverend Skinner should take the stand to explain his actions, but this was rejected, the defence insisting that there was no shred of evidence that Annie would suffer any pecuniary loss. Further antagonism arose when there was a suggestion that Reverend Skinner may have disinherited his grandchildren deliberately in order to secure compensation from GER, but this was vigorously disputed. Mr Bulwer pressed home his point that the Reverend Skinner could, at any time in the future, reinstate financial benefits upon Annie and her children. The jury retired and after thirty minutes returned to offer minimal damages of £150 (£17,500) for the widow and £350 (£40,500) for each child. There would be no celebration party that evening.

The Reverend Skinner died in 1881 and Annie remarried in 1883, having found herself a dental surgeon called John Brown, able then to resume her previously comfortable lifestyle and regaining her social standing.

# Thursday, 25 February 1875
# Alfred Page v The Great Eastern Railway Company

Alfred Page had waited a long time for this day. Having witnessed the violent deaths of both his brother and his good friend Russell Skinner, and having been unwell himself ever since, he was placing his trust in his lawyers, Messrs Metcalfe and Reeve to secure him a good settlement.

At the time of the tragedy, Alfred had recently invested in new business premises, an enormous warehouse, with plans to amalgamate his five or six existing workshops. It was here that, only two weeks following the crash, the Seventh Ward Liberal Association held a grand dinner, the space transformed into a banqueting room, shortly before the business was due to transfer all its equipment and stock there. The guest list included the great and the good from the Liberal Party, but sadly Alfred himself had to send his apologies. He had not yet recovered from his injuries. Jeremiah Colman, a guest in his official capacity as Liberal MP for Norwich, gave a speech in which he expressed his regret that Mr Page, who had generously placed the room at their disposal, was unable to join them, sending his warmest sympathy. He went on to chastise the management of the Great Eastern Railway, promoting his belief that the public would be better served if all railways, rich or poor, were handed over to the state, adding that, 'If the State can manage telegraphs, why could it not manage railways?'

Mr Metcalfe explained to the jury how, with the death of his brother George, Alfred was now the sole manager of the family currier business, in addition to his own brush company. Considerable losses had been sustained by both businesses and it was for these that compensation was sought. Mr Bulwer for the GER called for the account books from the currier business to be produced, while accepting the figure of £715 (£83,000) as an average annual profit from the brush business.

The discussion turned to Alfred's health. After ten days in the hospital, he was taken to his home in Sprowston, where he stayed in bed for some days. He had lost sensation in the right-side of his face and upper jaw and suffered from constant pain in his legs. At night he was disturbed by troubled dreams, returning time and time again to the moment when he cradled his dying brother in his arms. His health had always been good, apart from in the early spring, when, since a child, he had suffered from bouts of bronchitis. Since the accident, this infection had returned, attributed to exposure on the night of 10 September. He felt pain in the region of the heart, whereas before the accident he was scarcely conscious that he had a heart. From about November he had occasionally visited his business, but was unable to do anything more than sign cheques.

Mr Thomas Crosse from the hospital took to the stand, telling how Mr Page was generally a lively, light-hearted man, full of conversation and fun, but following the accident was depressed and nervous, suffering a recurring fear of sudden death. Mr Bulwer, once again protecting the

Company, expressed his belief that the plaintiff would perfectly recover in time; he had perhaps attempted to do too much too soon. The jury returned a verdict for £1,750 (£203,000)

Alfred's business continued to thrive, by 1881 employing fifty-three men, fifty-nine women and seventeen boys, a vast increase of 40 per cent in ten years. His father George died in August 1881 at the age of 80. Six years later Alfred himself died at home on 23 December, aged only 57. With his father living to such a great age, it is reasonable to suppose that had he not been involved in the Thorpe tragedy, Alfred may well have enjoyed a longer life. At his death, the scene at the house must have been frantic, for on the very next day, Christmas Eve, his youngest daughter Edith was to marry engraver William Spellor from Enfield. Alfred's widow Priscilla was now left to deal with the fall-out. Tragically for Edith, her father was not at the church to walk her down the aisle.

In 1895, Alfred's daughter Ethel married dentist Henry Freeman White, the youngest brother of Richard Wentworth White, who had also been injured that night in Thorpe eleven years previously. If Alfred had lived to attend this wedding, he and Wenty could well have been tempted to share first-hand tales of the accident, maybe over excellent Madeira.

# Saturday, 27 February 1875
# Job John Hupton v The Great Eastern Railway Company

At 29 years old, Eliza Hupton was now a single mother of three children, the eldest being 6, and the youngest just 6 months old. She had little choice but to claim compensation from the Great Eastern Railway. Job's mother had died in May 1874, leaving him the substantial sum of £170 (19,000) with which he planned to open his own leather business. Eliza had received the money the previous November and had been living off it since. Mr Bulwer, for GER, immediately objected that this information was not admissible. The jury found a verdict for £700 (£203,000).

The award meant that Eliza could move her children into more comfortable accommodation, remaining in The Rows. Two years after the accident, all three of her children were baptised together at St Nicholas Church, a final rejection perhaps of Job's strict Baptist roots.

# Saturday, 3 April 1875
# Reverend Charles Morse v The Great Eastern Railway Company

Charles was too poorly to attend his compensation hearing. At the age of 70, his injuries were taking a long time to heal. Instead he trusted his representative Mr Bulwer, on this occasion appearing for the plaintiff, to speak on his behalf. His wife Frances agreed to take the stand to explain to the jury what exactly happened to her husband on that dreadful night. Mr Bulwer took up the tale, the public gallery listening intently. Having called at the Rectory, Charles had made his way along Thorpe Road, oblivious to the dozens of others doing the same, arriving at Foundry Bridge, when a policeman stopped him. The two men went together to Tombland, knocking on doors of known surgeons, seeking immediate help, only to find them away from home, many helping at the scene of the accident. The policeman helped him to his front door, where Frances helped him up to his bed.

Frances took up the story. Her husband had looked appalling, one eye forced closed, his jaw appeared fixed, his right ribs were sore and his left leg was covered in painful scalds. She sent word to their local chemist, Mr Andrews, who willingly came to the house. He had been a saint, bathing the Reverend's bloodied head. Finding a large splinter, Mr Andrews had removed it with great skill, care and compassion. Her husband had complained of a painful elbow, impaired vision and difficulty in breathing. That night he barely slept, was quite delirious and constantly crying out 'It's here, it's coming.' From the following day, Mr Allen or Dr Bateman had regularly examined him, until he was well enough to travel to London a few weeks later to consult other medical men about his condition. By January, he had a 'stoppage of the bowels', able to take nothing but soda water and brandy. Even now he was constantly nauseous, unable to eat and having difficulty getting up and down stairs. He suffered from sleepless nights, had a shuffling gait and his usually excellent memory was failing. His voice was very indistinct and his right hand trembled continually. He refused to employ a professional nurse, meaning that all the responsibility for his day-to-day care fell upon Frances.

Mr Allen, a surgeon from the hospital, was cross-examined by the defence. He agreed that the Reverend was now much improved, but

148

sadly he believed that he would never be well again and that his life expectancy was poor. Spared of the injuries, Mr Allen estimated that he might have lived a further fifteen years or so, 'he had that appearance about him'.

The onlookers were completely swept away by this list of terrible ailments suffered by such a popular man of the cloth. It was difficult for the company lawyers to compete. Mr Metcalfe, in this case appearing for GER, addressed the jury. He wisely avoided pouring the usual scorn on the evidence of the prosecution witness or indeed the doctor. Instead he finished his address by appealing to the jury not to award heavy damages, 'as was sometimes done under the impression there was any amount forthcoming to be scattered profusely right and left'. (*Norfolk News*, 10 April 1875)

Ignoring the shocked whispers from the public gallery at this outrageous statement, his Lordship summed up, describing the jury as men of temperate and good sense and that he knew they would make a fair decision. The compensation was settled at £2,050 (£203,000).

The old man proved more resilient than at first appeared, living for a further ten years. Charles died on 1 May 1886. He had been married twice, fathered twelve children and served for forty-seven years as rector of St Michael-at-Plea in Norwich. The funeral eulogy in Hellesdon church must have taken some time.

# Thursday, 8 April 1875
# John Beart v The Great Eastern Railway Company

With the family patriarch gone, the business fortunes of the Bearts took an immediate turn for the worse. Details of the saga were publicly aired at the compensation trial held at the Sheriff's Court in Ipswich. It was a difficult day for all concerned with accusations and slanderous comments bandied around, every word recorded by the hacks in the public gallery. Mr James Bulwer, QC, recently elected Conservative MP for Ipswich, represented the family, with Great Eastern Railway appointing Mr Metcalfe QC to protect their interests; his brief as usual to keep the compensation as low as possible. Damages claimed were £5,000 (£581,000) a vast sum of money.

The proceedings opened with an instruction to the jury to focus on ascertaining the monetary loss to the deceased's family. Mr Bulwer, having given a compelling character reference for John, ramped up the drama with a story of possible foul play at the Norfolk and Norwich Hospital before his demise.

> Mr Beart had some time previously made a will, but must have forgotten it being in a state of great desperation, both bodily and mentally. While at Norwich, away from his family and friends, or anyone who knew about his property, a stranger was called in to make his will, and it was made under such circumstances that it could hardly be said to be a valid will, though probably it would be held to be such. However, unfortunately, the result of this will was that the wife, who had been living with him while he was in receipt of £800 a year, now had in consequence of his death, only about £50 a year. I do not know if the daughters had a legal claim upon any member of the family for one farthing, whereas before the accident they were living at home, and had a reasonable expectation of being dealt with as a kind and indulgent father would deal with children of whom he was fond.
>
> (*Ipswich Journal*, 8 April 1875)

The identity of this mysterious stranger at John's hospital bedside was never ascertained, and an extensive wrangle played out in the courtroom, with Mr Bulwer first claiming that John, who allegedly had 'never had a day's illness in his life', could well have lived a further ten years. The first witness called to give evidence was Mary Beart, John's widow, 58 years old and struggling with chronic creeping paralysis. Mary explained to the court that when they married, she and her husband had set up a modest business, renting Rowley House for £35 a year. She described how their fortunes had improved, moving into Crabbe House and expanding the business. As she spoke about her children growing up, it became clear that they were completely dependent upon gifts of money from their father, who seemed unable to refuse them anything. Mary explained how her husband, strong and active, still took a role in the business right up to the time of the accident.

Now it was the turn of son George Henry. He cut a pathetic figure as he admitted the difficulties he was now experiencing in obtaining credit from some of the principal houses with which his father dealt. He had no experience of buying groceries and was unable to estimate the optimum amount of stock to buy for the shops. He told the court that his brother in China had frequently received money from his father, as had his brother in India. If George wanted money he simply arranged it with his father, but he had no fixed stipend. It was true that the accounts were now showing a falling off in the business, and when cross-examined, George shamefacedly admitted that he did not know what income tax his father paid, nor that the capital was diminishing year on year. Henry John stepped up with similar concerns about how he might pay his personal expenses now that his father was gone.

Ada, fragile and ailing and no longer able to earn a livelihood as a schoolmistress, told the jury how she was now totally dependent upon her mother.

The legal gentlemen went on to discuss in depth the profits and losses of the businesses, with Mr Bulwer concluding that the jury was advised to accept the sum of £800 (£93,000) per annum as being accurate for the income from the business. He was not seeking vindictive damages against the GER, but only asked that the jury consider what the widow and daughters had lost by the removal of a kind husband and indulgent father. It was now the turn of Mr Metcalfe to speak on behalf of the Great Eastern. He informed the court that as of that date, 108 claims had been made against the Company arising from the Thorpe accident and of these, eighty-five had been settled without difficulty. However, there were in some cases, as in this one, expectations of such large sums of money that a jury had to be called in to decide what was reasonable.

The Under Sheriff summed up, addressing the jury for almost an hour. He pointed out that the family were no longer children, and that they might wish to consider seriously whether any compensation should be paid to the sons who are perfectly capable of supporting themselves. He admitted that the difficulties lay in the will, which was unfortunately worded and may need to be settled afterwards. The jury retired for a further hour, before returning to give their decision. Only four members of the family were to receive any compensation. The total award was £1,000 (£116,000) This was a disappointing result, the sum falling far short of their requested £5,000. John Beart would have been incensed.

On 13 April, the newspapers reported that the total amount of compensation claims against GER was now unlikely to exceed £40,000 (over £4 million), which would be a record sum for the company. About one quarter of that had already been paid, and there still remained five or six formidable claims, including those of Miss Ramsdale, Mr Gilman and Mrs Womack. Readers would be kept waiting until 1876 for the Womack case. But Mr Charles Gilman was due in court during the summer. Everyone looked forward to more revelations to come.

# 1 June 1875 – Sheriff's Court, King's Lynn
# John William Devonshire v The Great Eastern
# Railway Company

John Devonshire, 32, was a King's Lynn fish merchant, travelling to Yarmouth that night with his brother Henry. This was not the first time that John Devonshire had been in a legal tangle with the Great Eastern Railway. In 1873, he had taken action to recover losses arising out of the Company's delay in forwarding twenty-three baskets of smelts from Ely to London. But in the courtroom on this first day of June 1875, circumstances were very different. John was anxious, his fourth child was due any day and he was forced to be away from his wife Sophia. John explained how he had fallen into the river, but then gone to the aid of others. Later, at the hospital, he found it to be teeming with the injured and their families. He was forced to wait for more than three hours in his soaking wet clothes. Having spent the night on a ward, he was sent home to King's Lynn the following morning, suffering from pain in his back, across the loins and under the left shoulder. His own doctor attended him at home for about two months, half of that time spent in bed. It was six months before he could walk without difficulty. In his youth he had been an ordinary seaman, nimble, strong and active. But now he was constantly nervous, on occasion wracked with pain, and having difficulty sleeping on account of unpleasant dreams with random sensations of falling. He was always cold, sometimes feeling he was standing on ice, and his legs were numb. None of this had occurred before the accident.

Throughout this period he had not been able to pay proper attention to his fish business, and the jury was reminded that, as such, John was 'a fair and legitimate subject for compensation and for damages'. (*Lynn Advertiser*, Saturday, 5 June 1875) He owned wholesale warehouses in the North End of the town and his usual practice was to attend Lynn harbour personally to select and purchase fish, relying on his own judgement of quality and value. He would visit Yarmouth market every Friday, often boarding the boats to have first sight of the catch. In the season he purchased vast quantities of herring, taking them back to Lynn for curing. He also dealt in smelts, salmon, mussels, whelks and oysters. When the boats arrived at the harbour there was always keen competition among the traders, and only his personal presence could guarantee him success. John estimated his takings for the eight months before the accident as being between £800 (£93,000) and £900 (104,000). His annual return was normally something over £3,000 (£35,000), from which he could save £100 (£11,500), building a future for his wife and small children. Over the previous eight months, he had been obliged to order fish by letter, while employing one man at his shop and a boy at the warehouse. His income had dropped by about a third since the accident and he had willingly submitted his accounts to the Company for inspection.

Several character witnesses stepped up to speak highly of John Devonshire, including a baker, a hotel keeper and John's warehouse manager, all testifying that John was no longer the man he once was. Doctors returned to the stand, agreeing that all of John's symptoms were as a result of nervous shock, caused by the accident. He needed rest and care, time away from his business and some new occupation, free from anxiety. The plaintiff's case was closed.

The defence lawyers called their witnesses. It was Dr Fagge who stepped up to submit that he had observed all these aforementioned symptoms in other patients, reassuring the court that they all recovered within a short period. He would be not at all surprised if the plaintiff were well within three months. Fagge's colleague Mr Erichson agreed, stating that in his opinion there was no organic injury to Mr Devonshire's spinal cord, having examined him and finding no tenderness whatever. The plaintiff had certainly received a severe nervous shock, but he agreed with Dr Fagge that he should fully recover within a few months.

The accountant working for the company dismissed John's accounts, describing them as badly kept, showing an annual turnover of about £2,500 (£290,000), far less than Devonshire had claimed. The defence was quick to explain that the Company in no way wished to suggest that

John was attempting to deceive them. The summing up stressed that Mr Devonshire's health appeared to be improving, he could easily employ an agent to attend the fish markets on his behalf, and it was hardly the fault of GER if the plaintiff was a poor businessman. The jury returned damages at £350 (£40,500), far less than John had been hoping for.

John did eventually recover enough to return to work. However, in January 1880, Mr Harry Witt, the landlord of the popular Dock Hotel pub, died, leaving an opportunity for the Devonshire's to make a fresh start. In March they moved into the modest brick-built urban corner pub in St Annes Street, Lynn. John and Sophia had been the hosts for just three years when Sophia sadly died in 1883, at only 42. The following year John faced more tragedy, losing his eldest son Walter John, when just 11 years old. The incident was reported in the *Lynn Advertiser* of 19 July 1884. At around 6.00 pm one Tuesday evening, Walter and his younger brother Herbert were playing with a group of boys down at Fisher Fleet, a short tidal estuary where fishing boats moored. Walter and his friend Robert Booty, son of a fisherman, decided to take a dip. Young Herbert stood by and watched helplessly as his brother and Robert swam out of their depth, swept away by the ebbing tide, disappearing together under the black water. The alarm was raised but it was too late, the boys were drowned, their bodies dragged from the water after about thirty minutes. Walter's limp figure was taken to the pub, where his father had to endure the inquest held at his own home, where a verdict of 'drowned while bathing' was returned. Once he had lost both his wife and son, John may have found it intolerable to act the genial host, leaving the pub in April 1886, moving into a house in Norfolk Street with Herbert and returning to the fish trade. Over the following ten years John had a number of enterprises, including mineral water and concentrated fish manure. Once his son moved away to the West Country, John relocated to Swanage in Dorset, dying in 1908, aged 64 and buried within the sound of the sea.

# 1 June 1875 – Sheriff's Court, King's Lynn
# William Yaxley v The Great Eastern Railway Company

Following William Yaxley's dreadful experience alongside his friends Reverend Morse and Mr Gilman, he had spent a fortnight confined to bed with injuries to his legs and suffering from severe nervous shock. His case was quickly assessed, defence physicians once again expressing the opinion that the plaintiff would ultimately permanently recover, but they could not fix a time, maybe a year, perhaps two. The jury gave for the plaintiff, awarding damages at £600 (£70,000).

At the time of the Rail Disaster William's mother Elizabeth was 63 years old and still working as the landlady of the King's Arms in Botolph Street where he grew up. By 1891 William was widowed at 51 and had moved back into his childhood home to help his mother with the business. When she died just a year later, her son sold the pub to George Flowerdue. William died in the North Norfolk village of Walsingham.

# Ramsdale v The Great Eastern Railway Company

Ellen Ramsdale's compensation case was finally settled out of court in July, the newspapers barred from publishing the details. However the rumour circulated that GER had paid out damages of £5,000 (£500,000). This must have helped considerably with Ellen's ongoing medical expenses.

# Friday 6 August 1875 – Norwich
# Charles Gilman v Great Eastern Railway Company

On Friday morning at 11.00 am, His Lordship Mr Baron Bramwell, took his seat. The list for the day ran to no fewer than fifteen cases, three of those resulting from the Thorpe Collision. Having despatched a claim for damages resulting from non-repair of a baker's shop in Bury, the lawyers gathered expectantly for the much-anticipated case of Charles Rackham Gilman v Great Eastern Railway Company. As a respected Norwich solicitor, Charles would be aware Bramwell's reputation as being a great favourite of the Bar, kind and with good humour, efficient at dispatching with business. There was hope of a good result. However, having watched his two sailing companions, Charles Morse and William Yaxley, both recently fail to be awarded the compensation they'd hoped for, it must have been with some trepidation that the plaintiff entered the courtroom.

Charles, now aged 41, had always been a strong, healthy man, a sharp shrewd man of business and father of three children. Those in the courtroom that day who knew him before the accident, exactly eleven months ago, were shocked at how poorly he looked, appearing older than his years. They listened in horror as the lawyers and doctors described Charles to be 'a complete wreck', weak, unable to sleep, having difficulty reading or writing, suffering sudden attacks of 'absolute wretchedness', suffering from partial loss of memory and debilitating numbness in one leg. He could hardly walk, no longer able to handle his boat or his carriage. His lawyer, Mr Bulwer, first declared that he was only sorry that the case had not been settled out of court, so necessitating Mr Gilman to undergo this ordeal. But there had been significant differences of opinion in this case, which rendered a private settlement difficult.

Bulwer attempted to ridicule the findings of the Company's doctors, revealing that under the advice of Drs Fagge and Erichson, Mr Gilman had spent much of the past year travelling to the seaside in various parts of the country, including Ramsgate, Southend, Margate and Brighton, in a futile attempt to restore his strength. The plaintiff had been disappointed to have to resign from his legal practice and various previous offices, losing income amounting to around £2,000 (£232,000) a year.

Mr Gilman was called to the stand to recall his memories of the collision. Once he had been rescued from the roof of the carriage, he had been taken to the nearby home of his friend and fellow solicitor Captain Foster, where he received refreshment. He attempted to walk home, but after about 250 yards he could go no further. A cab was called to take him home, where a doctor attended to him. Mrs Sophie Gilman, Charles' wife of seventeen years, confirmed that her husband had been compelled to remain in bed for five or six weeks after the accident. She had accompanied him on the visits to the coast, but there had been very little improvement and he could never be left alone. Dr Bateman was called to conclude the case for the plaintiff, giving his sworn view that Mr Gilman was suffering from concussion of the brain and spinal cord. He very much doubted if he would ever be better than he was now.

The Company lawyers worked hard to denounce the horror stories as expounded by the prosecution doctors, referring to their notes taken when examining the plaintiff earlier that day, once again arguing that in their opinion Mr Gilman was improving. Had he not been for a short drive in his carriage only recently? Was he sleeping much better? In their opinion his brain was functional, if he could only attempt a little work, the stimulation might hasten his inevitable recovery. The learned judge advised the jury to offer reasonably substantial, though not vindictive damages, as although the Company was liable for the gross negligence of its servants, the accident had not been the fault of the unfortunate shareholders, out of whose pockets the money would have to come. Mr Gilman was awarded the sum of £6,000 (£697,000), representing three years of lost income. He left the courtroom to go home and rest. He'd heard enough.

# Saturday, 14 August 1875
# Thomas Hills v The Great Eastern Railway Company

For his appearance in court, 67-year-old Thomas Addison Hills had a journey of fifty miles from his home in Ely, near Cambridge. A skilled printer, publisher and bookseller, Thomas had been in business for forty years, working in partnership with his son Edward. As a young man he served his apprenticeship in an office in Huntington, subsequently making his way to Cambridge in 1827, where he gained employment as a printer at the Independent Press Office. There followed a period working at the University Press, before leaving for the cathedral city of Ely to set up a business on his own account. He had been most successful, able to live and work from a fashionable address in Minster Place, in the shadow of the great fourteenth-century lantern tower of Ely Cathedral, a landmark long-since much admired from miles around. Thomas was also known for his literary abilities, producing an excellent handbook on the cathedral, and held a number of prestigious positions within Ely society.

Called to the stand, Thomas explained that although he had waited for several hours to be rescued, once he had rested he had hardly felt any ill effects. However, two days later on the Saturday he found he could not walk properly and consulted his physician, who advised him to avoid work and prescribing sleeping draughts to aid restorative rest.

Following the pattern that had been set in these cases months earlier, the judge warned the jury that over the next few hours, several medical men would give evidence to the effect that Mr Hills would never recover, while the Company medical men would, he believed, say he would ultimately recover. They would have to make their own judgement. Dr Travers of Kensington described the condition of Mr Hills when he examined him in February: 'He complained of pain the lower centre of the spine, loss of power over the left leg and a feeling of pins and needles. Walking tired him very much and he was unfit for business.' (*Norfolk Chronicle*, Saturday, 14 August 1875) As part of his treatment, Mr Hills had spent time in Brighton, where he lodged with a Mrs Ingram. She gave evidence that during his time with her, the plaintiff's condition had deteriorated. He dared not go to sleep, showing signs of paranoia and anxiety. His walks along the sea front became more infrequent and of a shorter distance. Finally, Edward Hills testified that his father had previously been a most active businessman, of sound health. His father's share of the profits had been a minimum of £220 (£25,500) a year, with further income arising from acting as actuary to a savings bank, and a further £20 (£2,000) a year as crier at the Ely Court. With his father's enforced absence from the printing office, the business had doubtless sustained a pecuniary loss.

It was the turn of the defence and Dr Fagge snidely commented,

> I have never been able to make out that there was much the matter with the plaintiff, he moves briskly and I can only conclude there is no affection of the spine. It would be better if he were to do a little work rather than to make himself an invalid in Brighton, as it would distract his attention from himself. He will perfectly recover.
>                     (*Norfolk Chronicle*, Saturday, 14 August 1875)

The defence lawyer, Mr Parry, agreed with his colleague, pressing home his point with an added touch of sarcasm: 'If the plaintiff went to business, instead of morbidly thinking of his condition and listening to the cheering assurances of medical men that he would not recover, that he would in time perfectly convalesce. (*Norfolk Chronicle*, Saturday, 14 August 1875)

His Lordship gave his summing up, insisting that in his view the pain in the back was a genuine complaint, adding that Mr Hills was living on the ground floor of his home, for fear of the fatigue of getting upstairs. He was certainly entitled to damages.

The jury gave its verdict awarding a total of £800 (£93,000). If Thomas himself was less than satisfied with this result, at least the hospitality debt owing to Mrs Ingram of Brighton could be settled.

Despite his frail appearance, Thomas continued his busy lifestyle in Ely, founding the Savings Bank in the city, acting as its secretary for more than fifty years. For a long period he was Church Warden at St Mary's Church. Once retired he certainly did not slow down, but continued to take a keen interest in local affairs. He died on 16 December 1903, extraordinarily on the day of his 98th birthday.

To those looking on, either in person or through the words of the journalists, it must have become apparent that the compensation cases were a form of cat and mouse. The pattern set from the outset. A sum of compensation claimed by the plaintiff is, normally but not always, publicly announced. The prosecution then called witnesses to paint the worse possible scenario of the current state of health, finances and subsequent future, for either the bereaved family or the injured victim. The defence in turn played down the effects caused by the collision, casting doubt on the views of the prosecution doctors, while assuring everyone that the claimant simply needed time to adjust or to heal. The judge summed up, and the jury awarded a far lesser sum than first requested, pleasing the Company but disappointing the plaintiff.

If the Norfolk public were awaiting more gossip on the charming George Womack, then they had to be patient. His widow Emma had much to sort out. There was the business, the house, the servants and the children's future to consider. George's business and personal dealings were both complex and frustrating. Emma first had to sell the draper's shop. She consulted her Aylsham solicitor and a buyer was found in the form of businessman Donald Fraser. On 12 December 1874, as the city prepared for Christmas, an announcement appeared in the *Norfolk Chronicle*.

On behalf of the Executrix of the late Mr G.R. Womack,
I respectfully announce to you that I have disposed of the

Business hitherto carried out by him in NORWICH, and
have great pleasure in recommending you to his Successors,
Messrs. Donald Fraser & Co.

The transfer of ownership took place on Friday, 11 December, and with
the festive season approaching fast, Mr Fraser was anxious to entice
back George's customers.

We respectfully invite you to continue your favours to us
in the same old place. We shall always be found at home
and prepared to supply you with the Newest Goods, from
the best Manufacturers in England and Scotland. We have
engaged Skilful Cutters to Fit you well, and guarantee to
you our own personal attention at all times. Hoping to make
your early acquaintance and to secure your patronage. We
are, Yours respectfully, Donald Fraser and Co.

Emma was free.

# Friday, 14 April 1876
# George Womack v The Great Eastern
# Railway Company

It took a further sixteen months for Emma's case to reach the courts.
With the sale of George's business, Emma could afford excellent
representation in the guise of Mr Gates, QC, and her lawyer Mr Blofield.
The public was riveted and on 14 April 1876, Mr Gates opened the case
on behalf of Emma and her two children. She was seeking a sum of
£5,000 (£581,000) in damages. Mr Gates informed the jury that George
and his family had lived most comfortably, but that some little time
before his death had separated from his wife, moving to Yarmouth to
reside. However, he added, had George survived, the estrangement
would not have permanent, for just two days before the accident, George
had written to his wife appealing that she return to him, showing his
commitment by arranging to appoint Emma as his executrix and sole
legatee. Gates explained that Emma was not claiming for any loss

of society, or for outraged feelings, but as Great Eastern had already admitted responsibility, it was only right that Emma and her young children should be compensated for their loss of on-going income. To stress the point, Mr Gates revealed that the net annual profits of George's business had been between £800 (£93,000) and £900 (£104,000). The jury did not take long to award damages of £3,000 (£348,000). Again a disappointing result, but at least her nightmare was over. Four years later Emma married her cousin from London, Charles Arthur Middleton, a man thirteen years her junior. The couple left for a new life in Australia.

# Chapter 11

# Heroes

As further stories emerged about those involved in the tragedy at Thorpe-Next-Norwich, many of those who rushed to help became lauded as local heroes. Following church services, over afternoon tea, in the market place and around dining tables, their names were revered, as citizens discussed their courage and tireless efforts to help those in most need. Included amongst them were William Birkbeck, Captains Douglas, Foster and Herring, local brewer Henry Patteson, Michael Beverley, Thomas Crosse and John Baumgartner, many hitherto celebrated in this volume. But there are still four tales yet to tell, those of Dr William Hills, Dr Charles Owen, publican John Hart and boatbuilder Stephen Field.

## Dr William Hills (1828–1933)

Since his birth in February 1828 within the precincts of Guy's Hospital, Southwark, William Charles Hills was destined to become a medical man. He was the second son of Mr Monson Hills the elder, resident apothecary and cupper, a role he held for thirty years. William's father was a much respected senior figure at the hospital and in 1832 published a work entitled *A Short Treatise on the Operation of Cupping*, recommending that the essential instruments for collecting blood, such as a scarificator for collecting blood, glass cuppers, metal bowl and bloodletting knives, should be carried around in a discreet pocket-case, in order not to alarm patients. Known affectionately as 'The Governor', Monson was much loved and revered by both his students and the sick in his care, known for his kindness, patience and sympathy. He became a valued leader in the hospital's accident and emergency admission management, able to 'restore calm and decision to the troubled mind of the student.' (The Old Operating Theatre Museum Blog at oldoperatingtheatre.com)

Monson Hills married Sarah Lane in her hometown of Colchester in Essex in June 1822, starting their family in the busy community of Guy's Hospital in November 1823 with their first son, Monson Samuel Hills. Little Sarah was born two years later, followed by William Charles in 1828. Within ten years, four further siblings joined the family. Monson Junior was destined to follow in his father's footsteps, remaining at Guys and taking up the position of Cupper after his father's retirement. Meantime, William was educated at the renowned Merchant Taylor's School, followed by studies in Medicine both at Guy's and in Aberdeen, graduating as a MD in 1859. During his student years William lost both his parents in the space of two years. His father died in 1852, followed by his mother in early 1854. In the August following the death of his mother, William married a 42-year-old widow, Diana Elizabeth Reynolds, daughter of a solicitor.

William's first job was as House Surgeon in Surrey Dispensary, where he became interested in mental health issues, becoming senior assistant medical officer at the Kent County Asylum in Maidstone. In 1864, aged 33, he was promoted as Medical Superintendent at the Norfolk County Asylum at Thorpe-Next-Norwich. He and Diana moved into the asylum, immediately assessing what improvements might be made.

William's intent was to provide a more caring and therapeutic approach to his 400 patients by recruiting more specialist attendants and nurses. He was also determined to improve the budgetary situation, with plans to save costs and utilise the skills of patients. He was horrified at the state of the men's wards, where the straw mattresses were infested with fleas, resulting in early proposals to improve hygiene and reduce overcrowding. He quickly produced a revised laundry list and replaced soda and soap with 'Smiths' washing powder. Gas lighting was extended to include bathrooms and stairs. William was aware of the beneficial effects of music and he set out to create an attendants' band to offer 'treats to patients' more economically than outside entertainers.

On 21 June 1867 William's wife Diana died, aged 54. Less than two years later, on 7 April 1869, he remarried, this time to a much younger woman, Catherine Russell Scott, born in Carlisle, Cumberland in 1841. He brought his bride home to his comfortable quarters at the County Asylum. He returned to his work with a renewed vigour, and by September 1869, fifteen new single bedrooms, dormitories and attendants rooms had been opened, along with an additional day room, bathrooms and a dressing room. The women's rooms were supplied with white counterpanes and homely domestic fittings, all of which the lunacy commissioners found 'difficult to praise more highly' (*Mental Health Care in Modern England, The Norfolk Lunatic Asylum 1810-1998,* by Stephen Cherry).

William and Catherine lost no time in starting a family, their son Monson Odling Hills, born on 9 January 1870 and baptised in St Andrew's Parish Church. His baby sister Kate Alice arrived the following year. As matron, Catherine worked alongside her husband. William continued his ambitious endeavours, intent on providing more wards, facilities and space, again appealing to the lunacy commissioners for additional buildings. The authorities accepted that fifty more beds were 'absolutely necessary', but insisted on no additions to the asylum site. The challenges kept coming.

With so many problems and issues to deal with at the asylum, William's heroic efforts on the night of the railway disaster would soon be forgotten, stories hidden away for when the time was right to tell them, over a late night chocolate or a nip of whisky with friends. Meantime he had work to do.

Eleven years later, in January 1885, William enrolled his son Monson into the prestigious public boarding school of Charterhouse, near Godalming in Surrey, his parents hoping that their bright boy would eventually study medicine. Just over a year later, William and Catherine received the dreadful news that their 16-year-old son was severely ill and had been moved into the school sanatorium. Monson died on 15 February 1886. The school medical officer, Dr Clarence Haig Brown, the son of the headmaster, wrote in his report for Long Quarter 1886: 'The first death for some years has occurred in the school this quarter; its cause was pyaemia secondary to acute necrosis'. His father understood this to mean a form of blood poisoning as a result of the death of cells in growing bones. He wept.

Monson's body was returned to Norwich, where he was buried in Postwick Churchyard. Following the funeral, his father wrote to the headmaster's wife.

> I cannot allow another post to pass without sending a
> few lines to express my heartfelt thanks for all you have
> done in endeavouring to alleviate our sorrow. You have

displayed such tenderness and motherly feeling, together with such delicate and unobtrusive acts, that we are never likely to forget them. Although I am not a Carthusian, but a 'Merchant Taylor's' scholar, yet I am so in spirit and bound up in all that affects dear old Charterhouse. ... Two of his schoolfellows were present at the funeral, which took place in our pretty churchyard Postwick on Friday. There were upwards of 40 wreaths and crosses sent, of the most choice flowers and the scene was one that will not be easily effaced from the memory of those around the grave.

Mrs Hills added a postscript to her husband's note saying,

Your lovely and choice wreath was placed next to ours of violets ...

William and Catherine purchased a rose petal stained-glass memorial window to be placed in the school chapel alongside a plaque reading:

To the Glory of God and to the Loving Memory of Monson Odling Hills, only son of Dr W.C. Hills, Thorpe St Andrews Norwich who died at Charterhouse February XV 1886 aged XVI years. This window is erected by his father and mother.
(Quotations courtesy of Charterhouse Archive)

William's pioneering work at the asylum continued for a further six years, including taking official posts with both the Norwich Medical Chirurgical Society and the Medical Psychological Association. He was appointed as consulting physician at the Heigham Hall private lunatic asylum and wrote a number of valuable papers, published in *The Lancet* and other professional journals. William chose to retire in 1892, aged 64. William, Catherine and daughter Kate left the asylum and moved into the village of Thorpe, where Kate married in the parish church early in 1894. Her groom was Aubrey Blake, a Norwich solicitor. The couple lived in The Chantry, off Theatre Street, where their son Arthur was born in May 1899. On retirement, William had no intention of starting his own medical practice. However, such was the man that he found himself willingly giving free advice and assistance to grateful villagers.

He volunteered as a parish councillor in 1895. Three years later, when his wife Catherine passed away, the entire village offered sympathy and support to this generous and kindly man. William's health deteriorated such that during 1901, he left his home to move to the city to live with his married daughter and son-in-law, on which occasion the villagers presented him with an enormous silver inkstand.

William survived long enough to enjoy playing with his infant grandson before dying of heart failure, aged 73, in January 1902. His body was taken in an open hearse to All Saint's Church Postwick, where he was buried alongside his wife and son. The villagers of Thorpe gathered in large numbers to pay their last respects. A contingent of medical men travelled to the church, including many who had served at the asylum over the past decades. The floral tributes were numerous and beautiful, including a simple posy from 'Little Arthur', and a large cross composed of violets from his daughter, maybe emulating the tribute of violets chosen by her parents for her brother's funeral in 1886. William's generosity, spirit and demonstrable 'genial and sympathetic disposition' would doubtless be long remembered by his family, friends and colleagues.

# Dr Charles Owens (1846–1933)

After the collision, William Hills and Charles Owens remained firm friends. In the summer of 1881, when he was 35, Charles married 21-year-old Marion Isabella Hooley, the daughter of the vicar of Tharston, just two miles from Stratton St Mary. The couple moved into The Street in Long Stratton where they had five children. Charles was the GP in the market town for over fifty years, often travelling to patients in a dogcart drawn by a white horse. Elderly locals affectionately referred to him as 'the old doctor'. Charles held positions such as the public vaccinator, District and Medical Officer for a local workhouse, and Chairman of his Parish Council from 1895. In 1918 he was appointed Justice of the Peace and Commissioner for Taxes. Despite his advancing years, during the Great War he carried out work for various worthy societies, rewarded with a decoration for his work in the Volunteer Detachment, in which he held the rank of Brigade Surgeon and Lieutenant Colonel. Charles died in February 1933, at the great age of 87. His funeral took place at

St Mary's Church, Long Stratton, where his coffin was lowered into a grave lined with evergreens and white chrysanthemums.

# John Hart (1829–1898)
# & Stephen Field (1827–1904)

John Hart and Stephen Field shared much in common; their lives tracing similar paths. They were born within two years of each other; Stephen in 1827 in the rural village of Rumburgh, four miles from the market town of Halesworth in Suffolk, and John in 1829 in Norwich. Their fathers were born within a year of each other in the late 1790s. John's father James was a musician and Stephen's father Benjamin worked as a Pattern Maker in a foundry. As a young man, Stephen was drawn to the water, labouring at both Britcher's and Girling's Boatyards at Carrow Abbey from the early 1840s, acquiring the boatbuilding skills that would give him a living for life.

At 21 John was lodging with cordwainer Samuel Spalls, as an apprentice. Here he learnt the skills for making shoes and other articles from fine soft leather, a trade he continued for a further seventeen years.

Both men married their sweethearts within a few months of each other. Stephen was wed in the parish church of Thorpe-Next-Norwich in June 1849. Sophia Wright was a boot binder by trade and the daughter of a Norwich waterman. The groom and both witnesses signed with the mark of a cross. Only Sophia could write her name. During the following year, John married Harriet Hannah Spencer on 22 June in the church of St Julian in the city. The bride's father worked for a city brewery. Both couples produced seven children, Sophia within eight years and Harriet taking twenty-four years to complete her family.

Stephen and Sophia's first child, born in the same year as their marriage, was named Ann. Four further daughters and two sons followed. Tragically, in January 1860, Sophia died. Her death was recorded as the result of 'syncope', a sudden lack of oxygen to the brain, possibly caused by an underlying heart condition. The *Norwich Mercury* carried a death notice on 4 February: 'Recently, aged 31 years, Sophia the wife of Stephen Field, boatbuilder, King Street, leaving seven children to deplore their loss.'

The family was devastated and Stephen found himself as a single father, his youngest child Sarah, just a year old. Throughout the decade he kept himself busy, buying John Britcher's Boatyard, near Carrow Abbey, qualifying as a Master Boatbuilder, and building 16ft rowing boats, sea-going vessels, luxurious cutter yachts, 5-ton sailing boats designed for the Broads, and in 1865, developing the first Steam Wherry built in Norwich to be driven by a screw propeller. Named *The Alexandra*, this vessel was commissioned by Norwich Coal Merchant John Hart Boughen and was eventually launched on 10 March 1868, with much fanfare and celebration.

On 5 September 1868, the *Norwich Mercury* ran an advertisement offering for let the Three Tuns Inn in the riverside village of Thorpe-Next-Norwich, available due to the sudden departure of landlord Charles Miller, host for only one year. Also known as Thorpe Gardens, the property included upwards of five acres of land and had an enviable reputation. John Hart was interested. Maybe he was tired of the shoe trade, or simply longed for a change of scene and a better life for his family away from the noise and filth of the city. The inn was well known throughout Norfolk for its landscaped riverside gardens, warm hospitality and grand events, including the notorious and popular annual Thorpe Regatta. From as early as the 1820s, the pub had been sketched and painted by numerous artists, including by John Joseph Cotman, celebrated member of the Norwich School of Painters.

On 24 September 1868, landlord Charles Miller advertised his furniture, jugs, utensils, paintings, iron bedsteads and stock for sale by auction. The lots included twenty dozen bottles of port, sherry, champagne and claret, ten boxes of cigars and a 'Useful Brown Pony, Luggage Cart, Set of Harness, Wheelbarrow, Ferry Boat, Rowing Boat etc.' John and his wife secured the keys to the inn and moved in. The local press praised John in June 1869 for the sumptuous dinner served to members of the 'Ship Club', an old established tradesmen's club, meeting together to enjoy a long evening of entertainment, involving food, drinks, toasts and songs. It was a good start.

During that first summer of trading, John decided against holding the annual regatta, much to the chagrin of the locals. By August 1870, however, John and his wife were ready and arrangements were put in place. Sadly for John, his first regatta as landlord did not go without incident. Halfway through the programme of events, there was a pelting shower of rain, sending spectators running for protection in the crowded bar areas, under trees, beneath the leaking drinks' shelters in the gardens, and even under rowboats, turning them upside down to form cosy little huts. Once the downpour subsided, prolonged drinking led to some inevitable high-jinks and bad behaviour, culminating with the drinkers in the long room over the skittle alley hurling missiles, including a glass or two of beer, from the top windows onto the people below. Retaliation followed with bricks and drinking pots thrown skyward, breaking glass in the upstairs windows. Word obviously got out about the fun to be had. For the following two summers Thorpe was inundated with even bigger and worse behaved crowds. The final regatta was held in 1872 before John called it a day. He had simply had enough aggravation.

The Field family arrived in the village with a cart full of clothes, kitchen equipment and bedding sometime at the beginning of 1870, forced out of the city by industrial expansion on the river. Stephen Field was already well acquainted with Thorpe, having been part of a team for many years organising regular regattas on the water. He was also a skilled sculler and competitive rower, winning cash prizes and trophies. It would not be long before John and Stephen became acquainted. Stephen resumed his boat-building activities, initially from a site in Water Lane, developing a fleet of small boats, which he offered for hire.

The children in both families were now becoming adults, a number of them marrying in St Andrew's church in the village and setting up homes of their own. In 1871, Stephen was living with his four daughters and 16-year-old Stephen, who worked alongside his father in the family boat-building business. At the Three Tuns, John and Harriet worked all hours while caring for four boys, the eldest 14, youngest just 3. The children became great friends, enjoying the peace, safety and beauty of the river and surrounding countryside, so different from their city upbringings.

During the years following the railway disaster, John converted the skittle alley into a boathouse, from where he and his sons William and George began building vessels of all kinds, fully embracing the main occupation of the village. John also expanded his pleasure-boat hire business, in competition with Stephen, a perfect fit for the fashionable clientele visiting his riverside pub. Early in 1880, widower Stephen remarried. His second wife was Sarah Hughes, 49, originally from the village of Flint on the River Dee on the north coast of Wales. Stephen brought his bride into his village home, along with Sarah's 18-year-old niece. Over the next decade, despite being in his 50s, Stephen was at his physical peak, employing local men and working for some distinguished clients. Stephen's reputation as a skilled Master Builder spread far beyond Norfolk, resulting in a commission for a 5-ton Sailing Cruiser *Daphine*, ordered by a resident of Holy Loch in Argyllshire.

During 1885, John and Harriet made the decision to leave the life they had led for seventeen years as host and hostess of a busy pub. John's boat-building and pleasure-boat hire businesses were thriving, but Harriet was finding pub work more and more demanding. It was time to go. The new landlord, Barnabas Buck, took over the business in October. John and Harriet moved across the river, to a small bungalow on Thorpe Island, with a view across to their old pub. Their new home came with a piece of land on which they built further boat sheds, filling them with all the paraphernalia John and his sons needed, including planks of oak, teak and mahogany, mallets, hammers, chisels, nails, handsaws and planes. Only a year after leaving the pub, in August 1886, Harriet Hart died, aged just 58. The couple had been together for forty years. Three years later John, now aged 60, had matrimony on his mind. He married 44-year-old recently widowed Georgina Grey, originally from Reepham in Norfolk. The couple married in London under special licence, travelling back to Norfolk to set up home together on Thorpe Island, by this time referred to locally as Hart's Island.

While John was finding happiness again, Stephen was making major changes in his life and deciding to retire. He offered first refusal on his boat-building business to John, who was happy to help out, taking on Stephen's eldest son to be one of his team of craftsmen. Stephen never lost his love of the river and of sailing, continuing to skipper wherries and helping out in boat yards for as long as he was able.

In 1893, Stephen once again has to deal with family tragedy when his son Stephen dies in front of him. He was 38. No one could ever confirm exactly why he collapsed that day. There was a village rumour that later became a legend, concerning a silver half-sovereign given to him by John Hart as part of his wages. The story was that Stephen had immediately mislaid the coin, catching a chill when stripping down to search for it, then assuming he must have somehow swallowed it. John Hart strenuously denied any involvement and the doctor recorded Stephen's death as being the result of 'inflammation of the left lung'. Whatever the truth, Stephen's son was gone, leaving a wife and five children.

Five years later, John Hart was himself the victim of a mysterious death. In December 1898, aged 70, he lost his life under tragic circumstances. One evening a week or two before Christmas, John was enjoying a beer or three in the Buck Inn, seated in his usual chair, surrounded by friends and neighbours of over thirty years. This occasion was different however; it was a goodbye party. John and Georgina were due to retire from the boat-building business in just three days, planning a move to the North Norfolk seaside town of Cromer, leaving his empire in the capable hands of second son George. At around 10.30 pm, George joined his father for a quick nightcap, before the two men bade each other goodnight. George walked the short distance to his home in Chapel Lane. Gently inebriated, John boarded his moored ferry boat, sculling it downriver against an unusually high tide, heading for the opposite bank, a journey of no more than a few minutes. It might be that John had a couple more drinks than usual, but for whatever reason, as the boat drew up at the staithe outside his home and he attempted to alight, a manoeuvre he had completed successfully on hundreds of occasions, he lost his balance and struck his head on the woodwork. Momentarily stunned, he slipped silently into the rushing waters of the Yare.

Inside the house, Georgina was awaiting her husband's return. She heard the boat strike up against the wood, and when he did not come in she ventured outside into the black winter night to look for him. There was no sign of the ferryboat or of John. Georgina, although alarmed, thought she must have been mistaken. After all, hadn't her husband mentioned that he might row down to Norwich to join a friend? Georgina was fretful all through the night, but could do nothing until first light. At dawn, she hailed to a young lad on the Thorpe side of the river, urging him to summon George. On return to the house she catches sight of John's body floating in a stooped position, his coat billowing and his walking stick beside him, just at the spot where he normally moored up. Horrified, she attracts the attention of two passers-by, who 'borrow' a moored rowing boat and cross the river, dragging John's body onto the staithe. George arrives just in time to witness the scene, offering words of comfort to his stepmother while inspecting his father's body, noting that he has a severe bruise on one temple and that his watch had stopped at five minutes to eleven.

John's cap was found lying near to the river edge, and the ferry boat was discovered several yards downstream, trapped under the railway bridge. That evening, inside the Buck, the Deputy Coroner of Trowse Newton held an inquest over John's body, returned for the final time to his favourite drinking place. The verdict was accidental death. John's funeral took place on Tuesday, 20 December, his body removed from the bungalow at 2.00 pm, ferried over the river in the same boat from which he had met his death.

In his will John left his thriving business in the hands of his son George, including the house and land on the island, the boathouses and workshops, equipment, stock and order book. The company continued to operate as 'Hart and Son'. Three months after John's funeral, Stephen Field lost his wife Sarah. They had been married less than ten years. Stephen sets up home in Thunder Lane with his granddaughter, dying aged 76 in July 1904.

# Chapter 12

# Survivors

## Richard Wentworth White
## (1848–1924)

On the morning of Saturday 12, September 1874, 58-year-old Henry Freeman took breakfast in his lodgings at 10, Canning Place, Gloucester Road in Kensington, London, reading his copy of *The Standard* newspaper. He may have first looked at the front cover, scanning the densely packed columns of personal advertisements, before turning to page three, where a headline caught his eye:

> Fearful Railway Collision. Twenty Persons Killed and Many
> Injured. From our special correspondent in Norwich.

Press stories covering railway accidents were not uncommon, but it was the location of this particular one that concerned Henry. He had been born in Norwich in 1815 and although his work had later taken him to London, members of his immediate family continued to live in the East Anglian city. These included his eldest brother William Freeman and his younger sister Anne Maria, who was married to Norwich dentist Richard White. Henry read the article with interest, taking in the lurid details of the head-on crash in the village of Thorpe, the ensuing carnage and finally the list of the dead and injured. His worst fears were confirmed and he immediately put pen to paper, writing to William's wife Mary, at her home in Upper King Street.

> My dear Mary, What a terrible business this is on your
> railway on Thursday night, and by my paper this morning
> I see among the list of 'less serious cases', 'Mr R White,

Junior, dentist St Giles. Severe injuries to shoulder and contusions.'

I do hope the poor fellow is not much hurt, and what a miraculous escape from sudden and violent death.

Henry had every reason to be concerned. Wenty was the eldest son of Henry's sister Anne. Quite naturally Henry would have preferred to send his sympathies directly to his sister, but as he explained to Mary:

> ... the Whites have cut me entirely since my calamities and therefore I do not write to them but I should be very glad if William would go up to their house tomorrow morning to enquire how Wenty is going on and send me a few lines by tomorrow night's post reporting his injuries.

Henry was a timber broker and a troubled man at the best of times. In recent weeks he had been worried that his wider family may also disown him. At the same time he was concerned about the deteriorating mental health of his father, William Freeman. Above all, Henry found himself in a precarious financial position, as he had detailed in earlier correspondence with Mary, only a month before the rail disaster.

> I am quite ruined and as business holds out no prospect of improvement for me, I have made application to be admitted to Morden College, Blackheath, a nice retreat for broken-down merchants ... although I may have to work many months before there is a vacancy – not the finish to a long career of hard work that I might have expected, but far better than the work-house.
>
> (Norfolk Record Office,
> Freeman Collection, MC17/21/1)

The unexpected news about his nephew's injuries would have simply added to his woes.

In December that year Wenty's outstanding prosecution came up before the Magistrates. Speaking on behalf of him and his fellow defendants were some of the most eminent surgeons in the city, including Dr Eade and Dr Beverley. The judge dismissed the charges, however expressing his opinion that the Royal Society for the Prevention of Cruelty to Animals was justified in bringing the case.

For many years Wenty was regarded as one of the most sought-after wealthy bachelors in the city. He lived for some time on Thorpe Road, only a few hundred yards from the site of the accident. Once his father retired from the family dental practice Wenty took over as head dentist. His mother passed away in 1888, followed by his father in 1892, neither parent surviving to see their eldest son wed. However, Richard senior did live to see his son elected, in 1889, as the first ever Honorary Dentist at the Norfolk and Norwich Hospital, a role that Wenty held for nine years.

In 1884, when Wenty was 49, he married. His bride was 31-year-old Ethel Fitzgerald, the eldest daughter of a retired army major, whose family lived at The Hall in the village of Framlingham Pigot. The couple had two daughters, Rose and Nancy, before moving to Hampshire. In later life Richard and his wife returned to Norfolk to live in Framlingham Earl. In 1898 Richard dissolved the dental partnership and lived a comfortable retirement until his death in April 1924, aged 76.

His uncle, Henry Freeman, would have been satisfied and proud to know that his beloved nephew, having survived the railway disaster, lived a long and successful life. Sadly, Henry himself was not so blessed, dying aged 59, just a year after the accident, alone at his Kensington lodgings.

# Ellen Eugenie Ramsdale
## (1856–1925)

For a number of years there was little or no news about Ellen. Weakened by her terrible ordeal she would have needed time to recover, purchase and fit a prosthetic leg and then learn how to walk again. By 1880 her mother Mary, now 50, had moved to Thorpe and was living with her son Anthony at 2 Foundry Terrace. Around the same time, at Miller's Royal Photographic Studio at 182, King Street, Great Yarmouth, an engagement portrait was being prepared, resulting in a delightfully posed photograph of a confident, stocky young gentleman with a good head of hair and full beard, leaning protectively towards his fiancée, a slim, pale young woman, her full skirts hiding any hint of her missing limb. A little terrier dog perches under her right arm, no doubt intrigued by the camera. How Ellen Ramsdale and Dr Alex Mitchell first met is unknown, but on 4 March 1882, when she was 27 years old, Ellen's wedding was reported in the *Norfolk Chronicle*.

> On 28th February, at the Parish Church in East Dereham, by the Reverend W.T. Gidney, cousin of the bride, Alexander Mitchell M.D., Barton House, Great Yarmouth, to Ellen Eugenie, daughter of the late Robert Ramsdale of East Dereham.

Ellen's husband proved to be both accomplished and ambitious. Born two years after his brother James in Glasgow around 1848, he was the son of James Mitchell and Isabella Scott. James senior ran his own currier business, working in leather, at 65 Bridgegate Street, Glasgow. In 1851 when Alex was 3, the family was living in the fashionable St Andrew's Square, an affluent area dominated by the eighteenth-century church at its centre. By 1865 the family would be joined by siblings Thomas, Isabella, Roderic and Annie.

Possibly influenced by the extremes of wealth and poverty in Victorian Glasgow, and the high incidents of childhood illness and premature death, Alex choose to study medicine, both at Edinburgh and Glasgow Universities, starting his work experience at the London Hospital. He graduated from Glasgow in 1873, the same year as his father died, moving down to the fishing town of Great Yarmouth for a hospital position in Gorleston, before being appointed Medical Officer for Health for Great Yarmouth. It is likely that at the time of the railway accident, a year later, Alex and Ellen were not yet acquainted. Maybe she chose him as her physician when she was recovering from her 'life-changing' injuries and they fell in love? Ellen's disability may have been the reason why the couple had no children, but theirs proved to be a full and eventful marriage.

By 1891 the couple are living in Poplar in London, with Alex working at his practice in Regent Street, as well as taking up professional positions including surgeon for the C Division of the Metropolitan Police, honorary district surgeon to the Royal Maternity Charity and honorary physician to the Morley Home for Working Girls. His success meant that by 1901 the couple had relocated to the prestigious district of St James in Westminster. On Alex's retirement they left the city, taking a residence in the expanding South Oxfordshire village of Shillingford.

Mary Ramsdale's former lover and father of two of her children, Richard Charles Browne, had died, aged 63 in March 1893. His funeral at Saint Mary the Virgin Church in Elsing, caused quite a spectacle in the village. The newspaper reported many distinguished mourners, but there is no mention of either Mary or Charles' illegitimate son Anthony attending. Having neither a widow nor legitimate heirs, his estate passed to Mrs Catherine Louisa Hyde, Richard's younger sister. She inherited the sum of £3,664 (£425,000) plus Elsing Hall. There is no evidence that Mary Ramsdale or her two children by him, benefited in any way from Richard's will.

On 26 May 1912, Mary Ramsdale died at home in Blewbury in Berkshire. Less than twelve months later Alex died in Shillingford in April 1913, leaving his wife the sum of nearly £3,000 (£350,000). Ellen survived her husband by nearly twelve years, dying on 22 February 1925. Sometime in the intervening years, maybe unable to care for herself, Ellen moved down to Southsea near Portsmouth, lodging in the Sandon Private Hotel, located in South Parade, facing the sea. This small quality hotel accommodated thirty guests, offering residents all modern conveniences including electric light, bells and gas fires, along with comfort, cleanliness and excellent cuisine, all within one minutes of the pier, trams and shops. In 1924 the hotel came under new management, benefiting from redecoration and refurnishing, offering moderate winter residential terms from two guineas. It was here that Ellen died, aged 70.

It may be that during wet and windswept evenings, while dining at the Sandon Hotel in Southsea, Ellen regaled fellow residents with colourful accounts of those months she had spent, many years earlier, as the guest of the Three Tuns Public House in the Norfolk village of Thorpe-Next-Norwich.

# Sir Charles Gilman (1834–1911)
# & Sir Peter Eade (1825–1913)

Of the many survivors, two gentlemen in particular stand out for their exceptional contributions to Norwich life and prosperity. If both, or indeed, either of them had died that night in Thorpe, the lives of so many would have been all the poorer. Following the collision, Dr Peter Eade recovered quickly, his injuries being only slight, whereas Charles spent many months extremely unwell, friends fearing for his life, horrified by his weakened appearance at the compensation hearing. But Charles's health did ultimately improve, his vigour restored, just as the defence lawyer had suggested. The lives of these two men continued to run along parallel lines, both enjoying professional and personal good fortune, taking a prominent role in civic life, knighted by Queen Victoria, initiating and supporting public projects for the improvement of the city, lauded for their unceasingly generous philanthropy.

In 1882, Charles Gilman's reputation as a businessman of great energy and intellect resulted in an invitation to become a member of the City Council, the same year appointed as Mayor. It was during his final few months in this role, that he had the honour of hosting the Duke and Duchess of Connaught, invited to open the new Norfolk and Norwich Hospital buildings, finally completed after seven years in the making. Two years later, Charles was appointed as a Justice of the Peace and elected onto the Aldermanic bench, a great civic honour.

Charles continued as Secretary of the Norwich and London Accident Assurance Association, until the death of his father, Charles Suckling Gilman, in 1888. The senior management position was left vacant out of respect, until Charles took on the mantel in 1895, rewarding his son, Charles Storey Gilman with his former role of Secretary, a position he had held for forty years. The family firm was secure. In late 1896, Charles once again donned the mayoral robe and eighteenth-century gold chain of office. The timing was particularly gratifying as the following year was to be Queen Victoria's Diamond Jubilee. Charles successfully chaired the committee to plan the city celebrations, launching the Diamond Jubilee Fund, raising money to build the new Jenny Lind Infirmary for Sick Children.

On 20 June 1897, Charles and his wife were proud to witness 9,000 children assembling in the market place to sing the National Anthem.

As the final strains of the iconic music died, it was announced to the crowd that the dear Queen had conferred the honour of knighthood upon Mr Gilman, the esteemed Mayor of Norwich. A great cheer went up, reverberating off the Castle walls. There was much excitement in the streets of the city that day, with a floral procession, a 'costume' cricket match and a captive balloon making frequent ascents from the Cattle Market. Charles was invited to the royal residence of Osborne House on the Isle of Wight, during the following August, to attend his dubbing ceremony, a moment he counted among his greatest achievements.

Charles Gilman remained committed to his many charities, including The Jenny Lind Hospital, The Norwich Blind School, the Norfolk and Norwich Triennial Musical Festival and the Town Close Charity Trustees. For twenty-two years he was Chairman of the Conservators of Mousehold Heath. Sadly, in 1908, the year of his Golden Wedding Anniversary, Sir Charles became unwell and was cared for at his fine Victorian mansion, Stafford House in the Newmarket Road. His greatest disappointment was not being able to attend public activities. On Friday, 24 February 1911, a small piece in the *Eastern Daily Press* alerted readers that Sir Charles had fallen seriously ill and that his condition was giving cause for grave anxiety. A few hours later, he was gone. The entire city went into mourning. There was hardly a charity, institution or community that had not benefited from his quiet and orderly mind, his fierce determination or capacious bank account.

On 1 March, a lengthy funeral procession, accompanied by civic sword and macebearers, arrived at Christ Church in Eaton, where the service and interment took place. A photograph of a wreath-laden coffin featured in the middle of the front page of the *Eastern Daily Press*, the list of mourners taking up two columns of newsprint. Charles would be remembered as being 'kindly, courteous, generous, big-hearted and without a trace of bitterness in his difference of opinion with others'. Sadly, his friend Peter Eade, now aged 86, was unable to attend the funeral in Eaton, instead sending a wreath and condolences.

Sir Peter Eade had received his knighthood twelve years earlier than Sir Charles, travelling from Portsmouth aboard a commissioned steamer to Cowes, where he and others were met by the Home Secretary and driven to Osborne House in a convoy of royal carriages. On that first day of August 1885, Queen Victoria's son Arthur, Duke of Connaught, was assisting with the investitures. It is conceivable that the Prince and

Sir Peter, perhaps over tea served from a silver samovar, may have briefly discussed the railway disaster in Thorpe, the Duke having witnessed the aftermath at first hand.

Through his work at Norwich hospitals, alongside managing his private practice, Peter had soon become one of the best-loved doctors in the city.

And so began a lifetime of dedication and service to both medicine and to Norwich, his name closely associated with many of the city's milestones during the late nineteenth century and beyond. In 1876 he launched a campaign to establish open spaces and parks for the people, including the development of the 150 acre Mousehold Heath, with its panoramic views across his beloved city. Much later, he was proud to be present when, in 1886, the then Mayor, Mr John Gurney, opened the new road across Mousehold, dedicating the Heath for the free use of the people forever, afterwards attending a sumptuous luncheon at Sprowston Hall.

Private medicine was a lucrative business. Peter and his wife enjoyed a prosperous and privileged life. In 1877, he saw an opportunity to further improve his living arrangements, moving his wife and servants just a few hundred yards down St Giles, into one of the most prestigious houses in the city, Churchman House.

This magnificent Georgian building had been vacant since the Norwich School for Girls relocated to the Assembly House. This was a grand and much admired residence, most fitting for a man who would become Sheriff in 1880, a Knight of the Realm and Mayor in 1883, 1893 and 1895. On his first occasion as Mayor, the press and the public had great hopes for his year in office, the editor of the *Eastern Daily Press* commenting, 'Dr Eade is not wanting in public spirit, and he is sure to make a zealous public servant.' In May 1895, when the Mayor and former Coroner associated with the railway disaster, Edward Bignold, died unexpectedly, Sir Peter, then Deputy Mayor, was asked to step in for the remainder of the term. He did so gladly, nominating his friend, Sir Charles Gilman to be *his* Deputy.

Incredibly, throughout his life Peter found time for personal interests, including his collection of tortoises, bought from a street hawker and kept in his courtyard garden. He was said to find them intelligent, quiet and affectionate. He was a great advocate of temperance and a dedicated scholar and prolific writer, constantly turning out medical articles for journals, publishing local history books, notably on the hospital and on the buildings and residents of the parish of St Giles. He kept a personal diary, faithfully recording his activities and thoughts every night up to his death. He never threw anything away, collecting letters, manuscripts and cuttings concerning local, national and international events, building up a colossal collection of material in his office, with the aim of one day writing his autobiography. His ambition was fulfilled, but sadly not until after his death, when his friend Sydney Long took on the task. For fifty years Peter kept a rule to take a three or four week annual holiday with his wife, either to a favourite spot in the British Isles, or on the Continent.

Just a few of his greatest gifts to the city, which would endure for decades to come, included the opening of a city garden at Chapelfield in 1880. In the sixteenth-century the site was a piece of open ground used for archery practice and city artillery training. In the eighteenth century it was flooded to provide a reservoir for the city. In 1852 the Waterworks company agreed to give up its lease if the city corporation laid out the land as a public garden. It took a number of years for the scheme to come to fulfilment, with Peter at the centre of the improvement plans. From 1867 the area was enclosed, a Drill Hall erected and avenues of elms planted. In 1880 a magnificent pagoda appeared and the park opened to the public, by 1899 the amenities enhanced with a bandstand and children's playground. Chapelfield Gardens was only a short stroll from Churchman House, the Eades enjoying many evening strolls there when the weather was clement.

In 1883, when Peter was Mayor, the future of Norwich Castle looked to be under threat. Prison Commissioners wanted to rebuild and the plans took no account of the splendid history of the iconic structure. Peter was appalled, suggesting to the council that the city buy the castle from the Government. After all, a prison could be built anywhere. The authorities agreed, but only at a high price. Peter led a deputation to London to discuss the situation with the Home Secretary, negotiating the price down to £4,000 (£490,000), a mere quarter of the amount dictated in the Prison Act. The city secured the castle, a new prison was built on Mousehold Heath in 1887, and in 1894 the Castle opened as a museum for the enjoyment of all.

October 1905 saw the unveiling of a statue dedicated to the great seventeenth-century writer and philosopher Sir Thomas Browne, who had lived in the city for forty-six years up to his death in 1682. Sir Peter was a great admirer of Browne's work and chaired the Memorial Committee responsible for commissioning the work, set in the very centre of the city at the Haymarket. This was one of Sir Peter's most satisfying public achievements. He worked tirelessly to raise the necessary funds, with subscriptions received from all over the world.

On 25 September 1895, Sir Peter was given the Honorary Freedom of the City of Norwich at a ceremony in the Guildhall. The reception was held in the Castle Museum, when Sir Peter was presented with a portrait of himself, which he promptly donated to the Museum to be hung in its picture gallery. Sir Peter wrote later in his diary, 'This was one of the most memorable and gratifying days of my life.'

Sir Peter's funeral was held on 16 August 1915. The coffin was carried across the road from Churchman House into the parish church of St Giles, where he had worshipped for most of his adult life. But it was not his adopted city of Norwich that received his remains. Instead he was taken to Blofield to be interred in the quiet churchyard, alongside his father and sisters.

# Chapter 13

# Consequences or Lessons Learned

Following the release of the Board of Trade Report on the collision at Thorpe, it was evident that the formerly much admired Cooke and Wheatstone telegraph system was not, in fact, immune to human error. GER had been fortunate not to have any serious incidents on the single line out of Norwich in all of its thirty years. As a result, complacency had set in, rules were bent, regulations flouted and problems of punctuality ignored. The consequences proved catastrophic. There was an urgent need for a more secure system for use on single lines. Telegraph engineer Edward Tyer had devoted his life to the development of electrical appliances. As early as 1852 he had taken out a patent for an electrical signalling device operating on a railway engine. Its success led to him creating a plethora of further inventions, each one refining and improving the efficiency of railway signalling. By 1874 his electric block instruments were in widespread use, proving effective on double lines throughout the country. Following the Thorpe Disaster he turned his attention to single lines. The result was four years in the making.

In the meantime, when the new East Norfolk Railway Company single line from Whitlingham Junction (just yards from the site of the collision) to North Walsham, was opened on 20 October 1874, management immediately adopted the simple 'staff system'. If a driver did not hold in his hands the wooden painted stick, then he knew not to enter the section of line ahead. Out of respect for those who lost their lives in the Thorpe Disaster less than six weeks earlier, the inaugural trip was completed, unusually, without ceremony or noisy celebrations.

In March 1878 the Tyer Tablet System was finally patented. This system was considered foolproof, involving a set of circular thick metal discs, known as tablets, and a pair of tablet machines, installed one at each end of a single-track section of line. As a train arrived at a signal box to enter the single line section, the signalman would first use a bell code to telegraph their counterpart at the other end, requesting permission for the train to proceed. If granted, the far end signalman pressed a plunger on their instrument, releasing a tablet and locking the instruments at each end. The train could proceed with confidence. It was more complicated than earlier systems, doubtless resulting in some grumbling among the crews. But it worked, and the method was adopted all over the world. The last tablet to be used was in July 1994, on the New Zealand Rail Network.

On 29 April 1886, a meeting was held at the Guildhall in Norwich, with the purpose of forming a branch of the St John Ambulance Society, founded in 1877 in London. Among the medical staff on the committee were Michael Beverley, Thomas Crosse and Sir Peter Eade, each well aware that the rescuers at the collision, although willing, had no knowledge of basic techniques such as how to stem blood flow, apply dressings or support a fracture. Sir Peter rose to thank the Mayor for presiding over the meeting, stating that those most likely to benefit from this 'First Aid Society', would be agricultural workers, police, miners and railway men. He explained:

> Unfortunately severe accidents occur when a surgeon is not within reach of an injured person, at other times the patient is sent off directly to the hospital where he arrives in a dying state from loss of blood. This could have been controlled at first had anyone been present with such general knowledge as the St John society would teach. Not so long ago, I believe the usual, if not proper thing for ladies to do in the presence of an emergency, was to faint, or if not to faint, at least to scream loudly. I hope the time for this is now past, and that in the future by means of this association, many ladies as well as others would possess the knowledge which might enable them at times to be actively useful.
>
> (*Norfolk News*, Saturday, 8 May 1886)

The Association was an instant success, popular particularly with the wives and daughters of the gentry, delighted finally to be allowed have access to a worthwhile project. Even the royal princesses trained for certificates in the same way as everyone else. The lessons learned outside the village of Thorpe-Next-Norwich on that horrendous night, would have been invaluable in the progression of this pioneering movement.

Sir Peter had strong views on the probable cause of the Thorpe Railway Disaster. Writing in his autobiographical notes towards the end of his life, he recalled the letter he wrote to the British Medical Journal, shortly after the Thorpe collision, well before the findings of the Board of Trade Inquiry were made public.

> The immediate cause of the catastrophe was doubtless the error or misapprehension of some individual. But the fault in the background, the real radical error, is unquestionably, the unpunctuality of the trains, with the consequent necessity for varying the arrangements on the single line, and the necessary dependence, therefore, of safety upon the accuracy of individuals, or the exact carrying out of orders, which have varied from day to day according to the varying circumstances.
>
> (*The British Medical Journal*, 19 September 1874)

There are two positives arising from what was, at the time, the most serious railway catastrophe in this country. First, the rapid development of more stringent regulations for the use of single line tracks and, most notably, the courage, spirit and selflessness demonstrated by those heroes who came out to help at the Great Thorpe Railway Disaster of 1874.

# Select Bibliography

Many of the research findings for this book have been accessed from online sources at British Newspaper Archive and Ancestry. Equally invaluable was a facsimile of the rarely seen *East Anglian Handbook for 1875*, kindly donated by the Great Eastern Railway Society. The informative Board of Trade Inquiry Report of 1874 is available to download at railwaysarchive.co.uk. The archives at both Norfolk Record Office and Norwich Heritage Library were inspirational. I have been honoured to meet and correspond with descendants from a number of the victims of the disaster and with steam railway experts and enthusiasts. In addition, the following publications proved valuable background reading.

Ashelford, J., *The Art of Dress, Clothes Through History 1500–1914*, (The National Trust, London, 1996)

Batty Shaw, A., *Norfolk and Norwich Hospital: Lives of the Medical Staff* (Published by author as limited edition of 100, 1971)

Blanchard, G., *Writing Your Family History*, (Pen and Sword Books, Barnsley, 2014)

Burgess, E. and Burgess, W.E. (eds), *Men Who Have Made Norwich* (first published in 1904 from a collection of newspaper articles, reproduced by Norfolk Industrial Archaeology Society & Philip Tolley, 2014)

Bussey, D. and Martin, E., *Edward Boardman and Victorian Norwich*, (The Norwich Society, 2018)

Cherry, S., *Mental Health Care in Modern England, The Norfolk Lunatic Asylum 1810–1998,* (The Boydell Press, Woodbridge, 2003)

Dawson, A., *Travelling on the Victorian Railway*, (Amberley Publishing, Stroud, 2017)

Dawson, A., *Working on the Victorian Railway*, (Amberley Publishing, Stroud, 2017)

Drummond, D., *Tracing Your Railway Ancestors*, (Pen and Sword Books, Barnsley, 2010)

Eade, P., *Some Account of the Parish of St Giles, Norwich*, (Jarrold & Sons, Norwich, 1886, reprinted by ForgottenBooks.com, London)

Eade, P., *The Autobiography of Sir Peter Eade*, (Jarrold & Sons, London, 1916)

Eade, P., *The Norfolk & Norwich Hospital 1770–1900*, (Jarrold & Sons, Norwich, 1900, reprinted by Pranava Books, India)

Ellis, H., *Nineteenth Century Railway Carriages*, (Modern Transport Publishing Co. Ltd., London, 1949)

Foley, M., *Britain's Railway Disasters*, (Pen and Sword Books, Barnsley, 2013)

Gale, J., *The Coming of the Railway to East Anglia* (Melrose Press Ltd., Ely, 2015)

Garwood, C., *Mid-Victorian Britain*, (Shire Publications, Oxford, 2011)

Goodman, R., *How to be a Victorian*, (Penguin Books, 2014)

Goodrum, P., *Norfolk Broads, The Biography*, (Amberley Publishing, Stroud, 2014)

Gordon, D.I., *A Regional History of the Railways of Great Britain, Volume 5, The Eastern Counties*, (David and Charles (Publishers) Ltd., Newton Abbot, 1990)

Hibgame, F.T., *Recollections of Norwich Fifty Years Ago*, (Norfolk Press Syndicate Ltd., 1919)

Holmes, F., and Holmes, M., *Norwich Pubs and Breweries Past and Present* (Norwich Heritage Projects, 2011)

Holmes, F., and Holmes, M., *The Old Courts and Yards of Norwich* (Norwich Heritage Projects, 2015)

Holmes, R., *Soldiers*, (Harper Collins, London, 2012)

Kennedy, D., Sole Society, writing in Norfolk Roots Magazine about Frederick Sewell (Jan/Feb 2005)

Lambert, A.J., *Nineteenth Century Railway History Through The Illustrated London News*, (David and Charles (Publishers) Ltd., Newton Abbot, 1984)

Lloyd, C., Colonel *Unthank and the Golden Triangle*, (published by author, 2011)

May, T., *The Victorian Railway Worker* (Shire Publications, Oxford, 2003)

May, T., *The Victorian Undertaker*, (Shire Publications, Oxford, 2010)

Mingay, G.E., *Rural Life in Victorian England*, (Futura Publications Ltd., London, 1979)

Nuthall, T., *Thorpe St Andrew, A Revised History*, (Published by author, 2014)

Rajnai, M., *The Norwich School of Painters* (Jarrold & Sons Ltd., Norwich, 1985)

Wicks, W., *Inns and Taverns of Old Norwich*, (Published by author as limited edition, 1925)

Richards, J., and MacKenzie, J.M., *The Railway Station, A Social History* (Oxford University Press, 1986)

Rolt, L.T.C., *Red for Danger*, (Pan Books, London, 1960)

Sinclair, O., *When Wherries Sailed By*, (Poppyland Publishing, Norfolk, 1987)

Smith, G., *The Great Eastern Railway*, (Tempus Publishing Ltd., Stroud, 1996)

Tolley, P. (ed.) *Norfolk 1890*, (first published by British Industrial Publishing Company, Birmingham in 1890, reproduced by Norfolk Industrial Archaeology Society, 2016)

Tooke, C., *The Rows and the Old Town of Great Yarmouth* (Tookes Books, Great Yarmouth, 2007)

White, W., *White's History, Gazetteer and Directory of Norfolk, 1883* (William White, Sheffield, 1883)

Williams, N., *The Public Houses and Pleasure Gardens of Thorpe St Andrew* (published by author, 2019),

Wiseman, D. and Pointer, R., *Origins of the Street and Road Names of Thorpe St Andrew*, (published by authors, 2014)

# Index

Hart, John, publican and boat builder,
17, 18, 65, 67, 81, 93, 162, 167-172
Harvey, Colonel John, 4
Hawkshead, Cumbria, 120
Herring, Captain Henry L'estrange,
Thorpe-Next-Norwich, 68, 81
Hills, Monson Odling, 164, 165
Hills, Mr Monson, Apothecary, 162-3,
Hills, Thomas Addison, passenger, 72,
73, 157-159
Hills, Dr William, County Asylum, 18,
69, 71, 162-166,
Holroyd, John, railway servant, 51, 132
Hospital, Norfolk and Norwich, vii,
98-108, 111-119, 132, 148, 150,
152, 175, 178
Hotblack Beverley, Marion, 115,
116-117
Hotblack, John, 115, 116
Hupton, Job, passenger, 52-53, 71, 99,
100-101, 147

Inquests
Beart, John, 106
Betts, Mrs Eliza & son, 91-92
Betts, John, 103-104
Browne, Miss Susan, 102-103
Cassell, Frederick, 85-86
Clarke, Thomas, 82
Coote, Mrs Charlotte, 104-105
Faulkner, Miss Jane Ann, 108
Gilding, Mrs Sarah Ann & daughter,
42, 86-87
Hupton, Job, 100-101
Light, James, 83-84
Lincoln, Miss Susanna, 88-89
Murray, Miss Marianne, 84-85
Page, Mr George, 79-80
Prior, John, 82-83
Sewell, Frederick, 84
Skinner, Russell, 87-88
Stacey, Reverend Henry & Mrs
Mary Ann, 89
Taylor, Miss Mary Ann, 90-91

Ward, Robert, 85-86
Womack, Mr George, 78-79
Islington, Norfolk, 25

Jena, Germany, 38
Jenny Lind Infirmary for Sick
Children, Norwich, 113, 178, 179

Keeble, John, railway servant, 51
King's Arms Pub, Botolph Street,
Norwich, 46, 155
King's Head Pub, Thorpe-Next-
Norwich, xi, 6, 105
King's Lynn, Norfolk, 25, 65, 152

Lakenham, Norwich, 12, 16, 53, 86,
91, 92, 104
Liberal Association, Norwich, 146
Light, James, railway fireman, 13,
48-49, 62, 83
Light, Richard, 48-49, 84
Lincoln, Susanna, passenger, 35, 88-89
Lister, Professor Joseph, 115
Liston, Professor Robert, 111
Liverpool to Manchester Railway
Company, 1, 3
Long Stratton, Norfolk, 166-167
Lowestoft, Suffolk, 3, 10, 13, 40, 42-44,
49, 54, 57, 58-59, 64-66, 74, 82, 84

Medico-Chirurgical Society,
Norwich, 44
Metcalfe, Mr, lawyer, 143-146, 149,
151
Morse, Charles, Reverend, passenger,
44-46, 69-70, 148, 149, 154, 155
Mitchell, Dr Alexander, 176
Mousehold Heath, Norwich, 69, 179,
180, 181
Murray, Marianne Elizabeth,
passenger, 33-34, 72, 74, 84-85, 89

Navvies, The, 5
New Cut, The, 4-7

# INDEX